SOVIET MILITARY POLICY
SINCE WORLD WAR II

SOVIET
MILITARY POLICY
SINCE WORLD WAR II

William T. Lee
Richard F. Staar

Foreword by
William R. Van Cleave

HOOVER INSTITUTION PRESS   Stanford University, Stanford, California

Hoover Press Publication 330

Copyright 1986 by the Board of Trustees of the
    Leland Stanford Junior University
First printing, 1986
Manufactured in the United States of America
90 89 88 87 86   9 8 7 6 5 4 3 2 1

Library of Congress Cataloging in Publication Data

Lee, William Thomas, 1926–
  Soviet military policy since World War II.

  (Hoover Press publication)
  Bibliography: p.
  Includes index.
  1. Soviet Union—Military policy. 2. Soviet
Union—Armed forces. I. Staar, Richard Felix,
1923–   . II. Title.
UA770.L389   1986   355'.033047   85-46055
ISBN 0-8179-8301-5 (alk. paper)

Design by Zena Starfire

Contents

Tables

Figures

Acronyms and Weapons Systems Designators

AAM   An air-to-air missile. The AA-8 is carried on fighter aircraft to shoot down bombers and other aerodynamic targets, such as cruise missiles.

ABM   Antiballistic missile for defense against ICBMs and SLBMs.

ALCM   Air-launched cruise missile.

APC   Armored personnel carrier.

ASM   Air-to-surface missile, most, but not all, of which are ALCMs; a few include ballistic missiles launched from an aircraft.

ASW   Antisubmarine warfare.

ATBM   Antitactical ballistic missile.

ATGM   Antitank guided missile.

BMD   Ballistic missile defense.

BPK   Large ASW ship (*bol'shoi protivolodochnyi korabl'*).

C^3   Command, control, and communications.

CEP   Circular error probable; that is, the radius of the circle in which the RV is expected to impact 50 percent of the time. This is the basic measure of accuracy for all types of ballistic and cruise missiles.

CIA   Central Intelligence Agency.

CM   Cruise missile; that is, one that uses aerodynamic lift like an aircraft to travel from launch point to the target.

CPSU   Communist Party of the Soviet Union.

ECM   Electronic countermeasures.

FBS   Forward based systems.

FYP   Five-year plan.

GKO   State Committee for Defense
           (*Gosudarstvennyi Komitet Oborony*).

GLCM   Ground-launched cruise missile.

GNP   Gross national product.

ICBM   Intercontinental-range ballistic missile (SSM); for example, the SS-6, SS-7, SS-9 . . . SS-18 and so on for the USSR; Atlas, Titan, Minuteman, MX for the U.S.

INF   Intermediate-range nuclear forces.

IRBM   Intermediate-range ballistic missile; an SSM with a range between an MRBM and an ICBM; for example, the Soviet SS-20.

KGB   Committee for State Security
           (*Komitet Gosudarstvennoi Bezopastnosti*).

LCC   Launch control centers.

LRA   Long-Range Aviation/Air Force.

MAD   Mutual assured destruction.

MIRV   Multiple independently-targeted re-entry vehicle; two or more RVs carried by a single ballistic missile with a post-boost control system (PBCS or "bus") that guides each RV independently to an individual target.

MM   Minuteman.

MRBM   Medium-range ballistic missile; for example, the SS-4. In Soviet usage, an SSM with a range in excess of 1,000 kilometers is a "strategic" missile; an "operational-tactical" missile has a range of less than 1,000 kilometers.

MRV   Multiple re-entry vehicle; two or more RVs carried by a single ballistic missile. The RVs usually cannot be guided to attack separate individual targets, however.

MVD   Ministry of Internal Affairs (*Ministerstvo Vnutrennykh Del*).

NATO   North Atlantic Treaty Organization.

PK   Kill probability.

PMOC   Pay, maintenance, operations, and construction.

R&D   Research and development.

RV   Re-entry vehicle that carries the weapon payload (usually but not necessarily nuclear) of a ballistic missile that rises above the earth's atmosphere in the course of its trajectory and then re-enters. The interception of RVs involves two parameters: the radar cross-section and the speed of the RV. Neither of these parameters depends on the range of the missile. Hence, the RV of a missile we call strategic, the Poseidon, has a radar cross section larger and a speed slower than the RV of the Pershing II. The SA-12, called an ATBM, can intercept both the Poseidon and the Pershing II easily, but not the Mark 12-A from the Minuteman 3. (See SAM.)

SA-18   The eighteenth Soviet SSM to be deployed, in this case a large payload ICBM.

SAC   U.S. Strategic Air Command.

SAF   Soviet air forces.

SALT   Strategic Arms Limitation Treaty.

SAM   Surface-to-air missile. The SA-5 is designed to shoot down aerodynamic systems—and possibly also ballistic re-entry vehicles—operating at high altitudes and speeds. The best example of this category's inclusiveness is the SA-12, designed to intercept both aircraft and re-entry vehicles. (See RV.)

SA-N   A SAM installed on a naval vessel. The SA-N is the naval version of the SA-3, designed to shoot down aerodynamic systems operating at low to medium altitudes.

SDI   Strategic Defense Initiative.

SKR   Patrol ship (*storozhevoi korabl' raketnyi*).

SLBM   Submarine-launched ballistic missile; for example, the SS-N-6 has a range of nearly 3,000 kilometers and is carried on a "Yankee" or Y-Class nuclear submarine.

SLCM   A submarine-launched cruise, that is, aerodynamic, missile. The SS-N-3 has a range of nearly 600 kilometers (given an external source of information about the target's location) and is primarily designed to attack aircraft carriers and other types of ships.

SP   Self-propelled gun.

SRF   Strategic Rocket Forces.

SS-   Followed by a number, for example, SS-18; SS- designates a particular SSM weapon system.

SS-N-20 The twentieth naval missile system to be deployed, in this case an SLBM carrying a MIRV payload to intercontinental ranges. Missiles with the SS-N- designator are SSMs but are not necessarily ballistic. This designator is also used for SLCMs.

SS-N- A naval, that is, sea-based, surface-to-surface missile that may be ballistic or aerodynamic; range can vary from less than 100 to more than 10,000 kilometers.

SS-X- An SSM still in the development stage, usually being flight tested; the letter X designates the development stage for any type of missile; for example, SA-X-.

SSBN A nuclear-powered submarine that carries SLBMs.

SSM Surface-to-surface (ballistic) missile.

SSN Nuclear-powered submarine, most, but not all, of which carry some type of ballistic or aerodynamic missile.

START Strategic Arms Reduction Talks.

TASM Tactical air-to-surface missile.

TVD Theater of military operations (*teatr voennykh deistvii*).

VGK Supreme High Command (*Verkhovnoe Glavnokomandovanie*).

VPK The Military-Industrial Commission (*Voenno-promyshlennaia Komissia*).

V/STOL Vertical/Short Takeoff and Landing aircraft.

Foreword

Understanding the motivation, objectives, and nature of Soviet nuclear arms programs has frequently been a matter of projecting to the Soviets concepts and preferences of the United States, particularly when the subject has been either nuclear war or arms control. Western media, academic literature, and even statements by public officials describe Soviet nuclear policies in the terms with which we have fashioned our own policies, emphasizing mutual deterrence, parity, war avoidance, and negotiations.

Since the early 1960s, American sovietologists have argued that issues and policy disputes that dominate United States policymaking also dominate USSR decisionmaking; that Soviet nuclear policy and doctrine are the constantly shifting products of the internal balance between "hawks" and "doves"; that USSR nuclear arms programs can best be explained as copies of or reactions to American programs; and that, consequently, United States initiatives to limit and moderate arms policies and programs would very likely be reciprocated by a Soviet leadership beleaguered by economic and imperial problems.

Time and again, reality has confounded such interpretations and expectations. This book, by two eminent scholars of Soviet politico-military affairs, explains why. The book focuses on USSR *nuclear* arms policies and programs since World War II, traces the evolution of those policies and programs, describes their nature, and explains Soviet decisionmaking. It is sober and instructive reading for those who harbor the delusion that USSR arms programs are primarily reactions to our own and that "true" Soviet strategic (and arms control) principles and objectives are similar to, and consonant with, our own.

This book explains that Moscow's weapons programs are best understood and anticipated "as an attempt to satisfy the requirements of [Soviet] doctrine and strategy," which are based on nuclear war–fighting and damage-limiting objectives and the quest for nuclear superiority over the West. Officially established USSR doctrine and strategy can be determined—have, in fact, remained remarkably stable for over a quarter-century—and "clearly state both the reasons for and the objectives of the Soviet military buildup." Kremlin decisionmakers have deliberately and systematically established their own strategic policies and objectives, which are decidedly not mere mirror images of American ones, and they follow them assiduously. Only thus can the unremitting Soviet military buildup (its nature and its objectives) be understood.

In contrast to the United States, in the Soviet Union

> Senior politicians do not formulate military doctrine as a declaratory policy to which they intend to pay little, if any, attention in practice. The Defense Council or Politburo adopts a doctrine as the policy framework to guide its own subsequent actions—to judge and be judged by. Similarly, when the military establishment translates and expands the party's doctrine into strategy, and the political leaders approve that strategy, . . . the strategy subsequently provides policy guidance for decisions on weapons development, production, and deployment.

The book examines the Soviet military decisionmaking apparatus and USSR concepts of doctrine, strategy, and operational missions. It outlines the roles and missions of the armed services. Perhaps its most interesting and instructive part discusses the evolution of Soviet nuclear doctrine and strategy from its beginning (earlier than what has commonly been believed in the West) to the present.

What is striking is the early formulation of doctrine, its continuity, and the systematic determination with which Soviet leaders have developed the forces required by it. The authors report that "as soon as World War II ended, the USSR began a sustained drive to acquire balanced offensive and defensive forces designed to limit damage to the homeland and to fight and eventually win a nuclear war." For that matter, even the Soviet ABM program "started soon after the end of World War II and was approved by Stalin along with all of the other USSR nuclear strategy defense programs."

According to the authors, then, the Soviet Union was actually *ahead* of the United States in formulating a nuclear arms policy and the programs to support that policy. After World War II the United States wasted several years before it seriously turned to nuclear arms programs, policies, and strategies. Since that time, those American programs and policies have been modified several times, in important ways; they never seriously involved the USSR objectives "to limit damage to the homeland and to fight and eventually win a nuclear war."

The Soviet doctrine that exists today was refined and finally formulated during the 1950s and has undergone very few modifications since then. The same is true for USSR targeting goals and priorities for nuclear war, which are decidedly counter-force, not counter-city, *per se*. In the event of war, the Soviet objective would be not only to destroy the enemy's principal military forces and ability to fight but also to limit damage to the USSR. The Soviets have proceeded with determination to fashion the forces to accomplish those objectives. They have been prepared to work on such capabilities over a long period of time, pursuing them even when technical and operational feasibility remained well in the future.

Soviet doctrine, however, explains the forces the Soviets have developed and deployed, and the authors believe that doctrine will allow the United States to anticipate those now being developed for future deployment. Soviet doctrine requires a strong counterforce capability against enemy forces (particularly strategic nuclear, as seen by the USSR); a large, intimidating, strategic reserve force (to deter or limit enemy responses); and coordinated active and passive defenses against any enemy retaliation that could still take place.

The authors include a brief chapter on current Soviet nuclear programs and capabilities, but their purpose is more to explain the nexus between doctrine and programs than to detail programs. A copy of the most recent Department of Defense annual publication, *Soviet Military Power*, would complement this book very well. This publication details USSR programs that are clearly in line with the above objectives, thereby supporting the authors' main point. For example, *Soviet Military Power* notes that the SS-18 and SS-19 ICBMs are "specifically designed to attack and destroy [American] ICBM silos and other hardened targets"; that the new SS-24 and SS-25 ICBMs are both accurate and mobile, adding to the Soviet secure reserve forces; and that the USSR has a multifaceted program for defense against nuclear attacks.

The Soviets have never planned (nor do they today) nuclear policies and programs on the basis of the driving American concepts and precepts of strategic stability, parity, mutual assured destruction, and mutual deterrence. As the authors point out, "the Soviets consider deterrence to be one-sided. . . . Deterrence is stable when Soviet nuclear and non-nuclear forces are superior, not when they are equal to those of the West." Unlike the West, "the Soviets plan to fight a nuclear war like any other war would be fought, for political objectives, and plan to win it by military means." Soviet strategy is not a retaliatory, deterrence-only strategy. It makes no distinction between deterrence and fighting or defending the USSR in a war. It is explicitly directed at fighting a war and defeating an enemy with nuclear means, including disrupting, if not preventing, any enemy strike at the very outset of war.

It is clear from this book that, among military forces and capabilities, the Soviets place the highest priority on what they regard as "strategic" nuclear forces—forces for intercontinental and theater warfare and for defense of the homeland. This is in clear contrast to the United States, where the military assigns strategic nuclear forces a very low priority compared with non-nuclear general purpose forces, and where strategic nuclear forces command only a small fraction of the defense budget.

In this regard, the authors' conclusions are strongly supported by a recent CIA report to Congress, which concludes that "strategic forces will continue to command the highest resource priorities" in the Soviet Union. At the same time, this book will help one understand why that is the case, and why the CIA expects the resources committed by the Soviet Union to strategic nuclear forces to be increasing, unaffected by any economic problems:

> The Soviets are increasing their resource commitments to their already formidable strategic forces research, development, and deployment programs. We estimate that total investment and operating expenditures for projected Soviet strategic offensive forces (intercontinental attack and intermediate range) and strategic defensive forces (assuming no widespread ABM deployments) will result in a growth in total Soviet strategic force expenditures of between 5 and 7 percent a year over the next five years. (The rate would be 7 to 10 percent if widespread ABM defenses were deployed.[1]

The awesome USSR strategic offensive nuclear force programs are well known. Since "parity" in these forces was announced at the time of SALT I in 1972, the Soviets have outspent the United States by a factor of at least three to one on such forces and have introduced a plethora of new weapons systems, to the point that there is no single significant comparative index in which the USSR does not enjoy an advantage. What is perhaps less well known—but would be understandable upon reading this book—is that the Soviets have spent approximately an equal amount on their strategic defensive forces. Today, the USSR has an operational ABM system centered on Moscow, which is being modernized; a rich nationwide air defense system, which is also being upgraded to possess appreciable ballistic missile defense capability; a heavily financed research and development program for advanced ABM capabilities, both ground- and spaced-based; and an extensive civil defense and wartime sheltering program. As recent U.S. presidential reports have indicated, the Soviets have not been in compliance with the most important requirements of the SALT I or the ABM treaties and are most probably developing a base for a rapidly deployable nationwide ABM system.

The authors' logic mandates that we should expect such a deployment: Soviet doctrine, which is damage-limiting for the USSR homeland, determines Soviet force requirements, which then determine Soviet programs. In fact, the authors explicitly expect that distribution of the increased funding noted above will emphasize strategic defensive forces, including ABM. (One could also deduce other USSR programs by identifying gaps or weaknesses in the Soviet ability to carry out doctrinal requirements; for example, larger, less locatable strategic reserve forces, military space systems, and antisubmarine warfare improvements.)

Strongly supported by the evidence of Soviet strategic force programs, the authors' depiction of USSR objectives (and the determination to meet them) explains fundamentally the inability of the United States to accomplish its own arms control objectives. It also explains the failure of nuclear arms control. From the beginning of the Strategic Arms Limitation Talks (SALT), which since 1981 have been referred to as the Strategic Arms Reduction Talks (START), Soviet nuclear arms programs have been incompatible with the achievement of U.S. arms control objectives. Soviet aims at arms control talks have been very different from American aims. The Soviets will allow no arms control limitations to interfere with programs that are proceeding in accordance with their doctrine. Arms control talks and agreements, however, are useful in restraining United States programs and in helping to erase or prevent any American advantage in the nuclear balance. Chapter 10 explains this very well in terms of SALT I and the ABM Treaty.

The principal Soviet aims in SALT I were to stop the United States' ABM program, which would have made it more difficult for the USSR to achieve nuclear superiority and a strategic counterforce capability, and to buy the time necessary to surpass American ABM capabilities. A secondary objective was to obscure the counterforce, damage-limiting goals of ongoing Soviet strategic nuclear programs; the USSR goal was not to limit its own forces. To quote the authors: "Many would argue that, without SALT, Soviet strategic missile forces would be even larger. No evidence to support that argument exists. On the contrary, the USSR has sized its strategic forces to meet targeting requirements with a sufficient reserve . . . SALT or no SALT, the USSR strategic missile warhead inventory in the mid-1980s would have been about the same."

Soviet concern over the United States' ABM fifteen years ago also explains the currently strong Soviet opposition to the so-called Strategic Defense Initiative. American strategic defenses would threaten what the Soviets believe to be necessary in order to accomplish their doctrinal objectives and to represent a satisfactory nuclear balance. Of course, the USSR will by no means sacrifice or impair its own strategic defensive capabilities in an attempt to limit those of the United States. This book makes that clear, as do present Soviet strategic defense programs.

The authors include in their discussion USSR doctrine for theater and intercontinental warfare and theater nuclear force programs. Soviet nuclear emphasis on the theater of military operations (TVD) emerges clearly. There is one omission, however, of a contemporary nature; namely, the current "debate" over whether USSR doctrine for theater warfare (specifically, NATO Europe) has shifted from a nuclear to a conventional emphasis. For understandable (if not persuasive) reasons, there is a strong movement today in favor of a new conventional-emphasis posture for NATO, putatively to provide a defense that will "raise the nuclear threshold." Since obviously NATO has control over only its own threshold of nuclear use, and not the Soviet one, it is necessary to argue that USSR theater doctrine now also has a conventional emphasis and that in the event of war in Europe the Soviet goal would also be to raise and observe the nuclear threshold. The authors do not confront this argument directly, or even refer to it, but their position can perhaps be deduced from their emphasis on the nuclear orientation of USSR doctrine, the continuity of that doctrine, and the continued intensive modernization of Soviet theater and tactical nuclear forces.

The reader may also wish to consult recent Soviet publications emanating over the past two years from the Frunze Military Academy: *Tactics* by V. G. Reznichenko and the third edition of *Tactical Maneuver* by V. D. Sverdlov. Together, these books cast doubt on any recent departure from conventional emphasis in Soviet doctrine.

Richard F. Staar is an experienced scholar and prolific writer on Soviet domestic and international policies. To his scholarship he has added practical experience in negotiating with the Soviets as United States Ambassador to the Mutual and Balanced Force Reduction (MBFR) talks. William T. Lee has been a highly respected professional intelligence analyst of Soviet military policies, programs, and expenditures for thirty-five years. This book represents a valuable collaboration that adds a great deal to our understanding of USSR military aims and policies.

William R. Van Cleave
Director, Defense and Strategic Studies Program
University of Southern California

SOVIET MILITARY POLICY
SINCE WORLD WAR II

Prior to joining the Defense Intelligence Agency in July 1981, William T. Lee had written the basis for this book. Updating and consolidation has been the sole responsibility of Richard F. Staar. The only exception is the brief section concerning updated economic priorities appearing on pages 179–181. The coauthors, however, both agree upon and are responsible for the interpretation of all source material. Nothing in this book should be construed as representing the position of the Defense Intelligence Agency or of the U.S. Department of Defense.

1 / Introduction

"It just baffles me why the Soviets these past few years behaved as they have." This statement was made in early December 1980 by Walter Mondale, former vice-president and the Democratic party's nominee for president of the United States in 1984. Nearly a decade earlier, Henry Kissinger, the secretary of state during two Republican administrations, had questioned whether strategic superiority could be a meaningful concept in the nuclear age. These two men are not alone in sharing such attitudes. Across the political spectrum, American policymakers wonder what the USSR is up to each time it tests new weapons systems, makes significant additions to its forces in the field.

Few studies exist on the formulation of Soviet military policy—on how and why the USSR decides to produce the weapons systems that it does. Available analyses are diverse in both methodology and findings. Most can establish no doctrinal or strategic reasons that explain why Soviet forces are developing the way they do. Hence, most conclude that the process is dominated by factors such as the political style of the leaders, the image these leaders seek to project at the moment, and parochial bureaucratic interests. Many analysts explain USSR military policy and decisionmaking by concepts like "action-reaction," the "arms race" between the superpowers, and the exploitation of each new technology that comes along. One study lists "history, culture, and values" as the dominant factors influencing Soviet decisions on defense spending.[1]

The basic thesis of this book is that official military doctrine and strategy clearly state both the reasons for and the objectives of the USSR military buildup. The essence of Soviet military policy is to attain the forces required by its doctrine and strategy, the final objectives of which are to be prepared to fight and to win wars at all levels, including a nuclear war. This is not to argue that the Kremlin plans to launch a nuclear war either according to a timetable or at some future opportune moment. The evidence clearly indicates, however, that the USSR will be prepared to do so if its leaders ever think it necessary. If one grants the Soviets the premises of their military doctrine and strategy, the evidence argues that their military policy is rational.

We advance this thesis for three basic reasons. First, the historical pattern of USSR weapons acquisition makes little sense except as an attempt to satisfy the requirements of doctrine and strategy. Second, forecasts of future Soviet weapons acquisitions based on this thesis have been relatively accurate, whereas those based on other interpretations of USSR motives have proven incorrect. Third, in their professional communications the Soviets themselves place the requirements of doctrine and strategy—with due allowance for USSR perceptions of the existing threat—at the head of their list of motivations.

The complex and expensive process originates in top political leaders' policy directives that translate Soviet military doctrine and strategy into weapons systems and forces in the field. Consequently, we will begin this book with an outline of the ruling party's military policy and a brief summary of the decisionmaking process.

PARTY POLICY AND WEAPONS ACQUISITION

USSR literature credits the Communist Party of the Soviet Union (CPSU) with making the decisions on all matters of military policy, major and minor. The CPSU is said to take the initiative on all major technological innovations in Soviet weaponry—nuclear weapons, missiles, electronics, and other advanced technologies—and on the organization of the armed forces as well as on the formulation of military doctrine and the approval of strategy.

The uniformed political officers in the Main Political Directorate of the Soviet Army and Navy, headed by General Colonel[2] Aleksei D. Lizichev, provide us with some of the most informative discussions about the CPSU's military policy and the factors that enter into its formulation. The organization to which these officers belong functions both as a directorate of the defense ministry and as a department in the CPSU Central Committee apparatus. It is incorrect to suppose that all officers with military rank are spokesmen for the defense establishment. Their interests may be at odds with those of the party. The spokesmen for party policies and interests are political officers. Therefore, when reading Soviet military literature, it is important to know whether the author with military rank is a line officer or a political officer.[3]

The immediate past head of the Main Political Directorate listed the seven components of CPSU military policy as follows:[4]

- Developing the economic and technological base for defense
- Producing weapons, equipment, and matériel
- Training the entire population for defense of the homeland
- Elaboration of a military doctrine
- Determination of the basic directions for development of the armed forces and their branches and combat arms
- Training military cadres
- Developing and implementing principles for training and educating personnel

According to both political and line officers who write for the General Staff's journal, *Military Thought*, the top political leaders make all decisions on weapons acquisition and funding required to implement the CPSU's military-technical policy.[5] Directives or decrees on military-technical policy are issued in the name of the Central Committee, jointly by the party and the government at each CPSU congress and, occasionally, at Central Committee plenary sessions. These directives are said to constitute the basis for weapons system development, production, and deployment programs incorporated into each five-year plan, specifically the subplan for military construction.[6]

According to the above cited sources in Soviet literature, the Central Committee's directives on military-technical policy cover at least the following elements:

- Principal types of new weapons to be developed and procured
- Relative priorities
- Target dates for development and/or production
- General funding levels
- Expansion of research and development and of the production base

The factors that determine CPSU decisions on weapons acquisition are said by the same sources to include:

- Requirements specified by military doctrine and strategy
- Estimates of the military threat
- Assessment of the foreign political situation and probable future developments
- Service missions and training
- Technological constraints and opportunities and feedback between technology and strategy
- Economic capabilities and constraints, such as production technology and funding
- Research findings on the effectiveness of various types of military operations and weapons systems
- Adequacy of existing weapons relative to mission requirements and the adversary's weaponry
- Manpower resources, i.e., numbers and skills

Given estimates of the existing threat and the technological and economic opportunities and constraints, the central objective of the party's military policy is to provide the weapons required by military doctrine and strategy. Military doctrine has two components—political and military-technical. The military-technical component overlaps with military strategy in the following areas: [7]

- Questions of force development
- Preparation and utilization of the armed forces in war
- The most important applications (*napravleniia*) of military forces in combat
- Equipping the forces with weaponry
- Organizational structure of the services
- Development of military art
- Requirements for combat operations of troops and their combat readiness

According to a former defense minister, A. A. Grechko, this "side of military doctrine points out the ways, means, and methods for the armed forces to fulfill assigned tasks." [8] Essentially, the tasks of the armed forces to which Grechko refers are synonymous with the missions assigned to the services by Soviet military strategy.

This strategy formulates specific requirements for the force and weapons needed to meet policy objectives, to develop plans for combat operations, and to prepare methods and procedures for training the services and maintaining the requisite degrees of readiness. This is an interactive process between military and party hierarchies. As stated by the editor of *Military Thought*, "*guided by CPSU policy*, our military technical policy has the task of *ensuring superiority* over the aggressive forces of imperialism in the hardware of war."[9] (Italics added.) Another prominent military writer commented:

> At the same time, military strategy is an area of practical activity of the top political and military leaders in organizing the requisite composition and arrangement of the armed forces, their development, their equipping with weapons and military hardware, provision of other military supplies, planning of strategic utilization and mobilization deployment, the establishment of strategic forces, maintenance of these forces in a continuous state of combat readiness and, in case of aggression, purposeful utilization of the armed forces to perform the military-political and strategic missions of war, and the attainment of victory.[10]

Some of the specific functions of military strategy include:

- Working out war plans to achieve the goals set by CPSU policy
- Specifying the objectives of military operations and the forms and methods for conducting them
- Providing an appreciation of the objectives of military research and development programs and of the capabilities of the probable enemies' deployed forces
- Planning and controlling the uninterrupted flow of supplies to the armed forces
- Providing detailed performance specifications for weapons and matériel, production requirements and schedules, construction of facilities, and measures to protect and mobilize the economy in the event of war
- Training and organizing the armed forces to achieve the political objectives of a war[11]

Regarding future force requirements, strategy determines the missions assigned to services and major force components; weapons requirements (specific performance characteristics) for research and development organizations; the best choices of weapons systems and mixes, given the alternatives; the quantities to be produced; and the requisite time schedules for deliveries.[12] To determine these requirements, strategy involves estimating how enemy forces will operate and how effective they will be.

It is evident that the Soviet military budget emerges as a result of translating CPSU policies and objectives into strategic requirements to meet these objectives and then deciding how much can be spent. In the words of another writer:

> Strategy defines the volume and product mix for military consumption covering the immediate future, which also determines expansion of military production, the aim of which is to supply combat equipment to large units and units [sic], to create reserves of weapons, ammunition and other military supplies needed by the armed forces when war begins. This can be used as a basis in determining the volume of military expenditures in the state budget.
>
> A decisive role in determining the volume of military expenditures is played by policy. It estimates the international situation, defines the military-political aims and tasks of strategy, and also assigns targets to the economy.[13]

In brief, the critical bureaucratic actors in the formulation and execution of USSR military policy include decisionmakers in five agencies:

- The Defense Council—a de facto subcommittee of the Politburo headed by the general secretary of the CPSU, who is also commander in chief of the armed forces
- The defense industry department in the CPSU Central Committee Secretariat and possibly other components
- The Ministry of Defense
  a. The General Staff
  b. The Main Military Council directorates
  c. The military councils and staffs of the five combat services (strategic rocket forces, air and missile defense, ground, air, and navy)
- The Military Industrial Commission—essentially a subcommittee of the USSR Council of Ministers that manages military research and development as well as weapons production
- The USSR Gosplan—the central economic planning commission in the Council of Ministers

These organizations formulate the party's military-technical policy, translate policy into research and development and also production schedules in the five-year and annual economic plans, and subsequently manage the execution of those plans. This process can be summarized as follows:

• Each service of the Soviet armed forces probably formulates a weapons system acquisitions plan to carry out its missions.[14] Missions are specified by USSR military doctrine and strategy, integrated into a uniform plan for military operations in the event of war, and tested for feasibility in training and exercises. Each service has at least one senior military academy—the faculties of which perform a considerable amount of operations research—and possibly a number of research institutes. The services also have direct ties with scientific research institutes, design bureaus, and the series production plants of the industrial ministries that support them. In other words, resources and information needed to formulate the requirements for current and future weapons systems are in place.

• The General Staff probably reviews, coordinates, evaluates, and integrates the requirements submitted by the services and suggests innovations based upon its own analyses. In addition to the research and studies performed by service academies and institutes, the General Staff directly controls its own military academy, named after K. E. Voroshilov, to conduct operations research for all the Soviet armed services. It probably also has several research institutes as well as access to all research institutes and design bureaus of the industrial ministries, foreign intelligence, the USSR Academy of Sciences, and other sources of information and proposals concerning new weapons systems and technologies.

• The General Staff also probably integrates the draft plan for weapons acquisition that is reviewed in the Main Military Council chaired by the defense minister and is subsequently forwarded to the Defense Council through the Central Committee Secretariat—presumably by the department in charge of defense industries.

• Following instructions from the Defense Council, the Central Committee Secretariat produces a draft of CPSU military-technical policy. This document takes into account the political leadership's assessment of the internal situation, of research and development, and of economic opportunities and capabilities. In preparing this draft, both the Defense Council and the Secretariat have their own network of formal and informal channels to the weapons design bureaus and the Academy of Sciences, in addition to the inputs provided by the Ministry of Defense.

• The decree is then circulated throughout the party and the military and industrial bureaucracies for review, comment, and staff work. The USSR Gosplan, whose deputy chairman for military affairs is probably a general officer, costs out the proposed weapons development and production programs and examines overall implications for the Soviet economy.

 • After this staff review, the Defense Council and the Politburo make their final decisions, and CPSU military-technical policy emerges as the military construction component in the five-year plan. Results of this entire process become a constituent part of the five-year plan approved by each CPSU congress.

In effect, each annual economic plan requires a review of the five-year plan and a commitment to development and production schedules as well as corresponding resource allocations. Military policy is reviewed by the Central Committee, which also scrutinizes the long-range plan each year. Consequently, the five-year plan is modified during the course of implementation. In addition, foreign developments and technological innovations lead to special interim decrees on particular military technologies and programs. Although by no means immutable, the party's military-technical policy decrees and the five-year plans for military construction definitely provide the basic conceptual, bureaucratic, and resource allocation framework within which weapons system development and production occur in the USSR.

Whether the Military Industrial Commission (VPK) of the USSR Council of Ministers functions as a formal participant in preparing these plans is unclear. Its senior party member (Defense Minister D. F. Ustinov from 1976 until his death in December 1984) participated in formulating both CPSU military-technical policy and final decisions on the plans. Most likely, the primary mission of VPK is to manage the entire weapons development and production process once the Defense Council and Politburo have decided on the military construction component of the five-year and annual economic plans.

As described by both USSR political and line officers, decisions on weapons acquisition are rational in the sense that—given their perceptions of the existing threat and other factors listed above—Kremlin leaders have chosen to develop, produce, and deploy weapons systems designed to satisfy the requirements of their military strategy. The subsequent discussion of weapons system acquisition, particularly after 1960, should demonstrate our basic point.

This is not to argue that Soviet planners are always able to foresee the future better than others. In fact, they have been surprised repeatedly by unexpected U.S. technological developments. In every case, however, the USSR has responded to overcome these unanticipated developments as quickly as possible. Internal political power struggles, external crises, economic and technological constraints, and other factors notwithstanding, during the past four decades the Soviets consistently have attempted to acquire the military forces required to win a nuclear war against the NATO coalition.

On the USSR side, the origins of this process go back to an appreciation of the usefulness of nuclear weapons that was already well formed in the late 1930s. After the end of World War II, Stalin accelerated and expanded programs in most areas of contemporary military technology. This is discussed in Chapter 2.

2

From World War II to 1960

The years between the end of World War II and 1960 represented an exceedingly turbulent period in many respects. By 1948 Joseph V. Stalin had reduced USSR armed forces to about 2.8 million men and had given first priority to reconstruction of the domestic economy, with the objective of reaching the prewar level by 1950. On the other hand, the Soviet dictator spared no expense to develop those military technologies in which his country had been most deficient: nuclear weapons, radar, missiles, and jet engines. He also instituted construction of a large, essentially conventional, navy. Although the precise size and composition of his naval vision is subject to dispute, Stalin did have a large force in mind, and his development of a conventional navy seems to have had little relationship to efforts in the areas mentioned above.[1]

Although, in public, he deprecated the importance of nuclear weapons, Stalin appreciated the strategic significance of both nuclear weapons and the long-range bombers and missiles needed to deliver them. He recognized the importance of strategic air and missile defenses. The origins of almost all contemporary strategic and tactical USSR nuclear, missile, jet aircraft, and electronics programs go back to the days of Stalin. Perhaps this peculiar ambiguity between public positions and personal priorities can be best described by an outline of the history of Soviet nuclear weapons and ballistic missile programs.

Strategic Nuclear Weapons

Stalin and the Bomb

When Harry S. Truman told Stalin at Potsdam about the American success in testing a nuclear weapon, Truman thought this announcement would come as a great surprise. According to the president, the Soviet dictator showed little interest but expressed the hope that the United States would put the weapon to good use against the Japanese.[2] Of course, Stalin knew a great deal about the American nuclear weapons program as a result of espionage. More important, Soviet scientists had alerted him to the potential of nuclear weapons long before Albert Einstein's letter to President Franklin D. Roosevelt led to the Manhattan Project. The following milestones of the early Soviet nuclear weapons program are taken from an article by two political officers describing USSR weapons acquisition policy and published in the General Staff journal *Voennaia mysl'*:[3]

1. Nuclear physics work began on "a wide front" in the 1930s.
2. By the beginning of World War II, academicians A. F. Ioffe, I. V. Kurchatov, L. D. Landau, their students, and "other outstanding Soviet scientists and engineers had outlined the main directions in the resolution of the nuclear problem."
3. The German attack in June 1941 stopped the program. Major laboratories at Kharkov and Leningrad were lost or evacuated. Kurchatov and a great number of his coworkers were put to work on more immediate projects.
4. At the end of 1942, Kurchatov was again placed in charge of the nuclear program. "At his command, scientists were recalled from the army and other military assignments, from blockaded Leningrad and *places of occupation*." (Emphasis added.)
5. At the beginning of 1943, a CPSU Central Committee decision directed Kurchatov to organize "a new scientific establishment designated for research on the uranium problem" in Moscow. "Scientists and engineers of the most varied specialities were attracted to research in the field of the creation of nuclear weapons."
6. After Hiroshima and Nagasaki "the party Central Committee outlined the primary state task—to eliminate in the shortest period of time the monopoly of the United States in nuclear weapons."
7. To coordinate and direct the scientists, engineers, and industrial plants, the Soviets had "a specially created government organ,"

under the direction of B. L. Vannikov and assisted by A. P. Zaveniagin, V. A. Malyshev, M. G. Pervukhin, and E. P. Slavskii.

8. Development of nuclear propulsion systems for ships and submarines was carried on "simultaneously" with the development of nuclear weapons.

No doubt the USSR program was accelerated with information provided by Klaus Fuchs and other spies; how much will probably never be known. Clearly, however, the Soviets already realized the potential of nuclear weapons by the late 1930s. An article published in the *Saturday Evening Post* in 1939 described for the layman the first fission experiments at the Kaiser Wilhelm Institute two years earlier and the potential of weapons using uranium isotopes for yielding thousands of tons of TNT in explosive power. Stalin knew what his own scientists were exploring before World War II began. The program was re-established in late 1942, just as the battle for Stalingrad was reaching its climax; the extraordinary authority given Kurchatov could only have come from Stalin. Feigning disinterest to Truman, and subsequently playing down the military significance of nuclear weapons, was a pretense that Stalin adopted while he was doing everything he could to overcome the Soviet lag in the production of weapons and delivery systems. The USSR was behind not because the Generalissimo failed to appreciate either the political significance or the military potential of nuclear weapons, but because Soviet technology and industry simply could not compete with those of the United States in translating scientific experiments into usable hardware. American achievements added urgency to USSR efforts, but the Soviets did not start their program in reaction to that of the United States.

Stalin also assigned high priority to the development of long-range delivery systems—both aircraft and missiles—and to a variety of other technologies for the nuclear age. In order to have an initial delivery system for nuclear weapons, he personally gave the Soviet aircraft designer A. N. Tupolev just thirty-six months to manufacture a production prototype of the American B-29 from several that had landed in Siberia.[4] The schedule was met, and the USSR produced more than 1,000 of these aircraft, which it called the TU-4.

Early History of Soviet Ballistic Missile Development

Five years after becoming commander in chief of the Strategic Rocket Forces (SRF), General of the Army V. F. Tolubko published a biography of the first SRF commander, Chief Marshal of Artillery M. I. Nedelin, who had been killed in October 1960 by a Soviet ICBM that exploded on its launch pad. According to this account, soon after the end of World War II, Stalin himself established a supraministerial authority to develop long-range ballistic missiles for delivery of nuclear weapons. The highlights of the program were as follows: [5]

1. The missile authority may have been established in 1945 or as late as 1946. The core of this new organization apparently consisted of D. F. Ustinov (later to become a marshal of the Soviet Union and defense minister); S. P. Korolev; N. N. Voronov; Nedelin; and possibly Academician I. N. Kurchatov, who also was a key member of the nuclear weapons group. Other senior officers involved included marshals (of the Soviet Union) G. K. Zhukov, A. M. Vassilevskii, and L. A. Govorov.

2. The exact date of Nedelin's participation in the missile group is unclear. He probably became involved during April 1946, when he was appointed chief of staff for artillery, although it could have been as late as November 1948, when Nedelin took over the chief artillery directorate in the USSR Ministry of Defense.

3. In 1946 the first missile unit was formed from regiments of two Guards "Katiusha" units. Others were established later from artillery units that had distinguished records in the war.

4. Research on long-range rockets began at Korolev's design bureau in 1946, and the first flight test of a missile took place on 18 October 1947. Within a short period eleven more missiles were flight tested, and Korolev began working on a longer-range design with a larger payload. (This may have marked the beginning of the Soviet ICBM program.)

5. Nedelin participated in formulating the prospective plan for the first missiles put into production; coordinated the plan with the General Staff; and gave monthly reports to the minister of defense and to the USSR State Economic Planning Commission. Occasionally, the group reported directly to Stalin, who always remained well informed.

6. Missiles were deployed in the early 1950s, probably not long after Stalin's death. The referenced deployments probably represented a small number of units equipped with missiles in the 350 to 650 km range and possibly were considered part of the Supreme High Command reserve.

7. Sometime during the 1950s Nedelin formed a "particular organ of control—a special staff which occupied itself with developing the organizational-strategic basis of utilizing missile units."

8. Leonid I. Brezhnev was involved in the supraministerial group early, although the precise date is not specified. In 1952 he became a Central Committee secretary, and Tolubko describes his office as the

meeting place in which many of the most important decisions on the missile program were made. (No dates are given for these meetings.)

9. Preparation for the launch of the first ICBM began during April or May 1957 under a state commission headed by K. I. Rudnev, with Nedelin as his deputy.

10. When various types of missiles and nuclear warheads became available, there were three schools of thought about how to add them to the armed forces: (1) distribution among existing services (apparently with little change in the organizational structure), (2) restriction to the Soviet air forces and fleets, and (3) establishment of a new strategic service. According to Tolubko, the third option was supported by most members of the Central Committee, the government, and the military. When the SRF was formed in December 1959 by government decree, Nedelin became commander in chief.

11. A particularly important ICBM test took place the following April. There were some technical difficulties. Nedelin took responsibility for the launch. It was successful, and the missile was recommended for production and deployment.

Tolubko's only reference to Stalin's role is that he was always well informed on the program when Nedelin gave him progress reports. It may never be known whether or not establishing a long-range ballistic missile program parallel to the nuclear one was Stalin's idea, but he certainly reinforced it with all the resources of the Soviet state.

Other Strategic Weapons and Advanced Technology

According to Nikita S. Khrushchev, research and development of an antiballistic missile (ABM) defense began even as long-range ballistic systems were being conceived.[6] General of the Army (later Marshal of the Soviet Union) P. F. Batitskii subsequently provided corroboration. According to him, the ABM program started soon after the end of World War II and was approved by Stalin along with all of the other USSR nuclear strategic defensive programs—interceptors, SAMs, and radars.[7]

Whereas long-range ballistic missiles took many years to develop, it was possible to proceed faster with aircraft. The principal results of these efforts, however, did not appear until after Stalin's death. The rapidity of Soviet development of jet-powered medium and heavy bombers surprised the United States and led to talk of a "bomber gap." As soon as Tupolev had finished copying the piston engine B-29, he was ordered to develop long-range jet aircraft.

Stalin's nuclear weapons and missile programs provided the necessary technological base for results that began to appear by 1948–49 when radars and jet aircraft were being delivered to the Soviet armed forces in large numbers. Initially, most of this equipment went to air defense forces for protection of the USSR from American bombers. In 1948 PVO Strany, the national air defense forces, were separated from the ground forces, and in 1954 their first commander in chief was designated.[8] The Soviet air force and Chinese pilots (flying MIG jets) defended the air space over the Yalu during much of the Korean War. Deployment of the SA-1 at Moscow evidently began in the early 1950s, since two concentric rings of these air defense missiles reportedly became operational in 1954.[9]

Stalin and Soviet Nuclear Strategy

If Stalin understood the military potential of nuclear weapons,[10] why did he stifle discussion and formulation of doctrine and strategy for the nuclear age? Two reasonable hypotheses center on his megalomania and on his desire to cover up responsibility for the military debacle in the summer of 1941.

The number of victims of Stalin's paranoia between 1928 and his death in 1953 probably rivals the total casualties in most recorded wars of history through 1945. That he appointed himself chief and sole interpreter of Marxist-Leninist dogma is well known. Apparently, he also made himself chief military strategist of the USSR. An article in a Soviet military history journal, cited by Harriet Fast Scott, provides some insight.[11]

> In 1935 at the Frunze Military Academy, a military history department was formed. According to the department head, a 32-hour course of lectures was envisaged on the theory of strategy. The deputy commandant, in looking over the program, asked: "What is this strategy course? Strategy is Comrade Stalin's personal occupation and it isn't any of our business."

The article goes on to state that the academy commandant, Marshal B. M. Shaposhnikov, overruled his deputy and ordered the lectures on strategy prepared. However, they were never read. It is not surprising, therefore, that after World War II officers in the USSR armed forces were not permitted to discuss publicly the implication of nuclear weapons for Soviet military strategy.

Stalin had another reason for downplaying the importance of nuclear weapons: Their great destructiveness offered the potential for a truly decisive surprise attack that might be accomplished in a few hours. The issue could not be discussed, because Stalin had refused to heed warnings of German preparations to attack the USSR in 1941; as a result, the *Wehrmacht* achieved both strategic and tactical surprise and almost won the war that year. This, of course, Stalin could not admit. Hence, the debacle of Soviet arms in the first months and the vast loss of territory and population became one more example of the infallible Generalissimo's wise plan to defeat the Germans by withdrawing to Moscow and Stalingrad while preparing the victorious counteroffensive. He did not need any discussion of how nuclear weapons, coupled with long-range bombers and missiles, could have done in a few hours what German panzers and tactical aircraft almost accomplished in a few months.

Two Stalinist legacies for USSR military strategy are most apparent today. First, the Soviets continue to believe that no single arm or branch of service can win a war and that success requires integrated operations by all arms and services. Second, nuclear targeting strategy formulated in Stalin's time continues to dominate the development of USSR strategic missile forces. The SS-9 and the latest models of the SS-18 and SS-19 ICBMs are the direct products of a nuclear targeting strategy that emphasizes counterforce operations and rejects the targeting of the enemy population.

Critical advanced technologies were developed under Stalin as fast as the USSR's economic and technological resources would permit. The armed forces were doubled (to nearly 6 million men) during the Korean War. Nuclear weapons were developed, and a broadly based missile program was well on its way. Initial models of USSR jet fighters and radars were in production. Meanwhile, conventional armaments were not neglected. Professional military personnel could not write about the implications of the new weapons, however, and Soviet military doctrine remained frozen in Stalin's "permanently operating factors." [12] Judging from the speed with which articles on the implications of nuclear weapons appeared after the Generalissimo's death, however, a great deal of thinking must have been going on (even if writing about doctrine and strategy had been Stalin's sole prerogative). Nevertheless, the only identifiable weapons program his successors cancelled involved construction of a large conventional navy.

THE AXIAL PERIOD, 1953–60

The Initial Debate

Six months after Stalin's death in 1953, the editor of *Military Thought*, General Major N. Talenskii, published the first article challenging the validity of the "permanently operating factors" for the nuclear age and initiated a discussion of the implications of nuclear weapons for Soviet military strategy. The initial discussion of new strategic concepts in this journal lasted from September 1953 to March 1955, and most of it has become available to American scholars. During the next four to five years, however, the USSR hammered out its new military doctrine and strategy for the nuclear age in sources that are still not available in the West. The subsequent discussion is based only on arguments that surfaced frequently in the Soviet press during the late 1950s.

Most of the basic tenets of contemporary USSR military doctrine and strategy were formulated during the axial period 1953–60 but were not published openly until 1960–62. Consequently, almost all of the discussion on this subject is deferred to the next chapter. Here the focus remains primarily on the results of the initial debate in 1953–55, for which the evidence appears to be relatively complete. This discussion appears to have resulted in a consensus on the following points: [13]

- The "law of victory" is the objective of war.
- Victory is achieved only by decisively defeating the enemy militarily.
- The enemy can be defeated only by destroying his armed forces with decisive blows, executed according to a single strategic concept by all available forces and weapons.
- Victory is assured by the cumulative combination of military, economic, and moral-political potentialities.
- Victory in a nuclear war is best ensured by pre-empting the enemy's nuclear attack.

These tenets from the 1953–55 debate—particularly that victory is a feasible outcome of a nuclear war—are the foundation blocks of Soviet nuclear strategy to this day.

Even with the benefit of hindsight, it would be difficult to improve on Herbert S. Dinerstein's analysis of those portions of the discussions during the late 1950s that surfaced in the USSR military press and in speeches by Soviet leaders. [14] The process of formulating the new doctrine and strategy for the nuclear age had been largely completed before 1962, from which time the Kremlin dates the "nuclear revolution in military affairs." According to General of the Army Kurochkin: [15]

The process of change and basic revolutionary transformations took nearly seven years and was basically completed by the end of 1961. By this time a modern military doctrine had been formed, definite strategic views were formulated, and effective methods of preparing for and conducting operations and military actions by the formations of various branches of the armed services had been worked out.

Apparently, the first official statement[16] of the new military doctrine for the nuclear age that emerged from these discussions was made by Khrushchev in a speech to the fourth session of the USSR Supreme Soviet, initially published in *Pravda* on 15 January 1960 and subsequently as a pamphlet.[17]

Major Weapons Acquisition Programs During the Axial Period

While the USSR debated the doctrinal and strategic implications of nuclear weapons, jet aircraft, long-range missiles, and defensive missiles and radars, development and production of the new weapons proceeded as quickly as R&D organizations could develop prototypes and factories could produce them. Thus the axial period 1953–60 was not only the source of Soviet strategic nuclear concepts, but also the period during which the USSR established the scientific and industrial base for the development and production of successive families of weapons systems. These systems were designed to fight and win a nuclear war—both by the traditional means of defeating the enemy and occupying his territory and by the new approach of simultaneously limiting damage to the Soviet Union from the enemy's strategic nuclear weapons. Obviously, the size of that scientific and industrial base has now been expanded several times over, but the basic patterns of weapons system development and deployment have changed little, if at all.

During the axial period, weapons system development and deployment began to provide some damage-limiting capabilities. The first models of all-weather fighter aircraft—the MIG-17 and the SU-9—were produced for PVO Strany.[18] Understandably, deployment of the SA-1 was limited to Moscow because it was an extremely expensive first generation surface-to-air missile. Deployment of the SA-2, the largest and probably the most expensive single air defense procurement program in the world, began in the late 1950s.[19] Originally designed to counter only high-altitude penetrators, an SA-2 battery succeeded in shooting down an American U-2 high-altitude reconnaissance aircraft in 1960, and it has subsequently been exported to most Soviet allies and client states. As of 1985 both the SA-1 and SA-2 were still in the Soviet inventory,[20] although the SA-1 has been replaced largely by the SA-10. The SA-2 is still in service, but it is also being replaced by the SA-10. Several new model air defense radars for detection and surveillance were also deployed in large numbers during the 1953–60 period.[21]

Although the Soviet navy's damage-limiting missions apparently date from the late 1950s—including design and development—most of the hardware did not become operational until the following decade. In 1955–56 the USSR modified a Z-class diesel-powered submarine to carry two of the ground force's short-range missiles. Construction of the G-class (diesel) and H-class (nuclear) submarines armed with the 350 nautical mile–range SS-N-4 ballistic missile began in the late 1950s. More or less parallel to these SLBM programs was the Soviet navy's adaptation of cruise missiles to submarines—first, by modifying a W-class (diesel) to carry two missiles and, second, by constructing the J-class (diesel) and the E-class (nuclear) submarines armed with the SS-N-3 cruise missiles. (The SS-N-3 cruise missiles also have a range of up to 350 nautical miles.) The first four E-class boats (E-I) may have been intended to attack land targets, but the subsequent models (E-II) were assigned to anticarrier/antinavy missions.[22]

Considerable progress was made in strategic offensive capabilities for limiting damage to the USSR by counterforce operations in the Eurasian TVDs during the axial period. The Long Range Air Force (LRA) was equipped with some 1,000 Badger medium jet bombers, and initial deployment of SS-3 and SS-4 MRBMs began in the late 1950s. It was decided, however, not to produce a large number of heavy bombers, probably because ICBMs would become available before the heavy bombers could be produced and crews could be trained to use them. At the end of World War II, the Soviets had decided that missiles were far superior to aircraft for strategic strikes against fixed targets.

Priorities in the Eurasian TVDs and technological and economic constraints in 1957–58 led to decisions on strategic missile deployment that shaped both the realities and the perception of the military equation between the two superpowers until the mid-1970s. Originally, the USSR may have intended to deploy some significant number—say 50 to 150—of its first generation intercontinental ballistic missile (ICBM), the SS-6. Although this huge, awkward missile has been the workhorse of the Soviet space program for about two-and-a-half decades, it represents a very expensive and relatively ineffective ICBM. Probably because of this, in formulating the seven year plan (1959–65), the USSR decided to restrict the SS-6 to token deployment and to concentrate instead on the second generation SS-7 and SS-8 ICBMs. At the same time it gave priority to the deployment of the 700 medium- and intermediate-range ballistic missile (MR/IRBM) launchers—the SS-4 and SS-5—required to meet strategic nuclear-targeting requirements in the Eurasian TVDs. This set of decisions, combined with America's reaction of uncertainty and its fear that the Soviets would deploy hundreds of SS-6s in the early 1960s, led to the Minuteman and Polaris programs. Moscow had almost certainly not foreseen these programs when it made its decisions in 1957–58. These developments determined the strategic force balance of the 1960s and created a perception in the United States of the "missile gap," which, strictly speaking, only involved an ICBM gap.

To camouflage the decision that gave first priority to the Eurasian TVDs while the SS-7 and SS-8 ICBMs were being developed, the Soviet leaders, and Khrushchev in particular, engaged in a campaign of strategic deception designed to convince the world that the USSR was producing and deploying ICBMs in large numbers. This campaign contributed to the rapid deployment of Minuteman and Polaris by the United States, which exacerbated Soviet weakness in intercontinental strategic missiles. Khrushchev's October 1962 bluff over Cuba contributed a great deal to the mistaken Western perception that he was an advocate of minimum deterrence.

During the axial period the Soviets formulated their damage-limiting strategy, continued development of the military R&D base, and reorganized their armed forces and assigned each service its missions. However, they were able to acquire only the mere beginnings of the military capability required to satisfy their objectives. Concern for the proximate threat in the Eurasian TVDs determined the composition of USSR strategic forces through most of the 1960s and, combined with Soviet technological and economic constraints, confirmed American superiority in intercontinental strategic forces for nearly two decades. At the beginning of the axial period, Georgii K. Malenkov had stated that nuclear war would destroy civilization—that there could be no victors but only vanquished in such a war. This was and has continued to be the prevalent view in the West. Khrushchev rejected it, however, and affirmed the possibility of victory by means of a damage-limiting strategy. His successors have reaffirmed this objective and consistently sought to achieve the requisite military capabilities. Whereas there was much political and military turbulence during the axial period, the elements of continuity since that time are far more impressive.

National Economic Priorities in the 1950s

Economic priorities underwent several rapid shifts during the 1953–60 axial period. Some of these changes reflected the Soviet reaction to the Korean War. Others were related to the new political leadership following Stalin's death. Whether the USSR ordered the North Koreans to attack across the 38th parallel or simply agreed to provide them with all the necessary military and economic support is beside the point. Without approval and material aid from Moscow, there would have been no Korean War.

Through 1953 production of civilian machinery and equipment was frozen at 1950 levels. During these years almost all of the increase in output went to the military in the form of weapons. In order to mask rearmament programs, procurement was removed from the official USSR defense budget.[23] Total official defense expenditures rose from around 8 billion rubles in 1950 to around 11 billion rubles in 1955. Most of this increase occurred during the period 1951–53.

The evidence for change in the definition of the official Soviet defense budget during the Korean War was fairly straightforward, but it was almost universally overlooked by Western analysts. In the mid-1950s Khrushchev revealed that the USSR had increased the number of personnel on active military duty by nearly 3 million during the Korean War and that the average cost per active duty person was just over 1,000 rubles per year. Nevertheless, between 1950 and 1955 the official defense budget increased by only 3 billion rubles. This was hardly enough to pay for the increased manpower costs, much less the growth in other operating costs and military construction that necessarily accompanied partial mobilization. Procurement also increased rapidly during this period, so something—most likely procurement—was removed from the official defense budget.

Although many Western observers remained skeptical of the official Soviet defense budget, until the late 1970s most American academics continued to accept these figures as a valid measure of USSR defense costs (excluding R&D, which was assumed to be included in reported outlays for science). For approximately fifteen years (1960–74), the CIA estimated actual Soviet defense expenditures (using its direct costing or building-block method) to be essentially the same as the official defense budget (excluding military R&D, which the CIA—following the lead of Rand analysts—also erroneously assumed to be located entirely in reported outlays for "science").

Khrushchev's appointment as first secretary of the CPSU in September 1953 was widely interpreted in the West as signaling increased military expenditures. In fact, he reduced Soviet defense outlays by about one billion rubles during the period 1955–58 by cutting manpower, scrapping Stalin's conventional navy plans, and shifting the USSR defense effort toward missiles, electronics, and nuclear weapons. During the first three years of Khrushchev's ascendancy, military outlays declined from about 12 percent to about 9 percent, whereas consumption actually rose from about 60 percent to about 62 percent of Soviet GNP. In 1959 the rising cost of new weapons reversed the trend and drove USSR defense expenditures back up to 1955 levels, although, because of the rapid growth of the GNP during that period, the military's percentage remained essentially the same. In most years after 1959 defense expanded rapidly, and its share of GNP rose slowly but steadily. Since World War II the last period in which consumption increased as a percentage of GNP was 1955–58. Since then military outlays have risen consistently in USSR national economic priorities. This growth has been at the expense of both investment and consumption, but primarily of consumption.

In summary, the three basic characteristics of contemporary Soviet military policy that coalesced during the axial period 1953–60 were a war-fighting, damage-limiting strategy; development of the weapons systems required to achieve the objectives of this strategy; and (by the end of the period) a steady shift in Soviet national priorities toward the military establishment. The next chapter discusses the content of Soviet nuclear doctrine and strategy.

3

Soviet Nuclear Doctrine and Strategy from Khrushchev to the Present

At times, both traditional Russian and contemporary Soviet conduct have proven enigmatic to even the most perceptive Western observers. However, there is nothing enigmatic about the USSR's strategic concepts for the nuclear age as initially publicized between 1960 and 1962.[1] Soviet strategic nuclear concepts differ on a number of critical issues from prevailing Western concepts and from most of our conventional wisdom about their ideas.

Many in the West tend to view the concept of deterrence as mutual; that is, they see it as a condition that would make starting a war disadvantageous to all. Moreover, they tend to equate the stability of deterrence with parity in nuclear forces. The Soviets consider deterrence to be one-sided; they must make war unprofitable for the coalition of the United States and NATO. They believe they must strive for a situation in which the Western alliance will be incapable of circumscribing their options. Consequently, USSR and Warsaw Pact forces must make unreasonable the West's use of its deterrent capabilities while holding U.S. and NATO military and economic assets at risk to Soviet forces. Hence, according to the view from Moscow, deterrence is stable only when USSR nuclear and non-nuclear forces are superior—not when they are equal to those of the West. Additionally, the dominant Western perception is that nuclear war would have no political objectives in the traditional sense and could not be fought to either victory or defeat. The Soviets, in contrast, plan to fight a nuclear war like any other war, for political objectives, and plan to win it by military means.

SOVIET CONCEPTS OF DETERRENCE

Since 1956—when Khrushchev proclaimed that nuclear war between imperialism and "socialism," as personified by the two superpowers, is not fatally
inevitable—the USSR has elaborated its own concept of deterrence. When
the Soviets talk to one another, however, there is nothing mutual about it.
They modify the concept only if they are trying to influence foreign public
opinion. The USSR is quite serious about deterring an American nuclear attack, but it rejects any notion that the United States is equally justified in
seeking to deter a Soviet attack. Deterrence is to be unilateral; it is intended
to provide Moscow with a variety of options against the United States, but
free the USSR from the prospect of an American strike.

In the Soviet view, nuclear deterrence has three basic components: [2]

1. The general balance (or "correlation of forces") of political, economic, and military power and the socio-psychological characteristics of society and the population
2. Military doctrine and strategy
3. The military balance of forces

Only the latter two components will be dealt with here. Because the USSR
and its allies must deter the coalition of the United States and NATO from
launching a nuclear attack, any change in the general military balance of
forces in favor of the East strengthens deterrence; any change in favor of the
West increases the risk of war.

The foregoing is based on classic, tautological Marxist reasoning. First,
"capitalism" is driven to war by its internal politico-socioeconomic contradictions. Second, the rulers of capitalist countries recognize that Soviet-style
"socialism" is the heir-presumptive to the historical process. Therefore,
Western capitalists are driven by class hatred to make war on the East's "so-
cialists." The first attack took the form of intervention during the Russian
civil war. Between the two world wars the West engaged in various forms of
political and economic warfare against the USSR. During the Second World
War the "imperialists" again resorted to war against Soviet "socialism";
their paladin Hitler marched East in 1941. Because Hitler was on the wrong
side of the class struggle, he met with inevitable defeat. [3]

In the Soviet view, the Second World War represented a turning point in
history for three basic reasons. First, despite the enormous losses it suffered,
the USSR emerged much stronger politically, morally, economically, and
militarily. As one editorial stated: [4]

The victory of the Soviet people and their armed forces over the strike forces of international imperialism is of worldwide historical importance. This victory created favorable conditions for the development and victory of socialist revolutions in the countries of Europe and Asia, the formation of the world system of socialism, and successes of the national liberation struggle of peoples against the colonial yoke. All of this led to a serious weakening of the positions of imperialism and reaction to the strengthening and growth of the international forces of socialism and democracy.

Second, World War II proved that there are "no such forces in the world which can defeat socialism." Third, the USSR considers its rapid economic recovery from the devastation of this war as further proof of the superiority of the "socialist system" over the economic systems of "imperialism."[5]

The above reasoning explains why the Soviets believe that, despite their international politico-economic drive toward a nuclear war, "imperialism" is reluctant to engage the "socialist camp" militarily. Because "internal contradictions" among imperialist states have become more acute, the "imperialists" sense that another world war would be the graveyard of their system.

The "imperialists" are driven to exercise their lust for war against revolutionary and national liberation movements in the nation-states that have emerged from the pre–World War II colonial system.[6] In the Soviet assessment, the imperialists have lost virtually every one of these wars (and will continue to lose them) because the USSR is able to increase aid to the revolutionary and national liberation movements. The Soviet Union is also able to deter the imperialists from applying their full power against these movements. Failures in such wars exacerbate the "internal contradictions" among imperialist states and within the international imperialist system as a whole. Hence, the USSR's ability to extend the scope of deterrence beyond its own borders widens the "peace zone" and hastens the day when Moscow's protection may be able to cover the masses who struggle for peace and "socialism" within the bastions of imperialism.

According to the Soviets, this view of deterrence is corroborated by history. "All wars which the USSR had occasion to wage were forced, retaliatory and directed against repelling aggression."[7] Whose idea it was to invade South Korea may never be known, but the Soviets provided the war matériel. In a book they have even admitted that their air force participated in the fighting.[8] They continue to insist, however—and may even believe themselves—that the United States started the Korean conflict.

The USSR also rejects the proposition that its actions after World War II created NATO and led to the rearmament of West Germany. The Soviets believe that they installed communist regimes in Eastern Europe after that war to save those countries from imperialism. In other words, NATO and West

German rearmament had always been the twin objectives of imperialist statesmen. The USSR takes no responsibility for its contributions to the instigation of the cold war and to the creation of the military forces it most fears. According to the Soviet perception, the foregoing events were a natural manifestation of imperialism's innate aggressiveness and hatred of "socialism." As one high-ranking officer stated, "We proceed from the fact that the sole source of wars is imperialism." [9]

When the Soviets win a war they believe that they are not victors or conquerors like others but agents of history's justice against evil enemies who have outlived their time. "The class enemy was and remains the same—wicked and crafty, ready to commit any crime for the sake of his mercenary interests. Not having a future, he wants to take the future from all peace-loving peoples, above all from the peoples building a new world—the world of socialism." [10] The USSR military is not designed for ordinary predatory war but for a war "against forces which give rise to aggression and war. Victories of the Soviet Army are not simply victories of one force over another but an expression of the triumph of that which is new and advanced over that which is old and reactionary, a victory of true humanity and humanism over imperialist robbery and atrocity." [11] The invasion of Czechoslovakia in 1968 represented a "clear confirmation of the loyalty of the Soviet armed forces to their noble mission." [12]

As a Soviet political officer phrased it, peace is not something you ask of the imperialists; it is something you force on them by your own military power. [13] Despite pretense during diplomatic negotiations, the Soviet worldview excludes any acknowledgment of mutuality or equality of interests in matters of national security.

PRINCIPAL TENETS OF SOVIET MILITARY DOCTRINE AND STRATEGY

The new USSR military doctrine and strategy for the nuclear age made its initial appearance in four publications [14] during the period 1960–62. Essentially, military doctrine defines the nature of a future war, probable adversaries, Soviet objectives in such a war, general characteristics of the forces required, and policies for preparedness. [15] Military strategy specifies how the objectives of doctrine are to be achieved, what forces and weapons are required, and the interrelationships between military requirements and economic and technological capabilities. Additionally, it specifies military services and missions, principles of civil defense, resource and logistics requirements, and leadership and command of military forces and assesses the strategic views of the probable enemy.[16]

Doctrine is formulated by the highest political leaders, with input from the most senior military officers. Strategy is developed by the military establishment and subsequently reviewed and approved by the political leadership. Normally the Soviets use these two terms precisely, but the "military-technical" aspect of doctrine overlaps with the force requirements component of strategy.[17]

The following discussion begins with doctrine and proceeds through strategy. Most of the basic sources were published during the 1960s and have been referenced in a prior publication.[18] Additional citations are provided from *Military Thought* and from sources published during the 1970s. The principal tenets and objectives of Soviet military doctrine and strategy are the following:

- A war between the USSR and the Warsaw Pact on one side and the United States and NATO on the other would be a third and decisive conflict between Eastern "socialism" and Western "imperialism" for domination of the globe. Such a war would be an intercontinental, coalition war involving all the "basic" countries.[19]
- Such a war would be "just" for the USSR but "unjust" for the West. Like previous conflicts, it would be a continuation of politics by violent means. Because a nuclear world war would be so destructive, however, the USSR would not be justified in initiating it. The Soviets, therefore, reject any unprovoked "out of the blue" surprise attack on the "imperialists."[20] Revolutionary movements and "just" wars of national liberation, however, deserve and will receive USSR support.
- The growing power of the East makes it possible to deter a surprise attack by the West; hence, war is not "fatally inevitable." Nevertheless, deterrence may fail and the imperialists may in fact endanger some conquest of socialism. In such a case the USSR and its allies must and will "win" the war by completely defeating enemy military forces and occupying enemy countries in the continental TVDs.[21]
- To win the war, Soviet forces must limit damage to the USSR with counterforce strikes by strategic defensive forces—air, missile, space, ASW, and civil defense—and with additional strikes against surviving enemy forces. Strategic defensive operations are designed to ensure the viability of assets required to prosecute the war after the initial exchange. These assets include the politico-administrative system, essential economic units, military forces and facilities, and the general population.[22]

• The war may begin under a variety of circumstances, including that of a surprise attack on the USSR with either nuclear or conventional weapons. Most likely, the war will be relatively brief (a few weeks) but it could turn into a protracted conflict.[23]

• Soviet forces must be ready and able to pre-empt a U.S. or NATO attack on warning at any level of conflict. Pre-emption is the preferred option, but only on warning of an imminent Western attack. In the absence of a warning, USSR forces must be able either to launch under attack or to deliver a second response strike. In all of these circumstances the objective of the Soviet strike is to seize, or to regain and hold, the initiative and to limit damage to the USSR.[24]

• Soviet nuclear strikes—principally by the Strategic Rocket Forces (SRF)—will be decisive, but they cannot defeat the enemy completely or occupy Europe. Hence, the initial strategic exchange will be followed by a combined arms offensive—ground forces, frontal aviation, and navy, supported by the SRF, long-range aviation, and navy SLBMs—against enemy forces in the Eurasian TVDs and at sea.[25]

• The priority targets for all Soviet nuclear forces—strategic and operational-tactical—are the enemy's nuclear delivery systems and weapons; nuclear command, control, and communications; and air defenses. USSR strategic forces target enemy politico-administrative centers, military forces and facilities in the rear, and selected essential industries and transport-communications facilities. Operational-tactical missiles and aircraft target enemy military forces and facilities in the forward areas. Yields are matched with targets to ensure the required damage to the proper target but limit collateral damage to population, urban infrastructure, and other industry. The Soviets do not target the general population, but they may target selected elite groups.[26]

• The Soviet and Warsaw Pact armed forces and the economy must be prepared in peacetime for nuclear war. The first objective is to achieve "quantitative and qualitative superiority" in military forces.[27] This is the purpose of the party's "military-technical policy," as stated by the Defense Council and Politburo in CPSU resolutions and joint party-government decrees.[28] Preparation of the economy in peacetime includes creation of state and strategic reserves for personnel and matériel and measures designed to conduct repairs, rehabilitation, and recovery of the economy in the event of war.[29]

These tenets and objectives of USSR military doctrine and strategy constitute the core of its concepts on deterrence and the conduct of nuclear war. To the Soviets, the best deterrence is a force posture designed to fight and "win" a nuclear war—not one designed merely to punish the enemy for starting the war. In their view, the more the West perceives that the East has such forces and knows how to use them to fight and win, the more it will be deterred. Nevertheless, despite the unprecedented damage and destruction involved, the Soviets believe it would be feasible to win a nuclear war should deterrence fail for any reason.

Soviet military doctrine and strategy have changed little since the basic tenets were formulated in 1953–60. In those years the USSR expected a war between the two superpower coalitions to go nuclear from the outset. In response to changes in NATO doctrine, however, the Soviets modified their doctrine in 1964 to allow for the possibility of a conventional phase in a superpower coalition war.[30] During 1966–67 USSR military strategy was also modified to add launch under attack (on tactical warning of an enemy attack on its way) to the prior basic scenarios of pre-emption and the second strike.[31] Another modification of Soviet military strategy may have occurred in the late 1970s or may still be in process. The USSR could have perceived the possibility of "decoupling" a nuclear war with NATO from an intercontinental exchange as a result of alterations in United States declaratory policy and the shift in the nuclear balance in favor of the USSR that occurred during the late 1970s. With the exception of these three modifications, Soviet military doctrine and strategy have not changed since what the USSR calls the "nuclear revolution in military affairs" began ca. 1960. At present the only indication of another impending modification is a slight hint of a reduction in Soviet expectations that, if faced with defeat, NATO would escalate a conventional conflict to nuclear war.[32]

SUPERIORITY OF FORCE IN SOVIET MILITARY STRATEGY

Throughout the 1960s and into the early 1970s the USSR stated its objective to be "quantitative and qualitative superiority" in weapons and forces. To our knowledge, the earliest post–World War II statement to this effect appeared in the second edition of a book published in 1961 and edited by political officers; hence, it carried the policy imprimatur of the CPSU leadership.[33] All three editions of Marshal Sokolovskii's *Military Strategy* carried the following statement: "Therefore, the creation and constant maintenance of quantitative and qualitative superiority over the enemy in this means of armed combat and in the methods of its use represents one of the most important tasks of construction of the armed forces in the contemporary epoch."[34]

In the second and third editions of *Military Strategy*, the superiority objective was broadened to include all modern weaponry (rather than just the SRF) and tied to CPSU military-technical policy and the party's efforts to provide the necessary economic base. The second edition (1963) added the following short paragraph: "One of the most important questions is the problem of ensuring quantitative and qualitative military-technical superiority over the probable aggressor, that requires the presence of the corresponding military-economic base, the broadest enlistment of scientific-technical forces for the solution of this problem."[35] All three editions stated that the achievements of technical and numerical superiority over the enemy in modern weapons were "material prerequisites of victory." The second and third editions added five paragraphs linking the achievement of superiority in weaponry to the CPSU by means of its "military technical policy" and the party's unremitting efforts to develop the necessary heavy industrial and scientific-technical base.[36]

In this connection, a political officer stated the following:

> *Success in a nuclear missile war on the whole will depend on that correlation of forces which is established prior to the beginning.* The scales of efforts and methods of changing the correlation of forces during a war will be fundamentally different in comparison with those which were characteristic for wars in the past. In this connection, *already in peacetime there are being perfected the most important parameters of the material-technical basis for the combat potential of troops*—fire and shock capabilities, mobility and maneuverability, controlability, *and uppermost—the nuclear might of the armed forces.* . .
>
> First and foremost, account should be taken of the fact that the established correlation of forces determines the actual capabilities of the sides to exert influence on one another at a given moment with a determined degree of probability of success. In the process, *the advantage, in principle, accrues to that side which significantly surpasses the other in strength in the aggregate or in individual and more essential components of combat might.*[37] (Emphasis added.)

Volume 2 of the *Military Encyclopedia*—published in 1976 and edited by the late Marshal Grechko—contains this entry for "Military Superiority": "Soviet military doctrine . . . provides a program of action for ensuring military-technical superiority over the armed forces of the probable enemies."[38] To reiterate, doctrine is the province of the top CPSU political leadership. When Grechko edited the above, he was a full member of the Politburo. The foregoing statement could hardly be more authoritative.

Prior to 1972 and the signing of the ABM treaty, all Soviet open literature was remarkably candid in setting forth the principles and objectives of military doctrine and strategy. In the early 1970s informative discussions of these subjects gradually disappeared from open literature, but they continued in the issues of *Military Thought* available through 1973. Although the *Military Encyclopedia* remains a vast storehouse of useful information, some disinformation was introduced after Ogarkov replaced the late Marshal Grechko as editor.

Grechko, then defense minister, published two books—the first in 1971 and two editions of the second in 1974 and 1975.[39] The 1971 work repeated the standard tenets of USSR military doctrine and strategy; most of this material did not appear in the later work, however. Grechko's second book did not include anything contrary to what he had written in his first one or to what other Soviet authors had stated throughout the 1960s. It simply revealed little about the substance of USSR military doctrine and strategy.

In 1973 a book written by a group of line and political officers and edited by Professor General Colonel N. A. Lomov reiterated the Soviet position of the 1960s.[40] No similar book has been released to Western readers since that time, however. Two other volumes that may reiterate the same position are limited to internal circulation.[41] Throughout the 1960s informative discussions of USSR military doctrine and strategy appeared in *Communist of the Armed Forces*, the journal of the Ministry of Defense political directorate which is a department of the CPSU Central Committee. Since about 1972, however, articles in this publication have said little or nothing about these subjects.

The Institute of the USA and Canada was established in 1968. This so-called research center has been the source of a vast amount of clever disinformation, including the denial of the existence of a Soviet war-fighting strategy and a civil defense program. By definition, effective disinformation is a blend of fact, partial fact, and fiction. Despite its record and despite testimony by a former member that publicly identified it as a disinformation mill,[42] the output of this institute continues to be accepted uncritically in the West. Institute director Georgii Arbatov was promoted to full membership on the Central Committee at the Twenty-sixth CPSU Congress in 1981 in appreciation for his success in making the center widely credible.

Brezhnev initiated the current practice of denying that military superiority is a Soviet objective in a 1977 speech.[43] Volume 3 of the *Military Encyclopedia* was published in the same year, but with a new editor in place of Marshal Grechko. This volume and all subsequent volumes were edited by N. V. Ogarkov, whose performance in the SALT negotiations and as head of the government-wide *maskirovka* (deception) program was rewarded in January 1977 by appointment as chief of the General Staff and promotion to Marshal of the Soviet Union. The entry for "Military Doctrine" in volume 3 contains Brezhnev's denial of superiority as a USSR objective.[44] Ogarkov signed the entry on "Strategy" in volume 7 of the *Encyclopedia*, which appeared in 1979. He repeated what Brezhnev had said but denied that the USSR would ever be the first to use nuclear weapons.[45] In the same year Ogarkov published a long article in *Pravda* on the "myth" of a Soviet military threat to the United States and NATO.[46] This article contained another quotation from Brezhnev denying that superiority was a USSR objective.

Why, the reader may ask, are these statements judged to be Soviet deception? SALT could have caused the USSR to change its objective and settle for parity. Since elsewhere in this book Soviet statements are given a great deal of credence, why question these denials of the superiority objective? The answer is multipartite.

First, the omission of discussions about military doctrine and strategy from publications like *Communist of the Armed Forces* in the early 1970s can be considered a signal. The exclusion of most of this subject matter from Grechko's 1974 and 1975 editions and the absence of any subsequent work comparable to Lomov's 1973 book can be considered part of the same. The standard positions are not restated; nothing new is substituted for them, however. Although the Institute on the USA and Canada launched a large-scale disinformation campaign, there had been no sign of a struggle over such basic issues within the party or the military.

Second, the recommended literature at the end of the entries in the *Soviet Military Encyclopedia*, including the one for "Strategy" signed by Ogarkov in volume 7, references all of the basic works published in the 1960s and early 1970s. Any reader who proceeded from the *Encyclopedia* entries to the recommended reading would be educated in all previously published tenets of doctrine and strategy. The only difference would be that in the prior works superiority is affirmed time and again, whereas in the *Encyclopedia* it is reaffirmed in 1976 but denied from 1977 on.

Third, the entry for "Military Superiority" in volume 2 (1976) of the *Encyclopedia*—stating that Soviet military doctrine provides the basis for achieving superiority—lists Grechko's 1975 book as recommended reading. Superiority and victory are two of the standard objectives that survived in that book.[47] The entry for "Military Doctrine" in volume 3 (edited by Ogarkov) recommends, among other prior standard works, Grechko's 1975 book and the third edition of Sokolovskii's *Military Strategy*, which also enunciated the superiority objective.[48]

Fourth, as printed in *Communist of the Armed Forces*, Brezhnev's 1977 denial of superiority begins by saying that "superiority has not been stated as a Soviet objective in the past." This is simply not true, and everyone who has read the literature knows it.

Fifth, when volume 3 of the *Encyclopedia*, edited by Ogarkov, reversed volume 2 on superiority by quoting Brezhnev's denial, Brezhnev's statement denying the existence of the past was dropped.

Sixth, in his 1979 *Pravda* article on the "myth" of the Soviet threat, Ogarkov not only denied the superiority objective once again but also denied that USSR defense expenditures had been increasing in recent years. This, too, is a patently false statement.[49]

One recent example of artful disinformation operations by Arbatov's center is illustrative of the genre and of Western gullibility. An American reporter interviewed General Lieutenant M. A. Milshtein of the USA and Canada Institute, who is described as a "distinguished and widely respected authority on Soviet military history and practice." Among other things, Milshtein is reported to have said (1) that Marshal Sokolovskii's *Military Strategy* is not obsolete in general, (2) that it is obsolete on some points, and (3) that it is "certainly obsolete." Milshtein complained that Western authors continue to cite Sokolovskii but pay no attention to subsequent publications by marshals Brezhnev, Ogarkov, and Ustinov. (As has been pointed out, since the early 1970s these marshals have said little, if anything, about the content of USSR military doctrine and strategy. Except for their denial of the superiority objective, what they have said remains fully consistent with Sokolovskii.) Milshtein reportedly concluded the interview by saying that all this talk about Soviet efforts "to achieve victory" in a nuclear war "is simply not true."[50]

Ogarkov, however, did not censor the victory objective from the *Military Encyclopedia*, which has a primarily Soviet readership. This USSR objective appears twice in the entry for "Military Strategy" signed by Ogarkov himself:

> Soviet military strategy proceeds from the view that should the Soviet Union be thrust into a nuclear war *the Soviet people and their Armed Forces need to be prepared for the most severe and protracted trial.* The Soviet Union and the fraternal socialist states will be in this case, in comparison to the imperialist states, in possession of definite advantages: the established just goals of the war, and the advanced nature of their social and state systems. *This creates for them the objective possibility of achieving victory.* However, *for the realization of this possibility, there is the necessity for timely and comprehensive preparation of the country and the armed forces.*[51] (Emphasis added.)

USSR motivations for its disinformation campaign are obvious enough. When the Soviets were being open about their doctrine, strategy, and objectives during the 1960s, the conventional wisdom in the West was either to ignore this open literature or not to take it seriously. But in the 1970s the climate changed. More people began to read USSR publications, and the conventional wisdom of the 1960s was effectively challenged. Meanwhile, the Soviets came to appreciate the value of Western ignorance and misinterpretation of their doctrine and strategy. Shortly after SALT began, the USSR therefore first restricted and then virtually ceased to discuss its doctrine and strategy (except for the nonsense spread so effectively by Arbatov and his colleagues). High-ranking personages such as Brezhnev and Ogarkov also spoke out on a selective basis.

The reason for all this deception is straightforward. During the SALT era, the Soviets sought to lull the West rather than to intimidate it. The tactics differed, but the strategy remained the same. Khrushchev's tactical mistake in 1959–60 taught the USSR not to rattle missiles. Commercial exchange helped to finance the Soviet military buildup and to exacerbate "contradictions" in the Western alliance. Calming the West by asserting that superiority was not a USSR objective and that a nuclear war could not be "won" tended to depress NATO military efforts.

One can see this point by taking the opposite perspective. If SALT had caused the USSR to change its military doctrine, the new doctrine would have been announced. Four party congresses have been held since the SALT process began, however, and no hint of a new military doctrine has emerged. Moreover, there has been no indication that the Soviet Union is changing its military strategy to accommodate such a radically new doctrine.

THE SOVIET DEFINITION OF "VICTORY" IN A NUCLEAR WAR

The most basic difference between USSR and Western perceptions of the purpose and outcome of a nuclear war is that "victory" remains the fundamental Soviet objective. "Victory" is also the basic difference between USSR and Western criteria for acquiring nuclear weapons systems. As the fundamental principle of Soviet military doctrine—which is formulated and approved by the top leaders of the CPSU—"victory" has a long lineage in both the Soviet political and military establishments.[52] Between 1957 and 1960, Khrushchev said several times that "socialism" would survive a nuclear war but that capitalism would not. Until 1967 his 1960 speech to the USSR Supreme Soviet was cited by both political and line officers as the party authority on "victory" and complete "defeat of the enemy" in a nuclear war. Since then the same categories of officers have quoted from Brezhnev's speech on the fiftieth anniversary of the October Revolution.[53]

"Victory" encompasses both the objectives to be achieved by military operations in the course of the war and the consequent political characteristics of the postwar world. No single concise definition of what is meant by "victory" could be found, although Soviet sources provide a number of specific objectives the USSR would seek. Taken together, these objectives probably constitute a reasonable approximation of what is meant by "victory." The composite definition drawn from open literature is summarized below.[54]

- To maintain party control and continue to function politically, militarily, and economically after the initial exchange.
- To destroy the enemy governments that started the war
- To limit damage to the USSR so that it can recover
- To defeat and disarm NATO and to occupy all of Europe in as intact a condition as possible
- To disarm and neutralize the United States and the People's Republic of China
- To dominate the postwar world

In the postwar world "victory" would mean that Western political and economic systems would be liquidated; some form of Soviet "socialism" would become the worldwide political and economic system; and the USSR would dominate this postwar world.

According to the Soviets, one of the constituent objectives of "victory" would be to destroy the "imperialist" governments that would, by definition, have started the war. Because such an attack on the "world socialist system" would be the final act of imperialist aggression (the culmination of "imperialist" attacks on "socialism" beginning with the civil war [1918–21] and continuing through World War II and minor wars like Korea and Vietnam), a war between the two coalitions would be the final and decisive armed conflict; it would be required to end in the complete destruction of "imperialism."[55] In the Soviet view, the end of such a war could not be negotiated with the "imperialist" regimes that started it.[56]

The USSR expects that a war between the "imperialist" and "socialist" coalitions would continue for a few weeks and possibly longer. To conduct the war and to reap the fruits of final victory, the Soviets are determined to continue to function politically, militarily, and economically. Political and military control of not only the armed forces but of the entire society would be maintained, military units would be reconstituted, and the economy would be rehabilitated to support the war effort.[57] The continuity of party control and the USSR system is the most important condition of "victory" to Soviet leaders.

An essential element of the USSR concept of "victory" in a nuclear war is the plan to defeat and disarm the NATO countries and to occupy Western Europe in as intact a condition as possible so that its economic assets could be used to assist Soviet recovery.[58] Moreover, in the Kremlin's view, the total conquest of Europe would irreversibly shift the "correlation of forces" in the USSR's favor.

For the United States and the People's Republic of China (PRC), the apparent military objectives would be to disarm these countries and to neutralize them by preventing the reconstitution of their military forces. Presumably, the Soviets have considered the possibility of occupying both territories, but there is no evidence of any serious planning for occupation of the PRC. Soviet forces might well occupy Manchuria and border areas in the Far East and Central Asia, but it is difficult to imagine their occupation of China south of the Great Wall.

The USSR would seek to limit unnecessary collateral damage to the general population, industry, and urban infrastructure of the "imperialist" states for political, as well as military and economic, reasons.[59] In the Soviet perception, only the "capitalists" and the "ruling classes" constitute the enemy who would be criminally responsible for the war. To destroy the "toiling masses"—along with most industry and cities—would be to destroy the human and economic basis for the "socialist" world that would be intended to replace "imperialism" as a result of the war. Consequently, general destruction of the enemy's population and industry would contradict the basic USSR political objective in a nuclear war.

Although Soviet sources are not specific about their vision of the post–nuclear war world, three of their expectations are given in general terms. First, all Western political and economic systems, governments, and regimes would be destroyed by military operations, and popular uprisings would occur throughout the world. The "masses" would simply no longer tolerate the "imperialist" regimes that had "unleashed" a nuclear war. Second, as the leading nation of the victorious "socialist camp," the USSR would dominate the post–nuclear war world. Third, some form of Soviet "socialism" would be installed in every country of the world.[60] Just how closely the post-"imperialist" regimes would conform to the existing Soviet political, economic, and social order is not specified.

USSR military doctrine represents the views of the ruling party (specifically, the top leadership) concerning the nature, objectives, and consequences of a nuclear war. Therefore, when Soviet political and line officers state that the USSR objective is "victory," they are promulgating military doctrine as approved by the highest CPSU leadership. Political officers know the party views, and it is one of their duties to indoctrinate military officers. Any line or political officer rash enough to promulgate a Soviet nuclear war objective contrary to, or not a part of, approved military doctrine would invite severe consequences.

This interpretation is documented by a 1973 report on the fifth conference of CPSU organization secretaries in the Soviet armed forces. On the eve of this conference, the Central Committee approved two new documents: (1) a statute on political organs of the defense ministry and (2) instructions to CPSU organizations in the army and navy—that is, to political officers. Senior Politburo member Mikhail Suslov opened the conference with greetings from the party leadership. The account of the proceedings explicitly linked victory in a nuclear war to Lenin's "formulated law" (victory as the objective in any war), to a Brezhnev speech in 1967, and to the basic purposes of CPSU political work in the armed forces. "What is the main element in the party-political work for strengthening military discipline? It is that of propagandizing the Lenin behests and the party's instructions on the significance of high efficiency and discipline for troop combat readiness and for their *victory in modern war*." [61] (Emphasis added.)

Soviet discussions of "victory" as the objective in a nuclear war have been explained in the West both as mere slogans intended to maintain troop morale and as the USSR military establishment's rationale for large armed forces. This interpretation alleges that there had been a recurrent debate during the 1960s on whether nuclear war could or could not have any outcome short of mutual destruction of the participants. In this debate the "civilian" side was represented supposedly by retired military officer General Major Nikolai A. Talenskii and a number of civilians, including Georgii Arbatov and others associated with the USA and Canada Institute. The "military" side included a number of writers having military rank, most of whom contributed to *Communist of the Armed Forces*, the periodical of the political directorate and to *Military Thought*.

There are several objections to this interpretation. First, what is called a "debate" might simply have been the result of polemical interchanges with the Chinese. (In fact, two of the "civilian" deviants on this issue—Boris Dmitriev and N. M. Nikol'skii—were exonerated by two political officers on these specific grounds.) [62] There is therefore a simple, documentable explanation for why some Soviet civilians were involved in a drift toward a "pacifist" position on the outcome of a nuclear war in the mid-1960s: They became carried away in their polemics with the Chinese at a time when the latter were chastising the USSR for being afraid of a nuclear war and for being unwilling to use Soviet nuclear power to achieve political objectives. The alleged "debate" was not a debate at all; it was simply a case of inadvertent deviation from the party line that occurred in the course of countering Chinese charges. [63]

Second, at least half of the "military" participants in the alleged debate were political officers from the Main Political Directorate in the Defense Ministry, which is also a department of the CPSU Central Committee apparatus. When those men sign articles, they give their military rank; nevertheless, they remain party functionaries charged with—among other things—indoctrinating line officers. Political officers do not debate the party line; they propagandize it. General Major K. Bochkarev, one of the most articulate spokesmen for "victory" in nuclear war during the alleged 1965 debate, has been mistakenly identified as the "deputy commandant of the General Staff Academy" by a proponent of the alleged debate.[64] Bochkarev, however, does not appear to have held that position at any time before 1971 when he retired.[65] In fact, all of the available evidence on Bochkarev—his educational background, publications, and affiliations—indicates that he served as a political officer. The alleged military-civilian dichotomy in the so-called debate is not persuasive either.

Third, in interpreting Soviet literature, one should take into account both the patterns of USSR force development during the 1970s and the continuous shift in national priorities toward the military establishment over the past two-and-a-half decades. If the Soviets were interested only in "mutual assured destruction and mutual deterrence," as has been argued, they would not have concentrated so heavily on counterforce weapons systems or spent so much on strategic defense. If their goals were limited, they violated their own objectives by expending so much effort on acquiring the military power to destroy most American ICBMs and on building up ASW capabilities against U.S., British, and French SLBMs—not to mention allocating billions of rubles for air and civil defense. Conversely, if the USSR had been willing to settle for "mutual assured destruction," it should have disbanded PVO Strany, eliminated ASW and anticarrier forces, turned over civil defense shelters to the Ministry of Trade for food storage, and ceased many other aspects of the continuing military buildup.

If the Soviets had wanted only mutual deterrence based on mutual assured destruction, defense expenditures would now be down to 10 percent or less of GNP. Instead, they rose to 18 percent in the 1970s and may soon rise to over 20 percent as a result of USSR leaders' commitments to numerous and vast military programs in the 1980s. Because the Political Bureau controls the purse strings, the cost of these extremely expensive weapons systems can be explained only if this leadership is serious about winning a nuclear war. (Assured destruction would be much cheaper.)

The tenets of Soviet military doctrine and strategy have been institutionalized in the missions assigned to the various services of the armed forces and in the principal concepts for the conduct of military operations, as outlined in Chapter 4. As will be demonstrated in subsequent chapters, the pattern of weapons system acquisition fits the service missions and, hence, is driven by the requirements of doctrine and strategy.

ESCALATION AND LIMITED WAR

As pointed out above, until about 1964 the USSR expected a war with the NATO coalition to be nuclear from the outset. Later, in response to changes in Western concepts that were formally published in 1967 by NATO, it changed its doctrine to allow for a conventional phase. The Soviets have not been as responsive to Western concepts of limited nuclear war, however— specifically to such ideas as (1) forcing a negotiating pause in a conventional conflict by a demonstrative or limited use of nuclear weapons and (2) controlling nuclear escalation at several stages of nuclear warfare short of a massive exchange.[66] The common thread in all these Western concepts on the limited use of nuclear weapons seems to be that these weapons can somehow be used in a controlled manner, or in something less than a massive nuclear exchange, to force the other superpower coalition to the conference table if a war begins at the conventional level.

Western concepts about limited nuclear strikes designed to halt conventional or nuclear offensive operations and to force the Soviets to negotiate a settlement are not realistic for several reasons. First, as discussed earlier, the USSR would view any war between the two superpower coalitions as the last act in the historic struggle between "imperialism" and "socialism." The Soviet Union could not terminate such a "just" war by negotiating, because this would mean "imperialism" would remain to fight another day. Second, USSR conventional military superiority could not be reduced to equality (let alone inferiority) by a dozen—or even a few dozen—nuclear strikes. Third, Moscow has nuclear superiority in the Eurasian theaters, thanks largely to strategic offensive nuclear forces not included in SALT—Soviet IR/MRBMs and medium bombers.

Consequently, any U.S. or NATO limited nuclear strike that is not large enough to eliminate USSR superiority in both conventional and nuclear arms in Eurasia might well be ignored by the Soviets. Their juggernaut would continue to roll at either conventional or nuclear levels. Conversely, NATO nuclear strikes large enough to deny the USSR its objectives would probably be viewed by the Soviets as the prelude to massive nuclear attacks by all available Western forces. In this case, the USSR would pre-empt the attack with its own massive power in strategic and operational-tactical systems (or respond with its own massive power if it did not succeed in pre-empting completely). In both scenarios, U.S. or NATO limited nuclear operations either would be ineffectual or (more probably) would bring about the very catastrophe they were designed to avoid. American concepts of limited nuclear strikes are not the rules of the game by which the USSR is likely to play. Simply stated, from the Soviet point of view, the objective can only be victory.

4 / Missions and Operational Concepts

The USSR armed forces have institutionalized the missions of their services according to military doctrine and strategy. Certain operational concepts are critical to understanding development and procurement decisions and the ways in which force would be used in the event of war.

The critical operational concepts discussed in this chapter are rooted in Soviet experience during World War II and appear to have been firmly adopted by the late 1950s. The basic institutional structure of the USSR military establishment did not change between the formation of the strategic rocket forces (SRF) during 1959–60 and the amalgamation of air, missile, and space defense in 1980–81. Around the latter time, Long Range Aviation received the designation Strategic Air Armies which also includes some former tactical units. Land and sea-based strategic missiles became more lightly integrated. None of the above organizational modifications involved any basic change in missions.

MISSIONS OF THE ARMED FORCES

The Soviet armed forces comprise the following five combat services:

- Strategic Rocket Forces (SRF)
- Air Forces (SAF)

- Navy
- National Air Defense (PVO Strany), now Troops of Air Defense (Voiska PVO)
- Ground Forces (GF)

Soviet airborne units are not considered a "service," being directly subordinate to the High Command. In addition, there are organizations for civil defense and rear services and various types of special support troops, for instance, engineer, construction, chemical, and signal. Finally, the border guards of the Committee for State Security (KGB) and troops under the Ministry of Internal Affairs (*Ministerstvo Vnutrennykh Del*, or MVD) make up the balance.[1]

Each of the five services (along with civil defense and rear services) is headed by a deputy minister of defense. They are assigned one or more major missions during wartime. These missions form a cohesive set, all of which must theoretically be fulfilled in order to achieve "victory" at any level, including that of a nuclear war. Consequently, the five services have war-fighting, damage-limiting missions, supplemented by the evacuation, repair, and reconstruction functions of Civil Defense Troops, which undoubtedly would be assisted by MVD units.

The Kremlin probably views the world as six continental theaters of military operations (*teatr voennykh deistvii*, or TVD): three facing NATO, two in Central Asia and the Far East, and one "transoceanic." In addition, there are several coordinated but distinct oceanic TVDs in which the Soviet navy will conduct its strategic operations, both offensive and defensive.

USSR strategic missile and air forces will conduct strikes in each of the above TVDs. With few exceptions, Soviet intercontinental ballistic missiles (ICBMs) and intermediate/medium-range ballistic missiles (IR/MRBMs) are assigned targets in all TVDs. The same applies to the navy's submarine-launched ballistic missiles (SLBMs). Strategic aviation target assignments in the transoceanic TVD, if any, have been quite limited since the mid-1960s. This situation is now changing, however, as the Soviets modernize their heavy bomber force and equip it with long-range, low-altitude cruise missiles. Except for the purpose of excluding one-third of their strategic offensive forces from SALT constraints as a bargaining tactic, the USSR has never entertained the notion that "strategic" missiles and air strikes can be equated with homeland-to-homeland exchanges. The equation of "strategic" with intercontinental is an American concept that the Soviets do not share. All USSR missiles having a range in excess of 1,000 kilometers are strategic; shorter range systems are classified as "operational-tactical."[2]

In the Eurasian TVDs, particularly those facing NATO, the Kremlin envisages "operational-strategic" combined arms campaigns by the ground forces, frontal aviation, military transport aviation with airborne troops, and the navy, all supported by the strategic rocket forces, SLBMs, and long-range aviation.[3]

In the Soviet perception, the geographically proximate Eurasian TVDs pose as much or more of a threat as the transoceanic TVD. A senior USSR political officer has noted that the United States and its allies have some 6,700 military bases and installations throughout the world, most of them in Western Europe.[4] Soviet concern about the Eurasian TVDs is the primary reason that the medium-range bomber and IRBM gaps favor the Soviets, the heavy bomber gap favors the United States, and that the "missile gap" was really an ICBM gap. In every case in which the Kremlin has had to choose, it has given first priority to deployment of strategic systems designed for operations in the Eurasian TVDs.

It should also be kept in mind that geography divides the Soviet navy into four fleets, two of which (those in the Baltic and Black seas) can reach the open ocean only by passing through narrow straits controlled by NATO countries. In the Far East, offshore islands present a partial barrier; in the West, the Greenland–United Kingdom gap does the same. Although the Northern Fleet has the best access to the high seas, its bases are also far removed from the North Atlantic.

Taken as a whole, the USSR armed forces have three basic missions: strategic offense, strategic defense, and "operational-strategic" campaigns in the Eurasian and oceanic TVDs.[5] Concepts of strategic offensive and defensive missions are similar to those of the United States, although Soviet concepts of strategic defensive missions are more broadly defined. In addition to air, space, and missile defense, USSR strategic defensive operations include strategic antisubmarine warfare (ASW) against American SSBNs, operations against U.S. and NATO aircraft carriers, and management of the war ("civil defense"). The Soviet concept of an "operational-strategic"[6] mission is essentially a combined arms offensive, supported by long-range missiles and aircraft, that defeats and disarms NATO forces and occupies Western Europe. Naval operations in the oceanic TVDs, particularly interdiction of sea-lanes, may also be considered "operational-strategic."[7] The emphasis on offensive operations, defeat of the enemy, and occupation of his territory is fundamentally different from the operational strategy of U.S. and NATO "general purpose forces" in the North Atlantic alliance TVDs.

To achieve "victory," as the USSR envisages it, all parts of the combined arms operation must be accomplished successfully. Consequently, trends in the effectiveness of Soviet strategic forces are properly understood only in the context of their contribution to this notion of victory in war, that is, limiting damage to the homeland by enemy strategic forces, neutralizing the overseas enemy, and ensuring the victory of USSR "operational-strategic" campaigns in the Eurasian TVDs.

Strategic Rocket Forces (SRF)

Essentially, the SRF's mission is to carry out a targeting strategy that emphasizes counterforce strikes against enemy military forces (see Chapter 8). The USSR regards the SRF as the premier branch of service in the nuclear age for several reasons. First, it will deliver the bulk of the Soviet Union's destructive power in the form of nuclear strikes in the initial stage of the war, the results of which are expected to be decisive for the final outcome of the war. To limit damage to the USSR, the SRF must destroy the greatest possible number of the enemy's nuclear delivery vehicles and nuclear weapons in the initial strike. Second, the ability of the Soviet Union to seize and hold the initiative—or to regain the initiative if the enemy attacks first—depends primarily on the effectiveness of the SRF, particularly its counterforce strikes against enemy nuclear forces. Third, the success of the "operational-strategic" campaign to occupy Western Europe depends heavily on the SRF's capability to hit the most important NATO military targets and to destroy U.S. reinforcements.

All three editions of the authoritative book *Military Strategy* summed up the SRF's damage-limiting mission and its liabilities in this regard as follows: [8]

> *Protection of the rear area of the country and groups of armed forces from enemy nuclear attacks* (emphasis in the original) has the aim of preserving the vital functions of the government, of assuring the uninterrupted functioning of the national economy and transportation, and preserving the combat readiness of the armed forces. *These aims are achieved mainly by annihilation of the enemy's means of nuclear attack in the regions in which they are based. However, there is no guarantee that considerable aircraft and rocket forces can be annihilated at their bases, particularly at the start of the war with a surprise enemy attack.* (Emphasis added.)

This quotation highlights the two main themes in the Soviet evaluation of the SRF's mission. Counterforce strikes are essential to limit damage to the USSR and thus ensure ultimate victory. At the same time, the SRF cannot be certain of accomplishing everything because the opponent may launch on warning some of its missiles and aircraft. Moreover, enemy SLBMs at sea cannot be targeted by ballistic missiles. The Soviet navy must destroy enemy ballistic missile submarines or the country must be protected by ABM defenses or some combination of the two must exist. Consequently, victory in a nuclear war requires not only USSR counterforce strikes by strategic missiles but also the use of active and passive defenses.

Although the Soviets expect initial massive strikes by the SRF—supplemented by the navy's SLBMs—to be decisive in determining the war's outcome, they do not expect the initial nuclear exchange to conclude the war. In their view, this initial exchange will only set the stage for the subsequent combined arms campaign that will result in victory for Soviet and Warsaw Pact forces, preferably in the course of two to three weeks.

Strategic Air Armies

As the long-range component of the Soviet air forces, the five strategic air armies have a similar (yet somewhat more complex) damage-limiting mission than that of the SRF. Like the SRF and the navy's SLBMs, the first priority of Stategic Air is to destroy enemy nuclear delivery capabilities. However, because missiles are considered the more reliable means of eliminating fixed targets, Strategic Air would play a lesser role in the initial exchange. Its primary nuclear mission is to strike mobile and transitory targets not suitable for ballistic missiles. High on the list of mobile targets are enemy aircraft carriers. Hence, Strategic Air shares this damage-limiting mission with Soviet naval air force medium bombers, submarine-launched cruise missiles, and torpedo attack submarines.[9] Strategic Air Armies also perform reconnaissance in support of all other services.

If a major war begins at the conventional level—a possibility that the Soviet Union has considered likely since the mid-1960s—during that phase Strategic Air will constitute the primary strike force against enemy nuclear delivery systems, command and control installations, and weapons stockpiles. At present, ballistic missiles are not sufficiently accurate to be effective unless they carry nuclear warheads. Soviet targeting priorities are the same for the conventional phase as for a full-scale nuclear exchange.[10]

The Soviet Navy

The Soviet navy has a complex set of missions, including strategic offense and defense, support of "operational-strategic" campaigns in the Eurasian TVDs, sea-lane interdiction, power projection, and the traditional responsibilities for coastal defense.[11] During an initial strike, the navy's SLBMs will supplement the SRF's strategic attacks against fixed targets in all TVDs, cross-targeting with the SRF in some cases. The primary role of the SLBM force, however, appears to be that of providing a large, secure, reserve force after the initial exchange. Unexpended SLBMs would be used to support military operations after the initial exchange and would ensure that the Soviet Union would become the predominant, and probably the only, nuclear power in the postwar world. The SLBMs also provide a hedge against SRF losses to enemy counterforce strikes.

Although not specifically stated in the available literature, the reserve mission of the SLBMs can be inferred from several factors. First, the USSR places great emphasis on the availability of large reserve forces for any kind of military operation. Some of the SRF's missiles would undoubtedly be withheld as reserves during an initial exchange, but such reserves are vulnerable to enemy counterforce strikes; SLBMs at sea are not. Second, the long range of the SS-N-8, SS-N-18, SS-N-20, and SS-N-23 missiles permits these SLBMs to strike most of the United States from home waters protected by Soviet ASW screens, allowing the SS-N-6 missiles concomitantly to carry out strikes against most of the important targets in the Eurasian TVDs from protected areas. Third, the small portion of the Soviet SLBM force normally maintained on patrol in peacetime is probably a good indication that most of the Soviet navy's SLBMs would be withheld from the initial exchange—at least until after the SRF had suffered greater-than-anticipated losses to enemy counterforce strikes.

The Soviet navy's primary anticarrier forces are medium bombers equipped with various types of air-to-surface missiles, the submarine-launched cruise missiles (SLCMs) of its nuclear and diesel-powered submarines, and torpedo attack submarines. As noted, naval air will be supported by the Strategic Air Armies and, of course, by a variety of reconnaissance and surveillance systems. USSR anticarrier forces would seek to engage and destroy U.S. and NATO carriers beyond the range of enemy carrier aircraft to attack land targets in the Eurasian TVDs.

The strategic ASW team consists primarily of surface ships, nuclear attack submarines, and specially configured aircraft.[12] With few exceptions, major Soviet navy surface combatants built since 1960 have been equipped primarily for ASW operations. The most ambitious ASW nuclear-powered submarine is the high-speed, deep-diving, titanium-hulled Alpha class. Apparently, this class is now being supplemented by later models—such as the Mike class, which displaces about 9,500 tons (as compared to Alpha's 3,700 tons).[13] ASW operations encompass both destruction of enemy nuclear-powered guided-missile submarines and protection of Soviet ballistic missile submarines (SSBNs) from hostile ASW forces.

In addition to these strategic offensive and defensive missions, the Soviet navy has four other tasks: (1) support of operational-strategic offensive attacks in the Eurasian TVDs, (2) sea-lane interdiction, (3) the traditional responsibility for coastal defense, and (4) power projection. Navy support of the operational-strategic offensive by the ground forces, frontal aviation, and air transport aviation consists primarily of amphibious operations and

SLBM strikes. In the NATO TVDs, initial Soviet amphibious operations probably would be directed at Denmark, the straits connecting the Baltic and North seas, and the northern coast of Norway. Meanwhile, numerous guided-missile patrol boats, minefields, and land-based cruise missiles would provide coastal defense for the USSR.

Power projection appears to be an emerging mission for the Soviet navy, which has been increasingly active in various parts of the world over the past fifteen years. The four new classes of cruisers being built and the large aircraft carrier under construction will be most useful for that particular role in peacetime and during local conflicts; however, the primary global war mission of most of these new surface combatants would probably consist of protecting Soviet SLBMs and strategic ASW operations. The priority given to this mission is exemplified by Admiral of the Fleet Gorshkov's statement that it "has acquired the character of a State task."[14] The importance of ASW centers on preventing the launch of sea-based ballistic missiles against the USSR. The SRF have a set of weapons that can perform this mission against land-based ICBMs. The Soviet navy is striving for a similar capability against SLBMs.

Troops of Air Defense (Voiska PVO)

The mission of Voiska PVO is to defend the USSR from enemy air, missile, and space attacks in any scenario, preferably with the assistance of other services—but, if necessary, by using only its own resources. Specifically, Voiska PVO operations are designed to ensure the continuous functioning of the country's political-administrative system (party and government), essential economic units, and military forces and facilities. The Soviets recognize that they cannot prevent all damage from a U.S. or NATO strike. The task of defenses is to limit damage from such an attack to the greatest possible extent. Consequently, the USSR is willing to deploy and maintain systems whose individual effectiveness may be unacceptably low by American standards. The Voiska PVO approach is rather to layer each system on the next, so that together they may achieve as much attrition as possible.

Although initially constituted as an air defense organization, Voiska PVO have gradually achieved integration of the equipment necessary for two other missions: (1) defense against ballistic missiles and (2) offensive and defensive combat in space. For example, the USSR understands the term "air defense installation" to include the ballistic missile defense (BMD) mission.[15] Surface-to-air missiles such as the SA-5 may play such a role. Because of this Soviet interpretation of air defenses, the United States insisted that the 1972 treaty prohibit testing air defense equipment "in an ABM mode."[16]

Voiska PVO also operate equipment exclusively for defense against ballistic missiles such as the ABM system around Moscow. Voiska PVO also developed the flat twin transportable missile-engagement radar designed for use in conjunction with the Pechora-class radars and with the SH-8 high acceleration interceptor. In addition, Voiska PVO have charge over development of directed energy weapons. In 1984 the USSR announced that a high-energy laser device would be tested in space but did not mention its purpose or its organizational affiliation.

Voiska PVO must be prepared to go it alone without attrition of enemy forces by prior Soviet missile, air, and naval operations or to take full advantage of whatever degree of damage has been inflicted. The previously cited paragraph from Marshal Sokolovskii's *Military Strategy* recognizes that counterforce strikes cannot guarantee the total destruction of enemy nuclear delivery systems, although it presumes significant attrition. The paragraph continues:[17]

> Therefore, it is necessary to have the necessary forces and means for destroying great masses of enemy aircraft and rockets in the air in order that there be no nuclear attacks against important objectives within the whole territory of the country. This can be done by military operations for protecting the country from attack by enemy aircraft and missiles.

The conclusions to the book edited by General Colonel Lomov—published in 1973 after the ABM treaty and the Interim Agreement on Strategic Offensive Forces had been signed—stated that in view of the damage that would be inflicted from an enemy nuclear attack, active defense of the country had acquired "state-strategic significance."[18]

Given the perception that the United States will target the military forces, industry, and general population of the USSR, Soviet defensive priorities seem clear:

- Active defenses will attempt to preserve the essential political, military, and economic entities and the installations that cannot be relocated.
- Passive defenses (shelters and evacuation) will care for the party-government-military elite and essential workers.
- The general population will be evacuated and will receive as much collateral protection as the active defenses can provide in the course of defending the political system, the economy, and the military.

Four basic sources synthesize Voiska PVO defensive objectives as follows:[19]

- Economic assets—industry, transport and communication facilities, strategic reserve bases, and storage points—required to ensure the "uninterrupted" operation of the economy
- Political-administrative centers
- Key military installations, such as SRF launchers, strategic aviation and military transport airfields, and naval bases[20]

The order in which these defensive objectives are listed varies, and no firm hierarchy of priorities can be derived from generalizations available in Soviet literature. Nevertheless, some comments may be of interest.

Preservation of the elite—party, government, and military—is almost certainly the first priority assignment of both active and passive defenses; to a lesser extent, the same applies to the scientific and technical elite.[21] Defensive priorities for military facilities and economic assets are complex. It is not a question of whether "military" or "economic" targets have higher priority; it is more likely that defensive priority would depend on the contribution of each military facility and economic asset to Soviet war-fighting capabilities.

It is also interesting that strategic reserve bases and storage points are listed as priority assets to be defended. In general, the importance of stocks is overlooked by American military planners. The prevalent U.S. objective in targeting the USSR has been to kill people, knock down houses and destroy factories. In contrast, accumulation of the appropriate stocks in peacetime is an integral part of Soviet planning to fight, win, and recover from a nuclear war.[22] American planners assume that strikes against USSR industry would have certain precise effects. These assumptions may be unfounded, given our state of knowledge about the size, composition, and disposition of such stocks; the command and control channels for their use under wartime conditions; and the plans that exist for protecting them.

Normal peacetime inventories of raw materials and goods in various stages of production constituted nearly one-half of the Soviet GNP.[23] Most of these stocks are located with the factories or other economic assets that use them; consequently, they would be damaged to a greater or lesser degree if the factories and assets were attacked. Some consist of vulnerable materials—petroleum products, lumber, cloth; others (such as metals) would be largely usable after attacks designed only to collapse factory walls.

In addition to these normal economic inventories, however, there are specialized and centrally controlled supplies, or "untouchable" state reserves. These stocks—maintained for various emergencies, nuclear war among them—are not necessarily stored with other economic assets and are centrally controlled (probably by the Supreme High Command, or VGK) in wartime. Something is known about the functions of state reserves because they are used in peacetime to alleviate temporary shortages and bottlenecks and possibly to cope with seasonal demands for commodities like food and fuel. Obviously, these supplies are large.[24] Their financing is buried in the USSR budget along with weapons procurement (which may be considered part of state reserves in peacetime because it is funded by the same budget source). However, no reliable data are available on the size and composition of state reserves, the portion located with factories, or the amount stored at state reserve bases.

Reference to inviolable reserves is rare. Nothing is directly known about their size, financing, or location. Presumably these reserves are maintained for dire emergencies, such as severe natural disasters and war. Inviolable reserves do include military equipment to form new units and to replace wartime losses.[25]

Military functions of the USSR economy in wartime have been summarized by two Soviet officers as follows:

- Maximum satisfaction of material requirements for war
- Maintenance of the necessary level of production in the event of an enemy attack
- "Postwar restoration of the economy"[26]

Maintaining control is the first objective. "No matter how chaotic the panorama of a world nuclear war may be at first glance, direction and control cannot be interrupted."[27] Next in importance are (1) to maintain the necessary material reserves for essential economic activity; (2) to provide "clothing, footwear, and other emergency requirements" for the evacuated population; and (3) to repair the damage and start the process of economic recovery.[28]

Combined Arms

Supported by air and naval elements, the Soviet ground forces have three principal missions:[29]

- To maintain the territorial and political integrity of the "socialist camp"
- To expand the "socialist camp" by "defending the conquests of socialism" and providing assistance to "wars of national liberation"
- To conduct an "operational-strategic" offensive to defeat and disarm

NATO forces and to gain control of Western Europe in as intact a condition as possible while at the same time defending the USSR against attacks by the People's Republic of China (PRC).

In addition to defending the USSR itself from any invasion, Soviet ground forces (and supporting elements) must defend the communist regimes of Eastern Europe from dangers such as the uprising in Hungary (1956); the "quiet counterrevolution" in Czechoslovakia (1968); and, indirectly, the underground Solidarity trade unions in Poland. In the official Moscow view, all these events were the work of "antisocialist elements," aided and abetted by the "imperialists."

USSR forces also have an "international duty" to defend the "conquests of socialism" anywhere; they are currently performing this duty in Afghanistan. Moscow also provides advice, guidance, training, and assistance to revolutionary movements and to organizations fighting "national wars of liberation" throughout the world.[30]

In the event of war with NATO, Soviet and Warsaw Pact ground forces—supported by frontal and military transport aviation, airborne troops, and naval infantry—would mount a combined arms "operational-strategic" offensive. The politico-economic objectives will be to "liberate" Western Europe from the "imperialists" and to make the assets of Europe available to assist USSR recovery should the war involve a large-scale nuclear exchange with the United States.[31] If necessary, the Soviet combined arms forces will simultaneously repulse any PRC attacks and seize the border regions (and possibly Manchuria) on the Chinese side. They will probably not penetrate south of the Great Wall, however.

As noted earlier, the Soviets do not expect the initial strategic nuclear exchange to end the war but only to set the stage for the "operational-strategic" campaign against NATO and for related naval operations in the oceanic TVDs.

Civil Defense

Although civil defense troops are not considered a branch of service like Voiska PVO, their mission is essential to Soviet military strategy. Both editions (1974 and 1975) of the late Marshal Grechko's book on the USSR armed forces provide additional insights into the missions and functions of strategic defenses, including civil defense. According to this source, "ensuring the high vitality of the country's economy in the event of an aggressor's attack and the rapid transformation of the military-economic potential into real military forces has acquired great significance under contemporary conditions."[32] During peacetime the USSR must prepare its armed forces and its population for war. Among other things, this means accumulating sufficient stocks of strategic materials and equipment.

Grechko notes that bombing of industry during World War II was not very successful; repairs were effected rather quickly and weapons production continued to rise. In the nuclear era, however, the situation is different—*unless* prior measures are taken to ensure "stability" of the economy and defense of the population. Even so, "already at the beginning of the war there may be a sharp decline in industrial production" accompanied by disruption of transport, communications, and other systems. "And as is well known, it is impossible to conduct a war without a reliable and functioning home front."[33]

Grechko goes on to argue that in the nuclear era the entire economy and population must be defended. This requires both active and passive defenses. Civil defense "now emerges as a factor of strategic significance in ensuring the vital activities of the state." These measures are not entirely passive, particularly with regard to the population. According to Grechko, the objectives of Soviet civil defense in the nuclear age are:

- To train the population to organize activity under difficult circumstances
- To prepare the population to put out fires over large areas, fight floods, provide mass medical assistance to victims, clear obstructions, and build roads
- To rapidly restore energy networks and water supplies and repair damaged industrial and administrative facilities
- To wage hand-to-hand combat with the enemy, under some circumstances[34]

Grechko presents a grim, yet not hopeless, picture. Damage to industry and population losses in a nuclear war will be unprecedentedly severe. Life, the nation, and civilization can and will continue, however, if the proper measures are taken beforehand and if surviving human and material assets are mobilized and directed to restore the damage. As the late N. S. Khrushchev said some thirty years ago, nuclear war is not "fatally inevitable," and, in the USSR view, neither is the destruction of civilization after such a conflict.

The requirement for ABM defenses is implicit in Grechko's position. As previously noted, the Soviets recognized from the beginning the shortcomings of counterforce as a damage-limiting measure. Air defenses can defend against missiles only to the extent that they are designed as dual purpose systems. Civil defense can also do only so much. Grechko's concept of comprehensive protection for large segments of industry, the armed forces, and the population requires defense against ballistic missiles. Otherwise, all USSR damage-limiting forces and measures—acquired at great expense—will be worthless.

This argument also appeared in the 1974 and 1975 editions of Grechko's book, published two and three years, respectively, after the signing of the ABM treaty and one and two years, respectively, after Grechko had been elevated to the Politburo. The retention of the commitment to all types of defense and the implicit argument for ABM in both editions of Grechko's book are all the more impressive because a great deal of what the author wrote on Soviet military strategy in his 1971 paperback was expunged from the 1974 and 1975 editions.[35] This should have sounded a warning to American military planners.

Soviet civil defense includes plans for a rapid transition of the government and economy to wartime operations. The USSR has undertaken a 30-year program, involving hardened command posts and survivable communications. Plans for industrial production during a war have also been perfected. Approximately 1,500 hardened facilities and more than 175,000 personnel constitute the core of this system. The cumulative dollar cost of this effort over the past quarter-century has been estimated at between $28 and $56 billion, which may be understated by a large margin.[36]

SOVIET OPERATIONAL CONCEPTS

Since the USSR intends to fight wars by employing forces according to its own concepts of military operations, these operational concepts will be examined. They include:

- Centralized control and direction of operations by all forces in all TVDs
- Damage-limiting operations by strategic defenses
- Maneuver of strategic and other forces
- Provision of secure reserves and force reconstitution after the initial strikes
- Basic nuclear war scenarios and emphasis on offensive operations[37]

The Supreme High Command and the General Staff

The Soviets plan to direct and control the operations of all forces centrally ("from the top down") by the Supreme High Command (VGK) acting through the General Staff. In peacetime, the principal decisionmaking body on military affairs is the Defense Council, which consists of about five or six senior men on the Politburo (as of late September 1985 the latter comprised thirteen voting and five nonvoting members). In wartime the Defense Council, which includes the Minister of Defense (S. L. Sokolov), would probably become the State Committee for Defense (GKO), chaired by the incumbent general secretary of the party (M. S. Gorbachev). The general secretary would also head a group of about twelve senior military officers, constituting the Supreme High Command (VGK).[38] Thousands of senior party and government officials would provide staff support from hardened underground command posts outside of urban areas.

During World War II, the GKO held joint sessions with the full Politburo on the most important policy issues.[39] In the initial period of a nuclear war, there would be no time for such deliberations. Neither a decision to pre-empt on warning of enemy intent nor a decision to launch on tactical warning that an enemy attack had begun could await a meeting of the Politburo. Consequently, in a nuclear war most of the critical decisions would probably come from the GKO and the VGK and, in many cases, from the CPSU general secretary alone. Tables 1 and 2 show the probable composition of these organs as they may have been constituted in 1986.

The General Staff is the executive instrument of the VGK. Within the General Staff, the operations directorate is the focal point for implementing

TABLE 1   PROBABLE STATE DEFENSE COMMITTEE (GKO), EARLY 1986

Names	Positions
1. M. S. Gorbachev	CPSU general secretary; chairman, Defense Council
2. N. I. Ryzhkov	Chairman, USSR Council of Ministers
3. E. A. Shevardnadze	Foreign minister
4. V. M. Chebrikov	Chairman, State Security Committee (KGB)
5. S. L. Sokolov	Minister of defense
6. N. V. Talyzin	Chairman, State Economic Planning Commission (Gosplan); deputy chairman, USSR Council of Ministers
7. L. N. Zaikov	CPSU secretary for defense industry
8. S. F. Akhromeev	Chief of the General Staff

SOURCES: Richard F. Staar, *USSR Foreign Policies After Détente* (Stanford: Hoover Institution Press, 1985), p. 111; Alexander Rahr, comp. "The Composition of the Politburo and the Secretariat," *Radio Liberty Research*, RL 259/85 (Munich, 9 August 1985); *Pravda*, 28 September 1985, 15 October 1985, 7 March 1986.

TABLE 2   SUPREME HIGH COMMAND (VGK), EARLY 1986

Names	Positions
1. M. S. Gorbachev	CPSU general secretary; chairman, GKO
2. S. L. Sokolov	Minister of defense
3. S. F. Akhromeev	Chief of the General Staff; first deputy defense minister
4. A. D. Lizichev	Chief of Main Political Administration
5. V. G. Kulikov	Commander in chief, Warsaw Pact; first deputy defense minister
6. Y. P. Maksimov	Commander in chief of Strategic Rocket Forces; deputy defense minister
7. V. N. Chernavin	Commander in chief of Navy; deputy defense minister
8. A. N. Efimov	Commander in chief of Air Forces; deputy defense minister
9. A. I. Koldunov	Commander in chief of Voiska PVO; deputy defense minister
10. E. F. Ivanovskii	Commander in chief of Ground Forces; deputy defense minister
11. A. T. Altunin	Chief of Civil Defense; deputy defense minister
12. S. K. Kurkotkin	Chief of Rear Services; deputy defense minister

SOURCES: CIA, *USSR: Ministry of Defense Officials*, CR 85-11682 (Washington, D.C., 1 April 1985); *Krasnaia zvezda*, 22 February 1985; and *Pravda*, 12 March 1985; Alexander Rahr, "Personnel Changes Since Gorbachev," *Radio Liberty Research*, RL 243/85 (Munich, 30 July 1985); *New York Times*, 11 August 1985, Pravda, 1 February 1986.

decisions, verifying that orders are followed, and, in this way, controlling the Soviet armed forces. In the initial period of a nuclear war, the General Staff would rely heavily on war plans that had been prepared in peacetime and tested through military exercises.[40]

The role of the General Staff as the executive agent of the VGK has probably not changed much since the Second World War. At that time, it had the following assignments.[41]

- Formulation of concepts of strategic operations
- General support of these operations
- Organization and implementation of coordinated action among the branches of the armed forces and the fronts
- Readying of reserves
- Operations, strategic movement, and regrouping of troops

- Supervision over combat areas during operations
- Analysis of results from combat operations

In a contemporary nuclear war, the role of the General Staff would probably be even more extensive, including direct control over the operations of long-range forces and major units. In a sense, the strategic nuclear forces are at the personal disposal of the CPSU Politburo. This leadership makes the final decisions on targets to be hit, deferred, or avoided. The party leaders, acting through the VGK and the General Staff, constitute the "strategic echelon." Authoritative USSR military figures are quite specific in this regard: [42]

> The decisive means of achieving the goals of modern war are rocket and nuclear weapons with their unlimited effective range and tremendous destructive capabilities. This requires maximum centralization of control of the principal nuclear rocket weapons in the Supreme Command, particularly in the initial period of the war, for here and only here is it possible to decide correctly and most effectively questions concerning the objectives of nuclear strikes, targets for destruction, the power of warheads and means for delivering them to the targets, the type of explosive effect and the time for the delivery of such strikes, and finally the issuing of orders or signal dispatches. Only here can the authority be placed for pressing the button to activate the principal weapons of war. The Supreme Command has thus become not only a directing organ of supervision but also the immediate executor of principal missions of the armed conflict.

Another Soviet writer states that the "strategic command authority" (clearly the VGK, chaired by the CPSU general secretary) has the "decisive role" in planning, conducting, and coordinating "deep" strikes. This authority will perform the following functions: [43]

- Determine the objectives and priorities of the strikes
- Plan attacks and allocate forces to targets
- "Set other time (graph)" for execution of the strikes
- Organize cooperation and control

According to a unified operation plan, the Soviets envisage conducting these vast operations under the centralized control of the VGK and the General Staff: [44]

> A future war can be conducted successfully only when all strategic operations are strictly correlated on the basis of a common strategic concept or

plan with unified centralized leadership and if they are purposefully aimed at solving the general problems of armed combat . . . Strategic operations in a future nuclear war will consist of coordinated actions by all services of the Armed Forces, conducted according to a common concept, plan, and under a unified strategic leadership.

Here "strategic operations" are not confined to the nominally strategic force components but also include the ground forces' combined arms offensive that exploits strategic missile strikes to achieve the strategic objective of destroying remnants of enemy forces and occupying territory. Such coordinated, combined arms operations are considered "strategic operations in the theater" or "operational strategic" campaigns.[45]

Strategic Maneuver

Prior to, during, and after the initial exchange, the VGK would conduct strategic "maneuver" by Soviet strategic offensive and defensive forces.[46] For strategic missiles, such "maneuver" ordered by the strategic echelon would consist of trajectory maneuver, including (1) retargeting either within or between TVDs and choosing various options for the weight and extent of the strikes in each TVD by missiles based in silos; (2) movement to alternative field sites by IR/MRBMs; and (3) deployment of most SLBMs to nearby ocean areas protected by ASW screens. Maneuver of strategic defensive forces also involves actions such as relocating SAMs, interceptors, and radars from their normal peacetime sites and bases; concentrating these forces in most likely penetration corridors; and coordinating deployment of tactical SAMs and frontal aviation aircraft with strategic defensive forces.

Soviet military literature is clear that the concept of strategic nuclear "maneuver" applies to all services and is directed by the Supreme High Command:[47]

Now maneuver is interpreted above all as an organizational and quick shift or redistribution of previously planned nuclear rocket strikes by rocket troops and aircraft for the purpose of the decisive defeat of an opposing grouping of enemy troops, mainly a nuclear grouping, as well as the rapid transfer of forces and matériel for the purpose of creating the most favorable grouping for them for prompt and complete exploitation of the results of the use of weapons of mass destruction and completion of the defeat of the enemy . . .

Strategic maneuver is usually carried out in accordance with the plan and under the leadership of the Supreme High Command. Large groupings of strategic rocket troops, the air forces, PVO Strany troops, naval forces and ground troops can participate in it. It is carried out both within the theaters of military operations and among several theaters. The chief content of strategic maneuver is the redirection of nuclear strikes and nuclear groupings for the fast and complete destruction of large enemy groupings and the achievement of strategic results.

Although USSR sources are not explicit on the subject, Soviet strategic maneuver greatly reduces the armed forces' vulnerability to nuclear targeting. This means that many peacetime locations will lose much (or virtually all) of their value as nuclear targets.

Reserves and Force Reconstitution

The VGK designates certain peacetime units and weapons as reserve forces and matériel for use only at its direction. Other reserve forces would be created through mobilization. As already noted, some portion of the SRF missiles would probably be withheld as a reserve from the initial strikes. IR/MRBMs probably have several missiles per launcher and most, if not all, ICBM launchers have at least one refire missile.[48]

Large reserve forces and matériel stocks are required for the purpose of reconstituting losses to units of all military services incurred during the exchange until Soviet weapons facilities can resume production. As far as can be determined, reconstitution will take place throughout all branches of the USSR armed forces by drawing upon reserve stocks of weaponry accumulated in peacetime and by mobilization of reserve personnel. Factories will probably begin conversion to war production and step up weapons production on existing lines during the crisis period. Repair and rehabilitation necessary to resume production is scheduled to begin immediately at all factories and installations. Nevertheless, the Soviets recognize that a great deal of military production will be lost because of damage incurred in the initial exchange.

Little attention has been paid to USSR plans for reconstituting its forces after a nuclear exchange and in the course of subsequent operations. Even less research has been done on Soviet programs for peacetime stockpiling of weapons and matériel. Although confined to general principles, there is a considerable body of literature on these subjects from which this brief summary has been drawn.[49]

Basic Soviet Nuclear War Scenarios

The USSR envisages three basic scenarios for nuclear war: (1) pre-emption on warning of a U.S. or NATO intent to initiate imminent hostilities, with or without nuclear weapons; (2) a launch on tactical warning that American missiles or aircraft are on their way to attack; and (3) a second-strike situation in which the United States succeeds in attacking the Soviet Union, without warning of imminent intent or any tactical warning, and the USSR delivers an "answering blow."

The Soviets adopted pre-emption as their preferred option in the mid-1950s, and they have apparently seen no reason to change it. At the same time, however, the USSR recognizes that there might not be adequate warning, in which case it would be in a second-strike situation. Although the USSR would prefer to pre-empt, it knows that it cannot count on being able to do so.

A Soviet pre-emptive strike would seek to seize and hold the initiative. Second strikes or strikes on tactical warning are designed to regain the initiative and hold it during the nuclear war that would follow the initial exchange. In contrast to U.S. concepts, a second strike by the USSR is not designed simply to inflict an unacceptable level of damage. Rather, the Soviets see second strikes as military operations intended to reduce the enemy's ability to fight.

Emphasis on the Offensive

A question often debated in the West—whether U.S.S.R. armed forces are basically offensive or defensive—is meaningless from Moscow's point of view for the following reasons:

- There is no place for a defensive strategy in a nuclear war, because enemy bombers and missiles will attack targets throughout the country—not just in the border regions or at sea.
- "Victory" in the Soviet sense requires both offensive counterforce strikes on enemy nuclear capabilities and defensive operations to limit damage from surviving enemy nuclear forces.
- By definition, the United States and NATO would be the "aggressors" in any war with the USSR and the Warsaw Pact.

Consequently, in Moscow's view, the Soviet armed forces would be "defending" their own country and Eastern Europe in any war. These forces, however, would carry out their defense in a highly offensive manner. The USSR will "defend" its empire by annexing Western Europe and by neutralizing the United States and the PRC by means of strategic nuclear strikes.

In summary, the missions of the Soviet armed forces follow from military doctrine and strategy (outlined in Chapter 4). The major operational concepts discussed here form a consistent pattern. Everything is tailored to the purpose of fighting and winning a nuclear war, most of which will take place after the initial exchange. The USSR has no doubt that a nuclear conflict would be far more destructive than any previous war, but it does not regard a nuclear war as the apocalyptic end to civilization. Operationally, in the Soviet view the principal difference between a nuclear war and previous wars is that, while simultaneously defeating enemy forces and occupying their territory, the USSR would also defend itself from enemy nuclear strikes, maintain political and economic control, repair damage, and begin recovery. "Nuclear winter" is not a part of any Soviet operational concept for the conduct of nuclear war.

5

Trends in Soviet Strategic Forces in the 1960s

The Soviets date the completion of what they call the "revolution in military affairs" to 1960. As already discussed, by that time a new USSR military doctrine and strategy had essentially been formulated. Large-scale production of both fission and fusion weapons had begun, and sufficient numbers of strategic ballistic missiles deployed to form a new branch of service, the Strategic Rocket Forces (SRF). It was to become the primary military instrument for achieving the objectives of the political leadership's new doctrine. The industrial base to develop, produce, and deploy the combination of strategic offensive and defensive nuclear forces required by the new doctrine and strategy—to defeat the enemy but limit damage to the Soviet Union—had been established.[1]

Ambitions during the 1960s, however, far exceeded capabilities. First, the USSR's earlier political and military actions—subjugation of Eastern Europe, the Korean War, suppression of the Hungarian rebellion—and Soviet military developments—nuclear weapons, heavy bombers, Sputnik, and the ICBM—had aroused the United States. Consequently, during most of the decade the USSR found itself in a highly competitive environment for the acquisition of strategic weapons. Second, its technology lagged far behind that of America. Third, the Soviet industrial base still remained much smaller than that of the United States; nevertheless, it was expected not only to provide all the weapons required by the new doctrine and strategy but also, in Khrushchev's words, to "bury" the United States economically.

Fourth, USSR military planning seemed to be not very prescient in the early to mid-1960s.

Nevertheless, during that decade the Soviet Union made an enormous effort to acquire the strategic offensive and defensive weapons required to fight and win a nuclear war by defeating the enemy while limiting damage to its own territory. The pattern of weapons system acquisitions established in the 1950s was expanded during the 1960s to include all the elements of a war-fighting, damage-limiting force posture.

STRATEGIC OFFENSIVE SYSTEMS

By about 1964–65 the USSR had deployed more than 600 intermediate- and medium-range ballistic missile (IR/MRBM) launchers. Their missions were to disarm NATO (primarily its nuclear forces during an initial exchange); to ensure the subsequent defeat of surviving NATO forces by nuclear strikes in support of the Soviet and Warsaw Pact combined arms offensive; and to facilitate the seizure of Western Europe in as intact a condition as possible (so its resources could be used to support USSR recovery while "peace-loving" governments were being installed in all former NATO member-states). Another 100 or so IR/MRBM launchers were deployed against potential enemies on the USSR's periphery in Asia.

Because most of the targets in the Eurasian TVDs were soft, the IR/MRBM force with yields in the 150 to 500 KT range (or even lower) satisfied almost all damage-limiting requirements for strategic offensive forces in these TVDs through the 1960s. As shown in Chapter 8, the megaton weapons usually ascribed to Soviet IR/MRBMs by Western sources have little to do with USSR requirements. Equipping all Soviet IR/MRBMs with megaton weapons would only result in overkill (immense, unnecessary collateral damage), which runs counter to the objective of seizing Europe in as intact a condition as possible.

Meanwhile, deployment of second generation SS-7 and SS-8 intercontinental ballistic missiles (ICBMs) proceeded, although these systems provided inadequate damage-limiting capabilities. They were effective against U.S. Strategic Air Command (SAC) bases, naval complexes, and other soft military facilities. With accuracies (circular error probable, or CEP) of about 2,000 meters, however, even the largest fusion warheads that might fit into the SS-7 and SS-8 payloads could not destroy any significant number of Minuteman (MM) silos or launch control centers (LCC).

In about 1960, the Soviets initiated development of the SS-9. Its purpose was to limit damage to their own country by attacking hard targets throughout the "transoceanic" TVD, as they call the United States. During the early

1960s, the Minuteman LCCs probably looked like the perfect target. Destroy 100 LCCs, and all 1,000 MM silos would be rendered inoperable. The SS-9s probably were deployed for this purpose. Because USSR targeting strategy specifies two warheads for each target (apparently to ensure that at least one will arrive at its destination), SS-9 deployment plans in the mid-1960s possibly envisaged a force of at least 300 launchers in order to attack the LCCs, other hardened command-control targets, and provide some reserves.[2]

Development of the SS-11 took place parallel to that of the SS-9. The SS-11 was deployed to attack soft targets. Both systems became operational in 1966. Deployment of SS-7 and SS-8 ICBMs halted a year or two earlier; these older systems were ineffective against hard targets, vulnerable to U.S. attack, and too expensive to provide the bulk of Soviet soft target capabilities in the late 1960s and the early 1970s. Meanwhile, development of the SS-N-6 submarine-launched ballistic missile (SLBM) for the Y-class nuclear-powered ballistic missile submarines (SSBNs) must have proceeded in parallel with—or not more than a year or two behind—the SS-9 and SS-11 programs.

By the mid-1960s, the USSR evidently realized that it required MIRV technology for at least three reasons: (1) to attack each individual MM silo, (2) to inflict the requisite degree of damage on all soft targets, and (3) to provide a substantial secure reserve force. The Soviets apparently understood the degree to which the MM silos were internetted. They also knew that, even if all the LCCs were destroyed, missiles could be launched from SAC's airborne command post. The need to penetrate American ABM defenses may have represented a fourth reason for Soviet MIRV development in the 1970s.

Two USSR space shots in 1964, in which several satellites were placed in different orbits by the same booster, demonstrated the basic principles of MIRV technology.[3] In order to have met the observed flight test schedules, which began during 1972–73, development of the SS-16, SS-17, SS-18, and SS-19 ICBMs must have been approved by the Defense Council and Politburo in 1965–66 as part of the eighth five-year plan (1966–70). The effort expended to improve the accuracy of both the SS-18 and SS-19 indicates that these two ICBMs, like the earlier SS-9, were designed for a damage-limiting role—to destroy MM silos and other hard targets in pre-emptive attacks.

It is therefore probable that Soviet MIRVs were developed not as a reaction to American MIRVs but in parallel with them. They were designed to provide the USSR with the counterforce, damage-limiting capabilities against U.S. land-based ICBMs that could not have been achieved (within practical time, manpower, and cost constraints) by single re-entry vehicle

TABLE 3 TRENDS IN SOVIET SRF DEPLOYMENTS IN THE 1960s

SRF	1960	1961	1962	1963	1964	1965	1966	1967	1968	1969	1970
IR/MRBMs											
SS-3[a]	50	110	290	470	640	700	700	700	700	700	650
SS-4[a]	50	100	250	400	550	600	600	600	600	600	550
SS-5		10	40	70	90	100	100	100	100	100	100
SS-14[b]					Not reported						
SS-15[b]					Not reported						
ICBMs											
SS-6	5–10	55–60	80–85	105–110	204–209	224–229	299	489	699	1,049	1,427
SS-7	5–10	5–10	5–10	5–10	5–10	5–10	200	200	200	200	190
SS-8		50	70	90	180	200	19	19	19	19	19
SS-9		5	10	19	19	19	20	70	120	170	228
SS-11							60	200	360	660	970
SS-13											20
SRF total (rounded)	60	170	370–380	580	660–850	920–930	1,000	1,190	1,400	1,750	2,080

SOURCES: John M. Collins, *American and Soviet Military Trends Since the Cuban Missile Crisis* (Washington, D.C.: The Center for Strategic and International Studies, Georgetown University, 1978), *U.S.-Soviet Military Balance, Concepts and Capabilities, 1960–1980* (New York: McGraw-Hill, 1980); John M. Collins and Patrick N. Cronin, *U.S.-Soviet Military Balance: Statistical Trends, 1970–1983*, report no. 84-1635 (Washington, D.C.: Congressional Research Service, 27 August 1984), pp. 14 and 37; International Institute for Strategic Studies, *The Military Balance, 1971–1972* (London: IISS, 1971); Ray Bonds, ed., *Soviet War Machine* (New York: Chartwell Bros., 1977). None of these sources give system-by-system data prior to 1970, although Collins (*U.S.-Soviet Military Balance*) and Bonds (*Soviet War Machine*) provide the dates for initial operational capability from which the figures for the 1960s have been constructed to match reported data for 1970–71. The figures shown here are not always identical to those from any one of the sources, because these sources usually do not agree precisely with one another for any given system and year. Hence, these data represent what appears to be a reasonable synthesis of various sources for the 1970s and a plausible reconstruction of deployments in the 1960s.

[a] No data on SS-3 deployment are available. It is likely that a number of these missiles were deployed in the mid- to late 1950s. Consequently, the data shown for SS-4 deployment may include SS-3 launchers in the early 1960s. Collins (*U.S.-Soviet Military Balance*, p. 460) gives 1959 as the year for initial operational capability (IOC) of the SS-4.

[b] These designators (because no deployment figures have been reported) are assigned to the two mobile (mounted on a track vehicle) IR/MRBMs displayed in Moscow parades during the mid-1960s. One or both of these systems were deployed but probably on a very limited scale (Marshal I. Iakubovskii, "Fifty Years of the USSR Armed Forces," *Military Thought*, no. 2 [1968]: 28).

TABLE 4   SOVIET SLBM AND SSN CONSTRUCTION PROGRAMS, 1960–70

Program	1960	1961	1962	1963	1964	1965	1966	1967	1968	1969	1970
G-(Diesel)			23	23	23	23	23	23	23	23	20
SSBNs	4	7	9	9	9	9	9	10	14	19	22
H-I & II	4	7	9	9	9	9	9	8	8	8	8
H-III								1	1	1	1
Y								1	5	10	13
SSBN deliveries		3	2					1	4	5	3
Attack class SSN	6	11	18	24	29	35	40	45	49	53	57
E-I	2	4	5	5	5	5	5	5	5	5	5
E-II: Cruise missile		1	3	6	11	17	22	26	29	29	29
C-I & II									1	3	5
N	4	6	10	13	13	13	13	13	13	13	12
V-I: ASW								1	1	3	5
A											1
Attack classes deliveries		5	7	6	5	6	5	5	4	4	5
Total nuclear class deliveries		8	9	6	5	6	5	6	8	9	8
Nuclear powered Total[a]	10	18	27	33	38	44	49	55	63	72	79

SOURCES: Michael McGwire, "Soviet Naval Programs," in Paul J. Murphy, ed., Naval Power in Soviet Policy, Studies in Communist Affairs, vol. 2 (United States Air Force, 1978), p. 81; International Institute for Strategic Studies, The Military Balance, 1971–1972; Captain John Moore, RN, ed., Jane's Fighting Ships 1977–1978; John M. Collins, American and Soviet Military Trends Since the Cuban Missile Crisis (Washington, D.C.: The Center for Strategic and International Studies, Georgetown University, 1978), pp. 97–99 and 274–75; Ray Bonds, ed., The Soviet War Machine (New York: Chartwell Bros., 1977), p. 153. These sources differ slightly in the numbers reported for any given weapons system for various years; the number shown here represents a "best judgment" composite drawn from the various sources.

[a] Note that as SSBN numbers decline, there is a corresponding increase in SSN deliveries. As McGwire noted years ago, since the mid-1960s production of nuclear propulsion units has been fairly stable at the level required to construct approximately ten nuclear-powered submarines a year. McGwire's insight into Soviet nuclear-powered submarine construction programs has been confirmed by data reported during the 1970s in the annual posture statements issued by U.S. defense secretaries.

ICBMs. This point will be explored in Chapter 8, which analyzes the capabilities of Soviet strategic ballistic missile forces to destroy the targets specified by USSR targeting strategy. Here, it is sufficient to note that current Soviet capabilities to destroy most American missile silos and other hard targets were made possible by decisions made around 1965–66.

Trends in USSR land- and sea-based strategic missile deployments during the 1960s are shown in Tables 3 and 4. Because SSBN construction schedules are intimately related, Table 4 also includes construction programs for nuclear-powered attack classes of submarines (SSNs).

As the Soviets began to deploy large numbers of strategic ballistic missiles—first, SLBMs and IR/MRBMs and later, ICBMs and long-range SLBMs—they modified the missions of their strategic aircraft to concentrate on mobile targets and targets of opportunity in the Eurasian and adjacent oceanic TVDs. The USSR probably built about 2,000 TU-16 (Badger) medium bombers and deployed half that number, many with the naval air force. Heavy bomber inventories peaked at approximately 200 aircraft in the mid-1960s, and these were also adapted to the revised missions of Soviet strategic aircraft, which were largely confined to the Eurasian TVDs.

One new aircraft of this type—the TU-22 medium bomber—was introduced in the 1960s. It had a limited supersonic capability but, like the TU-16, an inadequate range to allow it to attack Western carrier task forces from Soviet airfields before the carriers reached waters from which they could support NATO. Consequently, the USSR began development of a medium bomber with a sufficient range—the TU-26 Backfire, introduced during the 1970s.

To penetrate air defenses and to increase effectiveness against naval vessels equipped with both conventional and nuclear warheads, the Soviets developed several air-to-surface missiles during the 1960s. Trends in strategic aircraft inventories during this period are shown in Table 5.

STRATEGIC DEFENSES

By the beginning of the 1960s Soviet national air, missile, and space defenses (PVO Strany) were characterized by a large inventory of interceptors, most of which were ineffective at any altitude during nighttime or in poor weather; an enormous investment in the surface-to-air missile (SA-1) defenses of Moscow; a burgeoning SA-2 deployment program; and several thousand early-warning and ground control intercept radars, whose technology, at best, could barely keep pace with the perceived threat. The USSR navy had just begun to acquire a fleet of diesel- and nuclear-powered cruise missile submarines and medium-range bombers equipped with suitable air-to-surface

TABLE 5   SOVIET STRATEGIC AIRCRAFT INVENTORIES IN 1970

	1970
Long-range aviation (LRA)	910
TU-95 Bear	100
MYA-4 Bison	90[a]
TU-16 Badger	550[b]
TU-22 Blinder	170[b]
Soviet naval air (SNA)	650
TU-95 Bear	50
IL-38 May	20
BE-12 Mail	60
TU-16 Badger	400[c]
TU-22 Blinder	60
IL-28 Beagle	60
Total	1,560

SOURCES: The 1970 data are from the International Institute for Strategic Studies, *The Military Balance, 1970–1971,* pp. 9–10; and Collins, *Statistical Trends: 1970–1983,* pp. 23, 37, and 79–80.

[a] About one-half are tankers.

[b] It is not clear whether some of these aircraft are tankers or whether additional tankers and reconnaissance models exist.

[c] One hundred of these were reported to be tanker and reconnaissance models.

missiles for anticarrier operations. It possessed neither the platforms (surface ships and submarines) nor the weapons and sensors to conduct strategic ASW operations. Some design work had been done, however, so lead ships and prototypes more suitable to the missions were on the way.

The general patterns in USSR strategic defensive programs appear to have been as follows:

• During the 1960s the Soviets made an enormous investment in all types of air defense weaponry—interceptors, surface-to-air missiles (SAMs), radars, and communications systems.

• Deployment of the Moscow ABM defenses in the mid-1960s was followed by the realization that the system could not cope with large and sophisticated attacks; hence, a "back to the drawing board" R & D effort began in order to develop an effective ABM system took place during the 1970s.

• Investment in ASW platforms was modest in the 1960s but accelerated at the end of the decade, when deliveries of ships and SSNs specifically designed for this mission commenced.

• A large investment in cruise missile submarines and medium bombers for the anticarrier mission was made in the early to mid-1960s. Subsequently, the emphasis has been on modernization with a slow, but relatively steady, growth in the number of platforms and missiles.

During the 1960s the USSR deployed a large number of air defense systems designed to defend the country against an aerodynamic threat under all weather conditions at medium to high altitudes. (See Table 6 for an approximation of the growth in interceptors, SAM launchers, and radar inventories.) Although the total number of interceptors declined from approximately 4,000 to some 3,200, the Soviets added roughly 1,500 new model aircraft to the PVO Strany interceptor inventory. Most of these aircraft were capable of supersonic flight; all had the latest radars; and all carried one or more types of air-to-air missiles employing radar, infrared guidance systems, or both. None, however, were effective at low altitudes (roughly 1,000 meters or less, and particularly, below 300 meters). By switching to low-level penetration tactics, SAC largely denied the potential effectiveness of Soviet interceptors and associated ground radars for more than two decades.

During the 1960s the USSR completed the SA-2 deployments (begun in the late 1950s) and deployed two new systems—the SA-3 and the SA-5. The SA-3 was apparently designed to counter the low-altitude threat, although its effectiveness was limited by offensive tactics and countermeasures. The SA-5 was designed to counter high-altitude threats, which, after the cancellation of the U.S. B-70 program, were limited to the "Hounddog" supersonic cruise missile carried on B-52s and the American SR-71. Evidently, the Soviets thought these potential threats—along with the possibility that the United States could resume development of the B-70 or a similar aircraft—were serious enough to justify proceeding with SA-5 deployments. Meanwhile, the capabilities that were built into the SA-5 to counter high-altitude aerodynamic threats created persistent and widespread concern in America that this missile either had also been designed to engage ballistic missiles or could be upgraded to become an effective ABM system.

Despite all the efforts devoted to new SAMs, interceptors, and ground-environment air defense systems during the 1960s, PVO Strany was probably no more capable of accomplishing its mission at the end of the decade than at the beginning. At least another ten years of development were needed before the Soviet air defense system could become effective against low-altitude penetration tactics, countermeasures, and the American short-range attack missile (SRAM), which was approaching deployment by the end of the 1960s.

During the early part of that decade, the USSR apparently convinced itself that ABM defenses would not be difficult. Khrushchev boasted of being

TABLE 6   SOME TRENDS IN PVO STRANY PROCUREMENT, 1960–70

INTERCEPTORS	INVENTORIES	
	1960[a]	1970
First generation		
MIG-15, -17, -19	3,700	1,350
Second generation		
SU-9/11	100	750
YAK-28	—	350
TU-28	—	150
SU-15	—	400
YAK-25	150	200
Third generation		
MIG-23	—	—
MIG-25	—	—
Interceptor inventory	4,000	3,200
SAMs		
SA-1	3,200	3,200
SA-2	1,000	4,600
SA-3		
(Launchers)	—	(900)
Rails	—	1,800
SA-5	—	1,100
SAM inventory (on-launcher)[b]	4,200	10,700
Early warning (EW) and ground control intercept		
(GCI) radars		7,000
ABM defenses		
Radars		
Early warning	—	several
Battle management	—	2
Engagement	—	several
Missiles	—	64
Antisatellite		
Radars	—	—
Launchers	—	—

SOURCES: Collins, *American and Soviet Military Trends*, pp. 144–47. No precise data are available on the number of early-warning ABM radars that may also provide space tracking. Various sources report the "Dog House" and "Chekov" radars as part of Moscow defenses, so apparently two battle management radars are involved. Precise numbers of Hen Egg engagement radars are not available.

NOTES: Parentheses signify that the numbers therein do not add to the totals.

[a] Rough estimates only.

[b] Numbers are for early SAMs on deployed launchers. The total SAM (missile) inventory could easily have been ten or twenty times the number shown here.

able to hit a "fly in the sky" in the mid-1960s, and the Soviets deployed the Moscow ABM defenses shortly thereafter. By then, however, they began to realize the inadequacy of their technology. Consequently—more or less in concert with the SA-10 SAM program to counter low-altitude penetration tactics—they started developing the so-called "X-3" ABM. Although the full configuration of the system is not yet known—perhaps because no agreement has been reached on a final design—the "X-3" appears to have much in common with the Nike-X, which the United States developed in the 1960s yet refused to deploy.

Apparently, the Soviet navy received its strategic ASW mission about or before 1960. Aside from developing the November-class SSN, little could be done to implement the assignment until suitable platforms, sensors, and weapons had been designed, developed, and constructed. Initially, two older-class surface ships were converted for the ASW mission. By the mid- to late-1960s new surface ships—Kresta-class cruisers, Moskva-class helicopter cruisers, and one new Victor-class SSN—specifically designed for antisubmarine warfare were being delivered by Soviet yards. Lead units of the Krivak class were under construction, and design was well advanced on other new ASW surface ships, such as the Kara-class cruiser. The first unit of the Alpha-class SSN was completed in 1970. But this strikingly advanced design—which must date from the early 1960s, if not earlier—evidently had many problems; it was not deployed until nearly a decade later. In summary, the USSR instituted a broadly based and expensive strategic ASW program in the 1960s, but it only began to deliver surface ships and submarines specifically designed for this mission at the end of that decade.

The anticarrier assignment of the Soviet navy probably dates from the early 1950s. By 1968 USSR shipyards had delivered thirty-one E-class SSNs and sixteen J-class diesel-powered submarines, all armed with SS-N-3 cruise missiles for anticarrier and other antishipping operations. Meanwhile, the naval air forces had received several hundred medium bombers armed with air-to-surface missiles designed for the same mission. In addition, the navy's anticarrier operations were to be supported by several hundred long-range aviation bombers. Consequently, by the end of the 1960s the Soviets had acquired formidable aircraft and submarine cruise missile capabilities to engage carriers and other U.S. or NATO surface ships.

Summary of Procurement Trends in the 1960s

Another way to look at the pattern in development and deployment of USSR damage-limiting forces during the first decade of the "nuclear revolution in military affairs" is to count the number and types of weapons systems procured for each major mission. Although the information available in the public domain remains incomplete, it is adequate for the purpose of studying the patterns of force development and relating those patterns to Soviet strategic concepts and objectives. Table 7 presents the major identifiable weapons systems and hardware items procured in the 1960s, some of which were developed in the previous decade. The total is nearly 100 systems. Of these, some twenty were procured for strategic offensive forces; another thirty-two (counting the Moscow ABM radars and the Galosh missile as one system) for strategic defenses; and the remainder for the ground forces, frontal aviation, and military transport aviation.

Because the first priority of USSR strategic offensive forces is to destroy the enemy's nuclear delivery systems, weapons stocks, and C^3 (command, control, and communications) systems, the bulk of military procurement in the 1960s was clearly designed for damage-limiting operations to fight and "win" a nuclear war. As has been pointed out, during this decade the forces fell far short of the capabilities required to perform their damage-limiting missions. Nevertheless, the objectives of Soviet force development in the 1960s seem clear, and they were fully consistent with the military doctrine and strategy worked out in the axial period and published during the 1960s.

According to the conventional wisdom in the West, the USSR accelerated strategic missile programs after the Cuban missile crisis. It is impossible conclusively to test this hypothesis on the basis of information available in the public domain. Given the long lead times of strategic missile programs, however, there is nothing in the historical record to support the hypothesis that any Soviet strategic missile development program was accelerated after the Cuban crisis (with the possible exception of the commitment to construct large numbers of Y-class SSBNs).

The perspective on trends in USSR strategic missile force deployments can be improved by considering the buildup in the warhead inventory instead of looking only at launchers. During the 1960s and into the early 1970s official U.S. sources compared American and Soviet strategic forces only in numbers of launchers. Since the beginning of the MIRV era the comparison has taken both launchers and warheads into consideration, although almost always without counting USSR reload missiles. Moreover, U.S. official sources and most Western analysts only count ICBMs and SLBMs as "strategic" missiles, despite the fact that (1) the Soviets consider their IR/MRBMs to be just as "strategic" as ICBMs; and (2) not all of their ICBMs are targeted on the "transoceanic TVD," that is, the United States.

In his posture statement for fiscal year 1980, for example, then Secretary of Defense Harold Brown reported "total warheads" for the SS-20

TABLE 7   SOVIET WEAPONS PROCUREMENT IN THE 1960s

Major mission	Number of systems	System designators
Strategic offensive	20	
ICBMs	5	SS-6, -7, -8, -9, -11
IR/MRBMs	2	SS-4, -5
SLBMs	3	N-4, -N-5, -N-6
SSBNs[a]	3	G, H, Y
Bombers	2	TU-16, -22
ASM	5	AS-1, -2, -3, -4, -5
Strategic defensive	35–36	
Air defense	18–19	
SAMs	3	SA-2, -3, -5
Interceptor	6	MIG-19, SU-9, SU-11, SU-15, TU-28, YAK-25
AAM	4	AA-1, -2, -3, -5
EW & GCI radar	5–6	Back Net, Bar Lock, Knife Rest, Cake series, Tall King
Missile and space defense	5	
Early warning		
Interceptors	1	Galosh
Radar	4	Hen House, Dog House, Chekhov, Hen Egg
Antisubmarine warfare	8	
Surface ships	3	Kresta I, Moskva, Kashin
SSNs	2	N, V-I
Aircraft	2	May, Mail
Missiles	1	FRAS-1
Anticarrier	4 (11)[b]	
SSN/SLCM	2	E-I & II, C-1
SLCMs	2	SS-N-3, -9
Aircraft	(2)[b]	TU-16, -22
ASMs	(5)[c]	Most ASMs listed under strategic offensive systems
Operational-strategic		
Ground forces	23–24 (25)[b]	
Tanks	4	T-54/55, T-62, T-64, PT-76
APCs	3	BRDM-1&2, BMP-1, BTR-60
SPs	2	ASU-57, -85
Artillery & mortars	6	S-23, D-30, D-20, M-155, M-46
SAMs	2 (3)[b]	SA-2, -4, -6
AA-Guns[c]	3	ZU 23/2, ZSU 23/4, ZSR 57-2
ATGMs[d]	3–4	AT-1, -2, -3, -4

Major mission	Number of systems	System designators
Frontal aviation	8	
Interceptors	2	MIG-21
Fighters-bombers	1	SU-7
Helicopters	3	MI-6, -8, -10
Transports	2	AN-12, -22, -26
Navy	10	
SAMs	1	SS-N-3
Missile patrol boats	3	Komar, Osa, Nanuchka
Frigates & corvettes	3	Petia, Mirka, Poti
GLCMs	1	SS-N-3
Amphibious landing	2	Alligator, Polnochniy
Total	96–98	
Strategic offensive	20	
Strategic defensive	35–36	

SOURCES: John M. Collins, "American and Soviet Armed Services: Strengths Compared," *Congressional Record—Senate*, 5 August 1977; John W. R. Taylor, ed., *Jane's All the World's Aircraft*, 1973–74, 1975–76, and 1976–77 eds.; International Institute for Strategic Studies, *The Military Balance, 1971–1972*; Edgar Ulsamer, "The USSR's Military Shadow is Lengthening," *Air Force Magazine* 60, no. 3 (March 1977): 36–46; and Colin Gray, "Soviet Tactical Airpower," ibid., pp. 62–71.

[a]Note that the G-class submarine is diesel-powered but was considered a strategic system by the USSR during the 1950s and 1960s.

[b]Parentheses indicate systems already counted under another mission.

[c]Antiaircraft guns

[d]Antitank guided missiles

on the assumption that one missile had three MIRVed warheads for each launcher.[4] The SS-4 and SS-5 IR/MRBMs were treated in the same manner; that is, "total" warhead inventory equaled the number of launchers.

This practice illustrates one of the basic differences discussed earlier between American and USSR strategic concepts. The U. S. has no serious concept about a nuclear war continuing beyond the initial exchange. The United States stocks only one missile per ICBM and SLBM launcher, plus a few spares. Because the Soviets expect the initial nuclear exchange to introduce "operational strategic" campaigns in the Eurasian and oceanic TVDs that will continue at least several weeks, they maintain more than one missile per operational launcher.

For IR/MRBMs, the Soviets apparently stock three or four rounds per operational launcher; hence, the nuclear warhead inventory is several times as large as the number of launchers in the Strategic Rocket Forces inventory.[5]

TABLE 8   ESTIMATE OF SOVIET MISSILE WARHEAD INVENTORY IN THE 1960s

	1960		1965		1970	
	On launcher	With possible refire	On launcher	With possible refire	On launcher	With possible refire
SRF	55–60	160–230	924–929	2,550–3,690	2,077	3,590–5,860
SS-4	50	150–200	600	1,800–2,400	550	1,650–2,200
SS-5	5–10	10–30	100	300–400	100	300–400
SS-6			5–10	10–30		
SS-7			200	400–800	190	380–760
SS-8			19	40–60	19	40–60
SS-9					228	230–460
SS-11					970	970–1,940
SS-13					20	20–40
Navy SLBMs	70	70–140	80	80–160	336	346–692
SS-N-4/5	70	70–140	80	80–160	80	90–180
SS-N-6					256	256–512
Total (rounded)	125–130	230–370	1,000–1,010	2,630–3,850	2,410	3,940–6,550

SOURCES: On launcher warhead inventory taken from the number of launchers, as given in Tables 3 and 4.

Early-model SS-7 and SS-8 ICBMs were primarily deployed on soft launchers, so these systems probably had several reload missiles per launcher. The United States discovered in the early 1980s that the USSR also stocked more than one round (plus the minimum spares stipulated in the SALT II Treaty) for at least some of its current model ICBMs with multiple independently targeted re-entry vehicles.[6] It would be surprising if the Soviet navy stocks only one round for each of its SLBM launchers.

Table 8 attempts to estimate the likely trends in the strategic missile warhead inventory. All strategic missile systems are included, and allowance is made for refire rounds. There is no definitive evidence that the USSR stocks more than one round per launcher for the SS-9 and SS-11 or for its SLBMs; considering the evidence on multiple rounds stocked for other systems, however, it would be surprising if the Soviets did not have at least some reloads. Indeed, if they stock more than one round for each silo-based ICBM, the total missile inventory may be more than twice the number of operational launchers.

MILITARY EXPENDITURES

Throughout the 1960s USSR military outlays evidenced the same basic trends that began at the end of the preceding decade. Total expenditures rose quickly, and procurement grew faster than other components. The periods of most rapid growth were 1959–63 and 1965–70. During the latter period, defense expenditures approximately doubled, and procurement nearly tripled. The Soviet economy as a whole performed well from 1965 to 1970 (somewhat better than during the previous five years), and the military expanded particularly fast. By 1970 defenses accounted for about 12 to 13 percent of GNP, as compared to about 9 percent only one decade earlier. Data for these trends are presented in Table 9.

The rapid growth in military expenditures during the 1960s was driven by weapons procurement policies. More than one-half of the increased expenditures for that purpose can be attributed to the growth of actual physical acquisitions: that is, numbers of missiles, aircraft, tanks, guns, and support equipment delivered by the factories. The remaining expansion reflected growth in technological complexity and sophistication.[7] At the end of the 1960s, Soviet weapons lagged well behind those of the United States in most areas of technology and were relatively simple by Western standards. Nevertheless, by 1970 their qualitative change—as compared with 1960—had became both expensive and substantial.

Most outside perceptions of what was happening to USSR military expenditures during the 1960s, however, were 180 degrees removed from the

TABLE 9   SOVIET DEFENSE EXPENDITURES IN THE 1960S
(BILLIONS OF RUBLES)

	1955 PRICES							1970 PRICES				
	1960	1961	1962	1963	1964	1965	1966	1966	1967	1968	1969	1970
Procurement[a]	5.9	7.4	9.3	10.8	11.4	12.4	14.4	8.1	10.6	13.2	15.9	18.1
Personnel, maintenance, operations, and construction[b]	8.8	9.4	9.7	10.3	10.8	11.2	11.6	14.7	15.3	17.1	17.9	17.9
RDT&E[c]	1.0	1.1	1.3	1.4	1.6	1.7	1.9	6.4	7.1	8.2	8.4	10.0
Total	15.7	17.9	20.3	22.5	23.8	25.3	27.9	29.2	33.0	38.5	42.2	46.0
Defense share of GNP (percent)[d]	9.4%					10.7%						12.6%

SOURCES: W. T. Lee, *The Estimation of Soviet Defense Expenditures, 1955–1975* (New York: Praeger, 1977), and "USSR Gross National Product in Established Prices, 1955–1975," *Jahrbuch der Wirtschaft Osteuropas* (Munich/Vienna: Gunter Olzog Verlag, 1979), pp. 399–429.

[a]See Lee, *The Estimation of Soviet Defense Expenditures, 1955–1975*, pp. 65–66, for mid-point of range. The difference between the estimates in 1955 and 1970 prices is primarily the consequence of a discrepancy in Soviet data for total machinery output prior to and after 1965–66. This discrepancy is believed to result from the inclusion of prototypes in procurement in the period 1960–66, using 1955 prices, and the exclusion of prototypes from the 1966–70 data using 1970 prices.

[b]The differences in 1966 are primarily the result of increases in wholesale prices for materials during 1967.

[c]Data in 1955 prices exclude prototypes; data in 1970 prices include prototypes and are the mid-point of the range.

[d]Lee, "USSR Gross National Product in Established Prices, 1955–1975," p. 145.

facts. With few exceptions, Western academics accepted the official "defense" budget, which almost doubled from about 9 billion rubles in 1960 to nearly 18 billion rubles—or about 5 percent of GNP—in 1970 (6 percent when R&D is added). The CIA made an immense effort to estimate outlays for the USSR military by costing everything it could see in dollars and then converting the dollars into rubles. As a result, the official U.S. government estimate of Soviet outlays for procurement and operations essentially matched the official "defense" budgets from 1961 through 1975. To these figures the CIA added an estimate for military R&D that clearly was not included in official USSR "defense" figures. The agency probably spent up to $100 million for personnel and a total of perhaps $400 million to $1 billion (including collection costs) to duplicate the official Soviet "defense" budget, which is published regularly each year in *Pravda* and other Soviet publications.

Furthermore, the CIA estimate of Soviet procurement (a constant 5 billion rubles per annum throughout the 1960s) was unconvincing. To reconcile the visible increases in weaponry with constant procurement outlays, agency analysts created the myth that military industries constituted a super-efficient sector of the USSR economy—so efficient that resources could not be transferred effectively from military to civilian uses. As a result, the economy allegedly functioned in a state of "fundamental disequilibrium."

According to the CIA, the military burden on the Soviet economy declined steadily throughout the 1960s, from about 10 percent of GNP in 1960 to about 6 percent in the 1970s. This pattern coincided with the American experience during the 1960s, except that for the United States defense held steady at 9 to 10 percent of GNP until about 1967. It then declined sharply to about 6 percent in 1970.

In 1976 the agency discovered that it had underestimated USSR military expenditures for 1970 by a factor of two; that is, 50 billion rubles as compared to the CIA's estimate of 24 billion rubles in 1970 prices. When the CIA doubled its estimates of Soviet defense expenditures, however, it was unable to correct their rate of growth. The revised agency estimates overstate USSR military expenditures prior to 1970 to the same degree that it previously had underestimated them.[8]

Although the Soviets shared none of these illusions and were allocating more and more of their resources to the military, they nevertheless found themselves in a difficult position at the end of the 1960s. After the first decade of an immense effort to acquire the military posture prescribed by the ambitious doctrine and strategy adopted around 1960, they remained outclassed in almost everything except numbers of men, guns, aircraft, tanks, and bunkers. Most threatening to USSR strategy was the U.S. decision to deploy an ABM system to protect American ICBMs and certain other military targets. Moreover, the limited ABM program approved in the late 1960s had the capability to expand into larger and more capable U.S. defenses that could impair or deny the counterforce, damage-limiting objectives of Soviet MIRV programs. The latter were under development in the mid-1960s, but they would not be ready for deployment until a decade later.

Although they lagged several years behind U.S. schedules, the MIRV programs in the USSR were still competitive, particularly because two of the new ICBMs—designated SS-18 and SS-19 by the United States and RS-20 and RS-18, respectively, by the Soviets—were designed to destroy Minuteman silos. In contrast, American MIRVs were expressly designed to be effective only against soft targets. This was because Washington policymakers of the mid-1960s viewed any threat to USSR silos as "destabilizing" to the strategy of "mutual assured destruction," imputed also to the USSR.

In the late 1960s, however, Soviet strategic defensive technology remained woefully noncompetitive with that of the United States; ABM technology was ten to fifteen years behind. Despite the immense investment during the 1950s and 1960s, USSR air defenses could not cope with SAC bombers penetrating at low altitude. In the meantime, Soviet shipyards had just begun to deliver new classes of surface ships and submarines specifically designed for the ASW mission.

Diplomacy came to the rescue of military strategy, however. This is the story behind SALT and the era of "détente," which Moscow called "relaxation of tensions" without any relaxation in its efforts to achieve military superiority and to change the worldwide "correlation of forces" in its favor. The Appendix provides a detailed discussion of USSR motivations during these talks.

In brief, the Soviets were forced to execute a strategic "turnaround" by negotiating the ABM treaty to buy time and catch up in strategic defense technology. At the same time the USSR had to reach an agreement on strategic offensive missiles that would allow deployment of sufficient SS-18s and SS-19s to achieve effective counterforce, damage-limiting capabilities against Minuteman silos and other hard targets in the United States. Soviet military policy in the 1970s—discussed in the next chapter—followed basically the same pattern of weapons acquisition as during the 1960s. Chapter 8 will demonstrate that the launcher and MIRV ceilings, which the Soviets obtained in SALT II, coincided with their strategic targeting requirements. This was not merely coincidental; the final ceilings were the result of careful planning and skillful negotiations.

6

The SALT Era:
Superiority or Parity?

If USSR military policy had changed as a result of the SALT process and détente, the evidence for any such modification should have appeared in three areas: doctrine and strategy, patterns of weapons acquisition, and national economic priorities. Recent disinformation campaigns to the contrary, the basic tenets of Soviet doctrine and strategy have not changed. This chapter will examine trends in USSR weapons acquisition and national economic priorities during the 1970s.

The salient trends in Soviet military policy over the past decade had the following objectives:

- To continue quantitative expansion of the armed forces along the lines of the 1960s while observing negotiated limits on launcher numbers

- To complete development of and to deploy three new models of MIRVed ICBMs, required for effective counterforce attacks on American ICBMs and for complete coverage of soft military and related industrial targets in the United States

- To acquire SLBM forces capable of making a significant contribution to the initial massive nuclear strikes on targets in all TVDs and also to provide a large secure reserve

- To continue modernization of strategic defense with the best technology available and, most importantly, to develop the technology required to be effective against U.S. strategic offensive forces

- To upgrade Soviet operational-strategic forces with additional firepower and advanced technology so that victory over NATO would be assured in either a conventional or nuclear war

STRATEGIC OFFENSIVE FORCES

SLBMs accounted for all of the growth in USSR strategic offensive missile launchers between 1970 and 1980. The SRF began and ended the 1970s with a total of some 2,000 launchers, about 1,400 of which were ICBMs. The Soviet navy's SLBM force, however, grew from about twenty-five nuclear-powered submarines (SSBNs) with fewer than 300 missiles in 1970 to some sixty-five SSBNs carrying about 950 missiles in 1980. These quantitative trends in the number of USSR strategic missile launchers during the 1970s are shown in Tables 10 and 11.

Quantitative growth in the number of warheads during the 1970s was much more rapid than the increase in launchers. By 1970 the Soviets had about 2,400 warheads on ready strategic ballistic missiles. Including refires, the number of warheads may have reached between 4,000 and 6,000. By the end of 1980 the USSR inventory had grown to 9,000 warheads on ready missiles, some 6,600 of which were on ICBMs. The number of refire missiles is uncertain, although the total strategic ballistic missile warhead inventory in 1980 could have been double the number on ready missiles, or up to 20,000 (about 13,000 of which would have been on ICBMs). Table 12 summarizes increases in the Soviet strategic ballistic-missile warhead inventory during the 1970s and shows the sensitivity of all such calculations to uncertainties about the number of refire missiles.

By far the most important trend in strategic missile forces during the 1970s was the improvement in accuracy of ICBMs. This provided the first significant increase in Soviet damage-limiting capabilities since the mid-1960s and, together with the quantitative growth in the number of warheads, gave the USSR its first margin of superiority over U.S. strategic missile forces. In the West, this margin of superiority is the perceived "window of vulnerability" (of American ICBMs to Soviet counterforce attacks beginning in the early to mid-1970s). This potential threat was concentrated in two of the MIRVed systems—the SS-18 and the SS-19. Development began in the mid-1960s, and flight testing commenced after the SALT I agreements had been signed. Ironically, the SS-19 was precisely the kind of follow-on to the SS-11 that the United States had tried to forestall by imprecise unilateral statements appended to the 26 May 1972 Interim Agreement on Strategic

Offensive Arms.[1] The Soviets knew what they were doing. The United States either did not or found out too late.

When development began in the mid-1960s, the design accuracy for circular error probable (CEP) of the SS-18 and SS-19 ICBMs probably equaled the CEP attributed to the first versions of these missiles (ca. 400 to 500 meters).[2] Combined with the reported yields, these initial models would have been effective against 1960s American ICBM silos, rated at about 300 pounds per square inch (psi). By the time these Soviet missiles began flight testing in 1972, however, Minuteman silos were being hardened to about 2,000 psi. Consequently, when the SS-18 and SS-19 ICBMs began to be deployed in 1974, they would not have been very effective against Minuteman.[3]

Within a remarkably short time the Soviets began testing new models of these missiles—designated SS-18 mod 4 and SS-19 mod 3 by the United States—which were reported to have CEPs of about 260 meters.[4] Armed with this type of accuracy and with warheads of about 500 KT, these later models could have been fairly effective; two such warheads detonated on a Minuteman silo give a probability of about 0.9 of destroying a silo hardened to 2,000 psi.

This rapid improvement in the accuracy of the SS-18 and SS-19 ICBMs was evidently made possible by exports from the United States to the USSR of precision ball-bearing machine tools.[5] The USSR had tried to buy these machine tools more than a decade earlier and nearly succeeded. Under the aura of SALT and détente, the second attempt succeeded. Consequently, the Soviets were able to offer a credible threat to American ICBMs by the late 1970s instead of a decade later, a threat that the U.S. government is (somewhat belatedly) attempting to counter at a cost of tens of billions of dollars. The export of these precision ball-bearing machine tools to the USSR was probably the most expensive foreign trade deal in history.

Trends in Western estimates of Soviet missile yields and accuracies are summarized in Figures 1 and 2. During the 1960s and 1970s the accuracy of USSR land-based strategic missiles at full range improved nearly ten-fold, from more than one nautical mile ($>$2,000 meters) to about one-tenth of a nautical mile (or 200 to 300 meters) for the most accurate systems—the latest SS-18 and SS-19 ICBMs.

The trend toward greater missile accuracy was not the product of bureaucratic inertia, the parochial interests of the military, action-reaction, or any of the other conventional Western explanations for Soviet behavior. Rather, this trend clearly represents another manifestation of the USSR warfighting, damage-limiting strategy. As shown in Table 10, the SS-18 and SS-19 account for about 75 percent of the ICBM warhead inventory, which fact also reflects the counterforce priorities of Soviet military doctrine and strategy. At the same time, the combination of improved accuracy and MIRV

TABLE 10   TRENDS IN SOVIET SRF DEPLOYMENTS, 1970–80
(LAUNCHERS)

	1970	1971	1972	1973	1974	1975	1976	1977	1978	1979	1980
IR/MRBMs											
SS-4	650	600	600	600	590	590	590	570	560	530	560
SS-5	550	500	500	500	500	500	500	480	420	350	350
SS-20	100	100	100	100	90	90	90	90	80	60	50
									60	120	160
ICBMs	1,427	1,489	1,547	1,547	1,607	1,607	1,557	1,477	1,398	1,398	1,398
SS-7	190	190	190	190	190	190	190	80			
SS-8	19	19	19	19	19	19	19	9			
SS-9	228	270	308	308	298	298	272	208	132	68	
SS-11	970	970	970	970	1,030	960	910	850	750	650	640
SS-13	20	40	60	60	60	60	60	60	60	60	60
SS-17						10	20	50	100	140	150
SS-18						10	36	100	176	240	308
SS-19						60	100	120	180	240	240
ICBMs MIRVed (SALT-accountable)						80	156	270	475	620	698
SRF total (rounded)	2,080	2,090	2,150	2,150	2,200	2,200	2,150	2,050	1,960	1,930	1,960

SOURCES: John M. Collins and Patrick N. Cronin, *U.S.-Soviet Military Balance: Statistical Trends, 1970–1983*, report no. 84-1635 (Washington, D.C.: Congressional Research Service, 27 August 1984); John M. Collins, *American and Soviet Military Trends Since the Cuban Missile Crisis* (Washington, D.C.: The Center for Strategic and International Studies, Georgetown University, 1978), pp. 97–99 and 274–75; Collins, *U.S.-Soviet Military Balance*, pp. 448 and 520; International Institute for Strategic Studies, *The Military Balance, 1970–1971* through *1979–1980*; Ray Bonds, ed., *The Soviet War Machine* (New York: Chartwell Bros., 1977), p. 153; U.S. Dept. of State, *SALT II Agreement*, Selected Doc. No. 12A (Washington, D.C., June 1979), p. 49; Harold Brown, *Annual Report FY 1980, 1981, 1982*; Michael MccGwire, "Soviet Naval Programs," in Paul J. Murphy, ed., *Naval Power in Soviet Policy*, Studies in Communist Affairs, Vol. 2 (United States Air Force), pp. 106–7; *Jane's Fighting Ships 1977–1978*; Harold Brown, *Department of Defense Annual Report FY 1980*, pp. 68–71 and 90–93; and Statement by Dr. Jack Vorona, Defense Intelligence Agency, to the Subcommittee on General Procurement of the Senate Armed Services Committee, *Congressional Record—Senate*, 96th Cong., 1st and 2d sess., 13 November 1979, pp. 16507–10. The figures shown here are not always identical to those in any one of these sources because all the sources do not usually precisely agree for any given system and year. Cronin and Collins, *Statistical Trends*, is the latest source and is taken to be the most accurate.

TABLE 11   Soviet SLBM and SSN Construction Programs and Inventories, 1970–80

Program	1970	1971	1972	1973	1974	1975	1976	1977	1978	1979	1980
G-(Diesel)	20	20	20	20	20	20	19	18	16	16	15
Total SSBNs	20	27	33	39	45	52	58	66	68	68	69
H-I & II	7	7	7	7	7	7	7	7	7	6	6
H-III										1	1
Y	13	20	26	30	32	33	34	33	31	30	29
D-I				1	4	9	13	18	18	18	18
D-II				1	2	3	4	4	4	4	4
D-III								4	8	9	10
Typhoon[a]											1
SSBN deliveries	6	7	6	6	6	6	6	9	4	1	2
Total attack class SSN	57	61	64	67	70	74	77	81	87	94	105
P								1	1	1	1
E-I	5	5	5	5	5	4	2				
E-II: cruise missile	29	29	29	29	29	29	29	29	29	29	29
C-I & II	5	6	7	8	9	11	12	13	14	15	17
Oscar[a]											1
N	12	12	12	12	12	12	12	12	12	12	12
V-I: ASW	5	8	10	12	14	15	16	16	16	16	16
V-II & III					1	1	2	4	6	9	12
A	1	1	1	1	1	1	1	1	2	4	6
Converted E-I and Y-class							3	5	7	8	9
Attack classes deliveries[b]	5	4	3	3	3	4	3	3	5	6	7
Annual nuclear class deliveries	11	11	9	9	9	10	9	12	9	7	9
Total SLBM tubes	289	401	497	589	673	765	842	947	973	978	993
G SS-N-5	60	60	60	60	60	60	57	54	48	48	45
H-I & II, SS-N-5	21	21	21	21	21	21	21	21	21	18	18
H-III										6	6

Y, SS-N-6	208	320	416	480	512	528	544	528	496	480	464
D-I & II, SS-N-8				28	80	156	220	280	280	280	280
D-III, SS-N-18 MIRV								64	128	144	160
Typhoon SS-N-20 MIRV											20[a]
SSBN subtotal	208	341	437	529	613	705	785	893	925	930	948
MIRV subtotal								64	128	144	180[b]

SOURCES: Michael McGwire, "Soviet Naval Programs," in Paul J. Murphy, ed., *Naval Power in Soviet Policy*, Studies in Communist Affairs, vol. 2 (United States Air Force, pp. 106–7; International Institute for Strategic Studies, *The Military Balance, 1971–1972* through *1979–1980*; *Jane's Fighting Ships 1977–1978*; Brown, *Department of Defense Annual Report FY 1980*, pp. 68–71 and 90–93; John M. Collins, *American and Soviet Military Trends Since the Cuban Missile Crisis* (Washington, D.C.: The Center for Strategic and International Studies, Georgetown University, 1978), pp. 97–99 and 274–75; *U.S.-Soviet Military Balance*, pp. 448 and 520; John M. Collins and Patrick M. Cronin, *U.S.-Soviet Military Balance, Statistical Trends, 1970–1983*, report no. 84-163S (Washington, D.C.: Congressional Reference Service, 27 August 1984), pp. 20, 43; U.S. Dept. of State, *SALT II Agreement*, Selected Doc. No. 12A (Washington, D.C., June 1979), p. 49; Ray Bonds, ed., *The Soviet War Machine* (New York: Chartwell Bros., 1977), p. 153; Statement by Dr. Jack Vorona, Defense Intelligence Agency, to the U.S. Senate, Subcommittee on General Procurement, *Congressional Record—Senate*, 96th Cong., 1st and 2d sess., 13 November 1979, pp. 16507–10; and *Soviet Military Power* (Washington, D.C.: The Pentagon, 1983 and 1984), pp. 55–60, 62–64, 95, 99 (both editions). These various sources differ slightly in the numbers reported for any given weapon system in various years. The numbers shown here represent a "best judgment" composite drawn from the various sources but closely following Collins (*Statistical Trends*), as updated by the 1984 edition of *Soviet Military Power*. There is a small discrepancy between the deliveries and inventories in Table 10 and the annual submarine production rates on pages 79 and 99 of the 1983 and 1984 editions of *Military Power*, respectively. Much, if not all, of this discrepancy consists of a few special-purpose support submarines.

NOTE: Brown (*Annual Report FY 1981*, p. 133) reports that Soviet general-purpose submarine construction had been at the rate of ten per annum. Note that as SSBN deliveries drop off, there is a corresponding increase in SSN deliveries. As McGwire noted years ago, since the mid-1960s production of nuclear propulsion units has been fairly stable at the level required to construct approximately ten nuclear-powered submarines a year for the Soviet Navy. Brown has confirmed McGwire's prior insight into Soviet nuclear-powered submarine construction programs. Evidently, Soviet shipyards constructed eight SSN attack classes in 1980, plus four diesel-powered boats (Admiral Thomas B. Hayward, "Navy Chief Details Loss of U.S. Edge from Soviets," *Aviation Week and Space Technology* 114, no. 6 [9 February 1981]: 35). Presumably the eight SSNs include the new Oscar cruise missile class, which, with the first Typhoon class unit and another Delta class boat, would total ten nuclear-powered submarines constructed in the USSR in 1980 (essentially the average rate established in 1968–70 and subsequently maintained).

[a] Deliveries in 1980 included one Typhoon and one Oscar class boat, which were launched but were not operational during that year.

[b] Note that as SSBN deliveries drop off, those for SSNs usually correspondingly increase. As McGwire noted years ago, production of nuclear propulsion units has been fairly stable since the mid-1960s at the level required to construct approximately ten nuclear-powered submarines per year. History has confirmed McGwire's insight in this respect, at least through the 1970s.

TABLE 12   GROWTH IN SOVIET STRATEGIC MISSILE WARHEAD INVENTORIES UNDER ARMS CONTROL AGREEMENTS

SRF System	1970		1980	
	On launcher	With possible refire	On launcher	With possible refire
SS-4/5	650	1,950–2,600	400	1,200–1,600
SS-20			480	1,440–1,920
Subtotal	650	1,950–2,600	880	2,640–3,520
SS-7	190	380–760		
SS-8	19	40–60		
SS-9	228	230–460		
SS-11	970	970–1,940	1,280[a]	1,280–2,560
SS-13	20	20–40	60	60–120
SS-17 (4 MIRV)			600	600–1,200
SS-18 (10 MIRV)			3,080	3,080–6,160
SS-19 (6 MIRV)			1,440	1,440–2,880
Subtotal	1,427	1,640–3,260	6,460	6,640–12,920
SS-N-5	81	81–162	63	63–126
SS-N-6	208	208–416	464	464–928
SS-N-8			280	280–560
SS-N-18 (3–7 MIRV)			800	800–1,600
Subtotal	289	289–578	1,607	1,607–3,214
TOTAL (rounded)	2,370	3,880–6,440	8,950	10,890–19,650

SOURCES: Launcher numbers are from Tables 10 and 11, with MIRVed payloads as indicated. Like Collins (*U.S.-Soviet Military Balance*, pp. 445–50) and Collins and Cronin (*Statistical Trends, 1970–1983*, p. 18), this calculation counts an average of five MIRVs for the SS-N-18. On the other hand, all ICBMs are counted with the full payload packages as shown. By the end of 1980 all of the SS-18/19 ICBMs may not have been retrofitted with the full MIRV payloads.

Although the USSR strategic missile launcher inventory can be monitored fairly accurately, it is impossible to construct an accurate table showing the trends because of the uncertainty concerning the number of reload missiles. The Soviets stock reloads for ICBMs deployed in silos, and they may limit these to one round. Similarly, it would not be surprising if U.S. intelligence someday discovers that Soviet SLBMs also have reload missiles. All USSR launchers are probably intended to be used more than once.

In the past the standard U.S.-Soviet warhead inventory comparisons in official U.S. government documents, such as the annual Department of Defense posture statements, have clearly been erroneous, because they counted only one missile per launcher on the Soviet side. See, for example, Brown, *Annual Report FY 1982*, pp. 53 and 66; this source is the most misleading, because the SS-20 has several reloads per launcher.

[a] It is assumed that one-half of the SS-11 force consists of the mod 3 version, carrying three MRVs. Although this missile is not independently targeted, in many instances it can probably account for two or three targets per missile because of the large number of military and industrial targets located near each other in urban areas.

FIGURE I   TRENDS IN ACCURACIES OF SOVIET STRATEGIC MISSILES

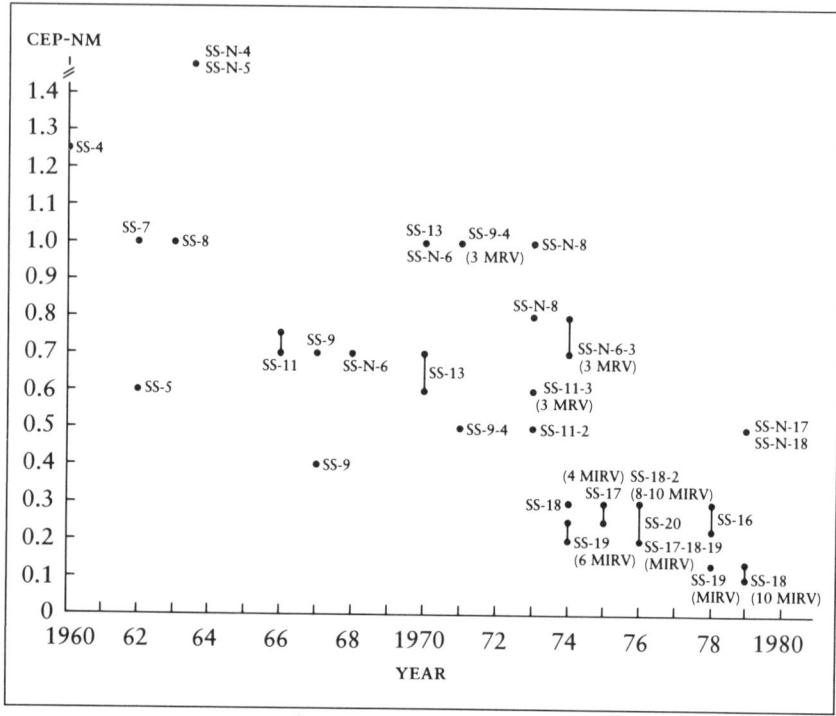

SOURCES: John M. Collins, *American and Soviet Military Trends Since the Cuban Missile Crisis* (Washington, D.C.: The Center for Strategic and International Studies, Georgetown University, 1978), p. 93, 101, 120 n. 69, and *U.S.-Soviet Military Balance: Concepts and Capabilities* (New York: McGraw-Hill, 1980), pp. 446, 453–56, 461; Congressional Budget Office, *Counterforce Issues for the U.S. Strategic Nuclear Forces* (Washington, D.C.: GPO, January 1978), pp. 13, 16–17; International Institute for Strategic Studies, *The Military Balance, 1979–1980* (London, 1980), p. 87; Walter Pincus, "U.S. Downgrades Estimates of Power of Soviet Missiles," *The Washington Post*, 30 June 1979; R. T. Pretty, ed., *Jane's Weapons Systems, 1979–1980* (New York: Franklin Watts, 1979), pp. 6, 7, 11, 12, 13; and Jeffrey Record, *Sizing Up the Soviet Army* (Washington, D.C.: The Brookings Institution, 1975), p. 40.

technology makes possible more effective strikes against soft targets with lower yields, as demonstrated by the declining trend in Western estimates of the yields for USSR strategic missile systems (see Figure 2). More effective strikes with smaller yields also reduce collateral damage, adding to the prospects for a viable postwar world. Soviet trends in strategic missile effectiveness are analyzed in Chapter 8. The observed trends in strategic missile force accuracy and yield composition during the SALT era are fully consistent with the objective of "winning" a nuclear war.

The trend in USSR strategic air forces in the 1970s was essentially one of modernization and modest growth. As the capabilities of the SRF against fixed targets grew, the strategic air forces concentrated more on strategic missions in the Eurasian and adjacent oceanic TVDs by both long-range aviation and naval air forces. Table 13 shows the trends in the number and mix of strategic aircraft during this decade.

Much has been made of the potential threat posed by the Backfire, introduced in the mid-1970s. If staged from Arctic bases and refueled, this bomber may have sufficient range to attack the continental United States. Yet the most probable reason for Backfire's range is to allow it to attack U.S. or NATO carrier and other naval forces at ranges that would isolate the Eurasian TVD battlefields from naval and logistic support. For the Soviets, assigning Backfire to attack targets in the United States would probably be a waste of a valuable military asset.

FIGURE 2   TRENDS IN YIELDS OF SOVIET
STRATEGIC MISSILE WARHEADS

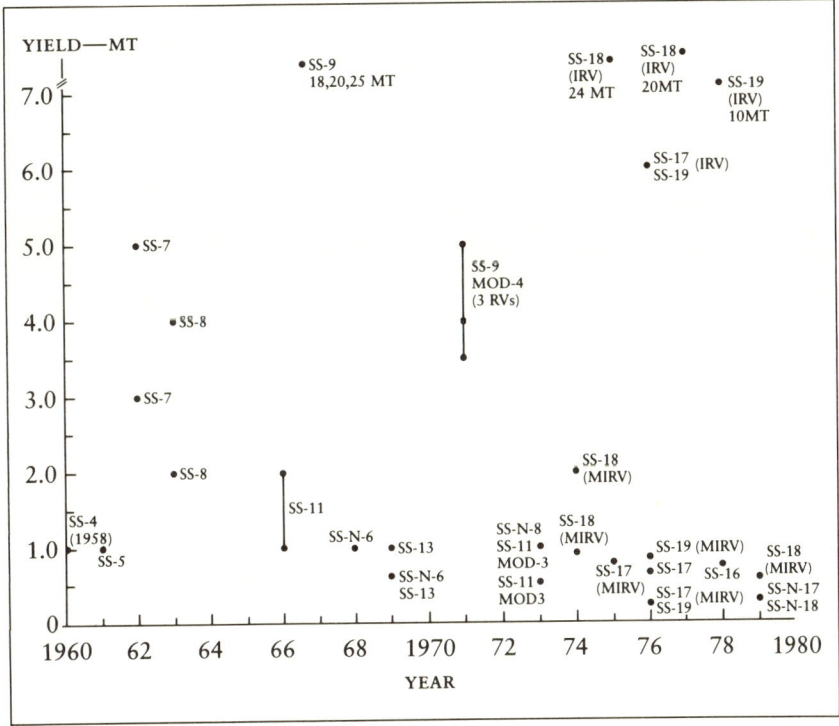

SOURCES: See Figure 1.

TABLE 13   SOVIET STRATEGIC AIRCRAFT FORCE TRENDS

	1970	1975	1980
Long-range aviation (LRA)	910	860	815
TU-95 Bear	100	100	100
M-4 Bison[a]	90	85	80
TU-16 Badger[a]	550	475	435
TU-22 Blinder[a]	170	175	125
TU-22M Backfire		25	75
Soviet naval aviation (SNA)[b]	650	730	745
TU-95/142 Bear[c]	50	55	80
TU-16 Badger[d]	400	430	395
TU-22 Blinder	60	60	45
TU-26 Backfire			75
IL-38 May[e]	20	55	50
BE-12 Mail[e]	60	100	100
IL-28 Beagle	60	30	30
Total	1,560	1,590	1,560

SOURCES: International Institute for Strategic Studies, The *Military Balance, 1970–1971,* pp. 7–10; ibid., *1975–1976,* pp. 8 and 9; and ibid., *1980–1981,* pp. 9 and 11 (rounded to the nearest five aircraft); and John M. Collins and Patrick M. Cronin, *U.S.-Soviet Military Balance, Statistical Trends, 1970–1983,* pp. 23, 37, 79–80.

[a]About forty of the M-4 bombers are configured as tankers. During the 1970s some 100 TU-16 aircraft were configured for electronic countermeasure (ECM) operations and approximately fifteen were configured as tankers. By the end of the 1970s about fifteen TU-22 aircraft were also configured as tankers.

[b]Does not include ninety fighter-type aircraft assigned to the Soviet navy in the mid- to late 1970s or some Forger aircraft carried on the Moskva and Kiev classes by 1980 (Collins and Cronin, *Statistical Trends,* p. 80). Collins and Cronin also report approximately 250 ASW helicopters in the Soviet inventory throughout the 1970s.

[c]Reconnaissance and ASW versions of this heavy bomber. According to Collins and Cronin (*Statistical Trends,* p. 80) fifteen TU-142 ASW Bears existed in 1975 and forty-five existed in 1980.

[d]All models. Throughout the decade about seventy-five to eighty-five SNA TU-16s were configured as tankers.

[e]ASW aircraft

STRATEGIC DEFENSIVE FORCES IN THE SALT ERA

Whereas the American government reacted to the ABM treaty and the SALT process by dismantling most of its strategic defenses and reducing R&D for others, the USSR continued to modernize and improve its forces and expand R&D programs in all areas of strategic defense. During the 1970s PVO Strany improved its medium- and high-altitude capabilities by developing new interceptors (SU-15 and MIG-25) and continued deployment of the SA-5 system. PVO Strany also did what it could to improve low altitude capabilities, while waiting for more effective systems to be developed, by expanding SA-3 deployments and introducing the MIG-23 interceptor. The Soviet navy greatly expanded its investment in surface ships and submarines designed for strategic ASW, even though the fundamental problem of locating U.S. or NATO nuclear-powered submarines in the open sea remained unsolved throughout the 1970s. Anticarrier forces were expanded and modernized with new cruise-missile submarines, such as the short-range, low-altitude SS-N-9 on the C-II class SSNs and the long-range SS-N-19 on the huge Oscar class SSN.[6]

Nothing in the pattern of strategic offensive or defensive force development in the 1970s indicates that the Soviets have abandoned "victory" as their objective or have concluded that it is neither possible nor desirable to field the forces required for meaningful damage-limiting capabilities in the event of a nuclear war. In fact, during both the 1960s and the 1970s, the patterns of strategic defensive force development provide what should be incontrovertible proof of USSR commitment to its warfighting strategy.

PVO Strany: Air, Missile, and Space Defense

During the 1970s numbers of PVO Strany interceptors declined from 3,200 to about 2,600 aircraft and then leveled off. Additions to the inventory between 1970 and 1980 totaled some 1,300 high-performance aircraft from three models: SU-15, MIG-23, and MIG-25. The SU-15 and MIG-25 continued the high-altitude tradition, whereas the MIG-23 Flogger had some effectiveness at low altitude. The MIG-23 is not reported to have a look-down-shoot-down capability, as was later developed for the MIG-25, but is evidently much less restricted than other PVO Strany interceptors when operating at low altitudes. Reportedly, the MIG-23 was the first Soviet interceptor capable of engaging a target lower than itself at any altitude.[7] A later model with improved low-altitude capabilities began arriving at PVO Strany in 1979–80. These aircraft now comprise about one-third of all strategic defense interceptors, and the technology is being retrofitted on earlier MIG-25 models.[8]

R&D on the SA-10—along with modernization of the SA-3 and continuation of SA-5 deployments—summarizes the thrust of PVO Strany's surface-to-air missile programs in the 1970s. Apparently, by the end of the 1960s the Soviets understood that large technological advances would be necessary to cope with U.S. bombers penetrating at low altitudes and armed with SRAM missiles. Most of the 1970s seem to have been devoted to developing the SA-10 system. The first SA-10 site became operational[9] at the beginning of the 1980s. The system is capable of defending against incoming missiles with a small radar cross-section at low to high altitudes.[10]

Meanwhile, the number of active SA-2 launchers was reduced by about 40 percent during the 1970s, presumably because (1) the SA-5 force took over the high-altitude mission as the number of launchers increased (from about 1,100 in 1970 to nearly 2,000 in 1980) and (2) the SA-10 units will probably be operated by former SA-2 units. The SA-3 low-altitude force has been modernized, and the number of missiles on launchers increased from 1,800 in 1970 to around 5,000 in 1980.

The pattern of Soviet interceptor development during the 1970s had been the same as that for the SAMs. They continued to deploy the best available technology, while developing the sophisticated look-down-shoot-down radar and missile technologies required to cope with low-altitude aerodynamic penetrators. The USSR devoted the decade of the 1970s to developing their AWACS aircraft (NATO designation—MAINSTAY), three interceptors (MIG-29, MIG-31, and SU-27), and corresponding air-to-air missiles with the capability of looking down into the ground clutter and intercepting aircraft and cruise missiles at low altitudes (below a few hundred meters). Deployment of these aircraft began in the early to mid-1980s. They represent an expensive revolution in Soviet air-defense technology.

Table 14 summarizes these trends in the deployment of major PVO Strany weapons systems during the 1960s and 1970s. Note the modest reduction in total interceptor inventories combined with large-scale modernization of more advanced systems, particularly MIG-23 and MIG-25 interceptors. Total SAM inventories increased somewhat; the emphasis was on modernization and technical improvements in existing systems, however, rather than on quantitative growth.

In addition, during the 1970s the Soviets probably made substantial investment in radars as well as data and communications systems for PVO Strany; no quantitative information on such systems is available in the public domain.

The USSR entered the 1970s about ten to fifteen years behind the United States in ballistic-missile defense technology. However, it devoted this decade to developing an ABM system, comparable to that which the United States relinquished in the ABM treaty and its aftermath and to begin deployment of this system around Moscow. At the same time the Soviets have pursued exotic technologies, like lasers and charged particle beams, that could lead to more effective ABM systems in the future.[11]

During the 1970s the Soviets developed or acquired three essential ABM technologies that were completely lacking at the beginning of SALT: (1) a small and "moveable" phased-array radar for local defenses; (2) two new ABM missiles, including one comparable to the U.S. Sprint designed for atmospheric interceptors; and (3) the "Ryad" computer, reportedly similar to the U.S. IBM 260/370 series.[12] The small ABM radar was installed on Kam-

TABLE 14   TRENDS IN DEPLOYMENT OF MAJOR
PVO STRANY WEAPONS SYSTEMS, 1960–80

	1960	1970	1975	1980
Interceptors	4,050	3,200	2,600	2,550
MIG-15, -17 Fresco	3,700	1,000	150	50
MIG-19 Farmer		350	200	—
MIG-23 Flogger B				650
MIG-25 Foxbat A			200	300
SU-9/11 Fishpot B/C	100	750	700	300
SU-15 Flagon D/E/F		400	850	800
TU-28 Fiddler		150	150	150
YAK-25 Flashlight	250	200		
YAK-28 Firebar		350	350	300
Air surveillance				
TU-126 Moss		9	9	9
SAMs (launchers/missiles)	4,200	10,700	11,800	12,520
SA-1	3,200	3,200	3,200	3,200
SA-2	1,000	4,600	3,500	2,800
SA-3 launchers		900	1,200	1,400
Rails/missiles		1,800	3,500	4,500
SA-5		1,100	1,600	1,900
SA-10 launchers				30
Missiles				120
Early warning and ground-control intercept radars		7,000	7,000	7,000

SOURCES: Collins, *U.S.-Soviet Military Balance*, pp. 463–67; John M. Collins and Patrick M. Cronin, *U.S.-Soviet Military Balance, Statistical Trends, 1970–1983*, pp. 30 and 32; International Institute for Strategic Studies, *The Military Balance, 1979–1980*, p. 9; and ibid., *1980–1981*, p. 10. These sources are in general agreement on total PVO Strany interceptor inventories and numbers of most models, except that *Military Balance* does not carry any MIG-19s for 1979–80 and lists a larger inventory of MIG-23s than Collins and Cronin. Collins and Cronin's total inventory apparently also includes most of the trainer aircraft listed in *Military Balance*. In general, Collins and Cronin's data are considered the most authoritative.

chatka at the Soviet ICBM test range in 1975 (presumably following prior development elsewhere).[13] Meanwhile, the USSR continued to advance its large phased-array radar technology. In the latter part of the decade four large radars of the Pechora type, reportedly having ABM battle-management capabilities, were constructed on the Soviet Union's periphery, evidently at sites already occupied by Hen House type large phased array radars. Moreover, given the lead times involved, the USSR must have decided in the mid-1970s to replace the ABM defenses around Moscow with the Pushkino type large phased array radar and the new missiles developed since the late 1960s.[14] Consequently, the ABM Treaty did not prevent Soviet leaders from committing resources to the programs and facilities that now provide the basis for rapid, nationwide deployment of ABM defenses. These implications will be developed in the next chapter.

In the 1970s the USSR also kept alive lingering American fears of the upgrading of SAMs to ABM defenses by testing these systems in an ABM mode. A series of tests of the SA-5 in an ABM mode ceased in the early 1970s, when the United States "brought up the tests to the Standing Consultative Commission as a possible violation" of the ABM treaty. Subsequently, the Soviets resumed this testing and also employed SA-10 radars against their own missiles "in an antiballistic missile mode." [15]

Other protests by the United States against USSR testing of air defense systems in an ABM environment and other R&D activity considered "possible violations" of the 1972 ABM treaty were treated with "a brusque or even hostile attitude" by Soviet representatives to the Standing Consultative Commission on compliance with U.S./USSR arms control agreements. [16] Obviously, the Soviets were attempting to conceal something.

During the 1970s the USSR also developed, and apparently deployed, a satellite interceptor system in line with the PVO Strany mission of air, missile, and space defense. [17] Development of this system has continued. [18] It is clear that the Soviets did not lose interest in missile and space defense as a result of the ABM treaty and the SALT agreements on ICBMs, SLBMs, and heavy bombers. Moscow's ABM defenses are being modernized as rapidly as the technology becomes available. Such developments have resulted in this 1980 statement from one U.S. official: "But it lends great credibility to NIE [National Intelligence Estimate] 11-3/8, which states that the USSR is capable of deploying a high-quality thick bank of ballistic missile defense systems within one year from the time the U.S. could detect that the deployment was unmistakable." [19]

Given the low level of effectiveness, long lead times, and extremely high cost of the Galosh system deployed around Moscow, it is hardly surprising that the Soviets did not try to defend the whole country with this system. But now that the USSR has developed the components of what appears to be a respectable, rapidly deployable ABM, why should it refrain from nationwide ABM deployments in the 1980s? Without a national ABM defense, all other Soviet war-fighting and damage-limiting measures—counterforce missiles, air defenses, ASW, and civil defense—would constitute a huge waste of resources.

Strategic Defensive Missions of the Navy

Antisubmarine Warfare (ASW).   As discussed earlier, during the 1960s the USSR reoriented its naval surface-ship building program to the strategic

ASW mission, even though delivery of new classes designed and armed for this mission would not begin until the latter part of the decade. Consequently, the magnitude of the effort to acquire a fleet of strategic ASW platforms was not apparent until well into the 1970s. In 1960 the USSR had no surface ships or nuclear-powered submarines (SSNs). By the end of the next decade the Soviet navy had acquired a fleet of strategic ASW platforms comprising approximately ninety major surface combatants of 4,000 tons and larger, nearly fifty SSNs, a considerable number of ASW aircraft and helicopters, plus V/STOL aircraft on large ASW cruisers. Finally, approximately eighty modern diesel-powered submarines—Tango and Foxtrot classes—can be used to augment ASW forces (in addition to anticarrier and other missions).

Whereas the Moskva was the only class of ASW helicopter cruiser deployed in the 1960s, three new classes designed for the ASW mission—Krivak, Kara, and Kiev—joined the fleet in the 1970s. The last one carries V/STOL aircraft as well as helicopters; Western writers often call it an aircraft carrier, although it is a carrier only in a technical sense. The Kiev class are primarily ASW cruisers; they do not represent Soviet attempts to compete with U.S. or NATO attack carriers.[20]

During the 1970s the USSR also developed four new classes of major surface combatants for deployment in the 1980s: Kirov, Udaloi, Slava, and Sovremennyi. The first two were probably designed for strategic ASW as their primary mission. The last two may have been designed primarily for an escort role—to protect ASW task forces. All of these new classes—like the Kiev, but unlike all prior ASW ships—carry an array of weapons to defend themselves against both Western surface ships and naval aviation.

Table 15 shows construction programs for major surface combatants that have strategic ASW operations as their primary wartime mission. Table 16 summarizes the growing inventory of major surface combatants and nuclear-powered submarines for the ASW mission. The Soviet navy also has a considerable fleet of small ASW surface combatants for operations in coastal waters.

During the late 1970s the USSR redesignated several of the less capable "large ASW ships" (BPK). Of these, only Krivak had been designed and built for the ASW mission. It was called a "patrol ship" (SKR), along with the smaller Petia, Mirka, and Grisha classes.[21] These redesignations in 1977–78 probably did not indicate any change in the primary mission; it is more likely that they reflected an appreciation for the limitations of the renamed classes in open ocean ASW operations, particularly as the new and more capable classes entered the fleets. In the future the redesignated classes may be assigned primarily to the ASW mission of protecting Soviet SLBMs in home waters; the new classes—most of which also carry advanced SAMs and antiship missiles to enable them to survive in a hostile naval environ-

TABLE 15   SOVIET NAVY CONSTRUCTION/CONVERSION PROGRAMS FOR MAJOR SURFACE COMBATANTS, 1965–80

Program	1965	1966	1967	1968	1969	1970	1971	1972	1973	1974	1975	1976	1977	1978	1979	1980
Destroyers	5	7	10	14	19	23	28	32	34	37	39	44	47	53	55	59
Kashin[a]	5	7	9	11	13	15	17	19	19	19	19	19	19	19	19	19
Kanin (conv)[a]			1	2	4	5	6	6	6	6	6	7	8	8	8	8
Kildin[a]				1	2	3	4	4	4	4	4	4	4	4	4	4
Krivak[a]							1	3	5	8	10	14	16	22	24	28
ASW Cruisers			2	3	5	6	8	9	12	13	17	19	22	25	27	29
Kresta I (conv)[a]			2	3	4	4	4	4	4	4	4	4	4	4	4	4
Kresta II					1	1	2	3	4	5	6	7	8	9	10	10
Kara									1	2	3	4	5	6	7	7
Kirov[b]																1
Udaloi[c]														1	1	1
Moskva		1	2	2	2	2	2	2	2	2	2	2	2	2	2	2
Kiev											1	1	1	1	2	2
Antiship cruisers and destroyers	4	4	4	4	4	4	4	4	4	4	4	4	4	5	6	7
Kynda	4	4	4	4	4	4	4	4	4	4	4	4	4	4	4	4
Sovremenniy[d]														1	1	2
Slava[d]																1
Total	9	11	16	21	28	33	40	45	50	54	60	67	73	83	88	95

SOURCES: *Jane's Fighting Ships, 1975–1976, 1979–1980, 1980–1981, 1982–1983;* International Institute for Strategic Studies, *The Military Balance, 1979–1980, 1980–1981;* Collins, *U.S.-Soviet Military Balance,* pp. 505–14; John M. Collins and Patrick M. Cronin, *U.S.-Soviet Military Balance, Statistical Trends, 1970–1983,* p. 43; Michael MccGwire, "Soviet Naval Programs," in Paul J. Murphy, ed., *Naval Power in Soviet Policy,* Studies in Communist Affairs, vol. 2, pp. 103–7; Arthur D. Baker III, "Soviet Ship Types," *U.S. Naval Institute Proceedings* 106, no. 11 (November 1980): 111–17; *International Defense Review,* no. 4 (1981): 377; and *Soviet Military Power, 1984* (Washington, D.C.: The Pentagon, 1984), pp. 63–68. In many cases, units are listed by year launched. Fitting out and sea trials generally take one to two years. These sources are in general agreement on ship numbers and construction rates for all classes except Krivak. This table accepts Collins and Cronin's (*Statistical Trends,* p. 98) figure with two additional units in 1980 for a total of thirty-two. Classification as cruisers or destroyers follows *Jane's* rather than Collins because of the larger size of the new ships. Similarly, Krivak is listed as a destroyer rather than a frigate because of its size (3,000 ton displacement) and armament.

[a] Soviet designation is "nuclear rocket cruiser" (ARK). Krov's complement of Hormone helicopters, SS-N-14 ASW missiles, and variable depth sonar indicate the ASW mission. Unlike earlier classes, however, Kirov's SAMs and cruise missiles are designed to give this class the capabilities to operate in a hostile air and surface ship environment.

[b] Redesignated in the late 1970s but with apparent change in primary wartime mission. Number launched.

[c] Udaloi is an ASW successor to the Kara class. Soviet designation not available. Number launched.

[d] Sovremennyi and Slava are primarily equipped for antiship operations. May serve as an escort for other new classes. Soviet designation not available. Number launched.

TABLE 16   TRENDS IN SOVIET ASW SHIP AND SSN INVENTORIES, 1960–80

	1960	1971	1975	1980
Large ASW ships (BPK)[a]				
Kresta II		1	7	10
Kara			3	6
Former large ASW ships (BPK)[a,b]				
Destroyer classes				
Kashin		17	19	19
Kanin[c]		2	7	8
Kildin[c]		4	2	1
Krivak		—	10	28
Cruiser class				
Kresta I		4	4	4
Antisubmarine cruisers (PK and ARK)[a]				
Moskva		2	2	2
Kiev				2
Kirov				1
Total surface ships		30	54	81
ASW SSNs		9	19	35
Viktor I		8	16	16
Viktor II & III			2	13
Alpha		1	1	6

SOURCES: Arthur D. Baker III, "Soviet Ship Types," *U.S. Naval Institute Proceedings* 106, no. 11 (November 1980), pp. 111–17; and John M. Collins and Patrick M. Cronin, *U.S.-Soviet Military Balance, Statistical Trends, 1970–1983*, pp. 85, 90, 97, 98 (except for one Alpha launched in 1970).

[a]Soviet designation. BPK is the translation of the Soviet designator for "large antisubmarine warfare" ships. The Kiev and Moskva class ships are designated "antisubmarine cruisers" by the Soviets. As noted in note (a) to Table 15, the Soviet designator for the Kirov class is "nuclear rocket cruiser," but her armaments indicate ASW as the primary mission; see Captain James W. Kehoe, USN, and Kenneth S. Brewer, "Their New Cruiser," *U.S. Naval Institute Proceedings* 106, no. 12 (December 1980): 121–26. Arthur D. Baker III ("Soviet Ship Types," ibid., p. 114) indicates that both Blackcom-1 and Udaloi "probably" have been designated BPK by the Soviets. *International Defense Review* (no. 4 [1981]: 377) cites Rear Admiral Sumner Shapiro, director of U.S. Naval Intelligence, on Udaloi as an "ASW warship" and Kirov as a "multipurpose command" ship.

[b]According to Baker (p. 112), in 1977–78 the Krivak class was redesignated from BPK to missile "patrol ship" (SKR). The other former BPK classes were evidently redesignated "rocket cruisers" (KR).

[c]Not originally designed or weaponized for the ASW mission. Kanin is a conversion of the Krupny class; Kildin, of the Kotlin class.

ment—may be assigned to open ocean operations against enemy SSBNs, along with five SSN classes configured for ASW operations and supported by ASW aircraft.

Meanwhile, the USSR reportedly began building a new class (Babochka) of large ASW hydrafoils.[22] During the 1970s the Soviets also invested billions of rubles in the Victor II and III and the titanium-hull Alpha class nuclear-powered submarines for ASW missions. Meanwhile, in the 1970s, the USSR developed four new classes of nuclear-powered attack submarines: Oscar, Mike, Sierra, and Akula. All were much larger than their predecessors and deployed in the 1980s. This is another reason to doubt that the reclassification of several former BPK classes in the late 1970s represented any downgrading of strategic ASW as a primary wartime mission.

At the end of the 1970s the West was surprised to find that a Soviet submarine designated as the Alpha class was moving at speeds in excess of forty knots and at depths of 600 meters or more. The first Alpha was launched in 1970, but nothing was heard about further construction of this class for some time. The 1977–78 edition of *Jane's* listed Alpha's speed at sixteen to eighteen knots and commented: "A program which apparently has come to a halt and whose purpose is unclear. Probably no longer operational."[23]

A decade earlier—probably about the time construction started on the first Alpha—two Soviet admirals described the advantages of high-speed, deep-diving submarines for ASW operations. One of them wrote:[24]

> The hydrologic features of seas and oceans are such that their capabilities for the use of detection devices are increased considerably when the submarines are in the area of the axis of the deep-water sound channel (at a depth of 600 to 1,200 meters); the conditions for the use of acoustic navigational means are also greatly improved at this depth. It is possible that, as a result of this fact, the capabilities of submarines will be improved for the secret tracing of enemy submarines and surface groupings, and also for long periods of pursuit while remaining undetected.
>
> Submarines with a great maximum depth of submersion can easily maneuver on a vertical plane; on the one hand, this increases their offensive capabilities and, on the other hand, increases the ability to make greater use of the enormous layer of water for their own protection.

The author predicted that large numbers of deep-sea submarines would appear in the future.

Shortly thereafter, the other admiral described the characteristics of a nuclear-powered ASW submarine as follows:[25]

1. "Optimum curve of a drop-shaped hull" for better location and contour of propellers

2. "Optimum" length-to-beam ratio of about 7 to 7.4

3. "Reactors with natural circulation of the coolant" to eliminate coolant pumps and their noise

4. Smaller and speedier than its quarry—the SSBN—and 1.5 times faster in changing depth

5. Direct action turbine (without gear reduction) to reduce noise and counterrotating, coaxial propellers

6. Much greater depth for concealed search, higher speed of silent movement, use of water strata for concealment, reconnaissance of water strata conditions, ability to sit on the bottom in case of accident or combat danger

Five years later a Soviet navy captain published a somewhat similar article extolling the virtues of high-speed, deep-diving submarines as a means of combating SSBNs, which he expected to be armed with much longer-range missiles than at that time. The author noted that advances in metallurgy and new, high-strength materials "are certainly not ignored by submarine designers. Today their attention is focused on titanium alloys, glass, ceramics, synthetic, and other materials of low specific weight" that permit nuclear-powered submarines to go deeper and stay down longer.[26] The writer also expected these SSNs to be highly automated, which would radically change the size and composition of the crew.

Whether the Alpha class meets all of the specifications and capabilities stated in these articles is not clear. Alleged speed and operating depths appear to accord with the expectations of both admirals cited above. Alpha has a titanium hull, yet is reported to be noisier than U.S. nuclear-powered submarines.[27] The 9,500-ton Mike class is a prime candidate for a second-generation quieter model, because it evidently was designed by the same Soviet team.[28] Meanwhile, the Alpha is a serious attempt simultaneously to incorporate a number of major technological advances into a high-performance ASW submarine. Considering that the design goes back to the beginning of the 1960s, if not earlier, it represents a technologically audacious project.

Development and construction of Alpha class SSNs represented an enormously expensive program and one more example of continued Soviet dedication to meeting the requirements of their war-fighting, damage-limiting strategy as rapidly as their technology and resources permit. The appearance of the much larger Mike class signals continued Soviet dedication to technologically advanced, extremely expensive, titanium-hulled SSNs for anti-submarine warfare.

Despite the investment in ASW ships and submarines, the critical problem for these USSR strategic forces at the end of the 1970s was the same as at the beginning: finding the enemy SSBNs in the open ocean. Little has appeared in the public domain on any progress (or lack thereof) toward its solution. The following intriguing but enigmatic 1976 item appeared in an American trade magazine: "Washington—Soviet Union is in an advanced stage of developing satellite-borne sensor systems that will permit detection and near real-time tracking of U.S. and North Atlantic Treaty Organization ballistic missile submarines." Eight years later Soviet submarines were linked to ocean surveillance satellites that can provide almost real-time detection and data sufficient to attack distant mobile targets.[29]

From the late 1960s to the mid-1970s Soviet literature contained many indications of interest in advanced acoustic and nonacoustic detection for tracking systems that might be adapted to submarine, aircraft, and spacecraft platforms against enemy submarines in the open ocean. An article discussed the problem of finding American SSBNs that patrol thousands of square kilometers of ocean and employ various concealment tactics. The writer recognized that "essential first and foremost are reliable methods of submarine searching and tracking." His discussion of acoustic search and tracking was followed by an observation about nonacoustic technology: "thermal, magnetic, radioactive, and other fields from around a submarine . . . can be fairly effectively detected, recorded and sometimes classified as well, with the aid of the latest shipborne and airborne search gear and equipment carried by special ASW submarines."[30]

In his book on Soviet seapower published in 1976, Admiral Gorshkov discussed the importance of ASW as "a State task" or mission. He went on to say that the "cardinal solution" to this problem would not be found in existing technologies (presumably acoustics), which were approaching the limits of their potential effectiveness. Rather, the admiral expected the answer to be discovered in "new principles" of ASW, presumably nonacoustics.[31] In the meantime, Soviet ASW forces may prove much more effective at protecting their own SLBMs, the primary secure reserve of ready strategic missiles than in locating and destroying U.S., British, and French SSBNs.

Anticarrier and Antinaval Forces. During the 1960s the USSR invested heavily in the navy's other strategic defensive mission—anticarrier operations. Over approximately the same period that the United States launched forty-one SSBNs, the Soviets built thirty-two nuclear-powered cruise-missile submarines (E-I and E-II classes) and sixteen diesel-powered submarines carrying the same SS-N-3 cruise missiles. The USSR navy was also equipped at this time with some 400 medium bombers—mostly armed with air-to-

TABLE 17 TRENDS IN SOVIET ANTICARRIER/SHIP SUBMARINE AND AIRCRAFT FORCES

	1960		1970		1980	
	Boats	Launchers	Boats	Launchers	Boats	Launchers
Cruise missile submarines	4	20	55	366	64	464
W-class (diesel)[a]						
J-class (diesel)	2	8	16	64	16	64
E-I & II class	2	12	34	262	29	232
C-I & II class			5	40	17	136
P-class					1	8
O-class[b]					1	24
Nuclear-powered	2	12	39	302	48	400
Torpedo attack submarines						
N-class	4		12		12	
	Aircraft	Missile loadings[c]	Aircraft	Missile loadings[c]	Aircraft	Missile loadings[c]
Soviet naval air force (SNA)	not available		380	700	395	750
TU-16 Badger			320	640	280	560
TU-22 Blinder			60	60	40	40
TU-26 Backfire					75	150

SOURCES: John M. Collins, *U.S.-Soviet Military Balance, Concepts and Capabilities, 1960–1980* (New York: McGraw-Hill, 1980), pp. 501–4; Ray Bonds, ed., *The Soviet War Machine* (New York: Chartwell Bros., 1977), pp. 90, 92, 110–11, and tables 10 and 12. Most of the tanker and reconnaissance models are from John M. Collins and Patrick M. Cronin, *U.S.-Soviet Military Balance, Statistical Trends, 1970–1983*, p. 80.

[a] A few W-class boats were fitted with cruise missiles in the mid-1950s but were probably retired in the late 1960s.

[b] Probably not operational until 1981–82.

[c] Missile numbers are not inventories but representations of standard aircraft loadings—generally, two for TU-16; one for TU-22; and two for TU-26 (which may also carry only one AS-6).

surface cruise missiles—for the anticarrier mission (see Table 13). Over the same time period that the United States made an enormous investment in strategic offensive submarines, the USSR allocated roughly comparable funds to submarines and aircraft for strategic defense.

During the 1970s Soviet anticarrier forces remained the third priority, although they were modernized and expanded somewhat. The SS-N-12 cruise missile replaced the SS-N-3 on older units and was fitted on new surface combatants. By the end of 1980 the USSR navy had about sixteen "C" class SSNs. The first unit had become operational in 1967, armed with the supersonic SS-N-7 cruise missile, for a total of about fifty cruise missile-carrying SSNs. Meanwhile, naval air was being modernized with the Backfire medium bomber carrying anti-ship cruise missiles; about seventy planes were in service by the end of 1980. The total during the decade averaged about 450 aircraft (see Table 11). Quantitative aspects of the buildup in Soviet naval units for the anticarrier mission are summarized in Table 17.

The most striking new development has been the Oscar class submarine, which reportedly incorporates the titanium hull technology of the Alpha and is armed with twenty-four SS-N-19 supersonic cruise missiles with a range of 300 nautical miles.[32] This development may indicate that the anticarrier and antiship mission is higher on the list of Soviet naval priorities during the 1980s than it was from the mid-1960s to the late 1970s.

Figure 3 summarizes 1960s Soviet naval construction for major combatants of 4,000 tons or greater and for submarines by five-year plan (FYP) period, with submarine construction programs distributed by major type and mission. Note the following trends:

• Construction of submarines has been relatively constant, totaling more than 300,000 tons over three FYPs.

• Construction of major surface combatants of 4,000 tons or greater—mostly designed and equipped for the ASW mission—has risen in each FYP, particularly during the tenth FYP (1976–80).

• SSBNs have dominated submarine construction during three FYPs, but less in 1976–80 than in previous (eighth and ninth) FYPs.

• Construction of SSNs for ASW has risen steadily over the course of four consecutive FYPs.

• Construction of diesel-powered submarines continues at a slow but stable rate.

Figure 4 summarizes USSR naval construction programs during the 1960s and 1970s by major strategic mission, offensive and defensive. Despite the huge nuclear-powered ballistic-missile submarine (SSBN) construction program that began in the mid-1960s and continued through the 1970s, more tonnage was built for the navy's strategic defensive missions before and after SALT. Even during the peak period of SSBN production, more tonnage had been delivered for strategic defensive missions than for strategic offensive missions.

If one could translate these data from tonnages into rubles, the effort placed on strategic offensive missions in the 1970s might well exceed outlays for strategic defensive surface ships and submarines. Nevertheless, the fundamental point would remain: The USSR navy's strategic defensive missions have been neither cancelled nor neglected since the SALT process began.

FIGURE 3   TRENDS IN SOVIET MAJOR NAVAL COMBATANT
CONSTRUCTION (TONNAGE BY FYP)

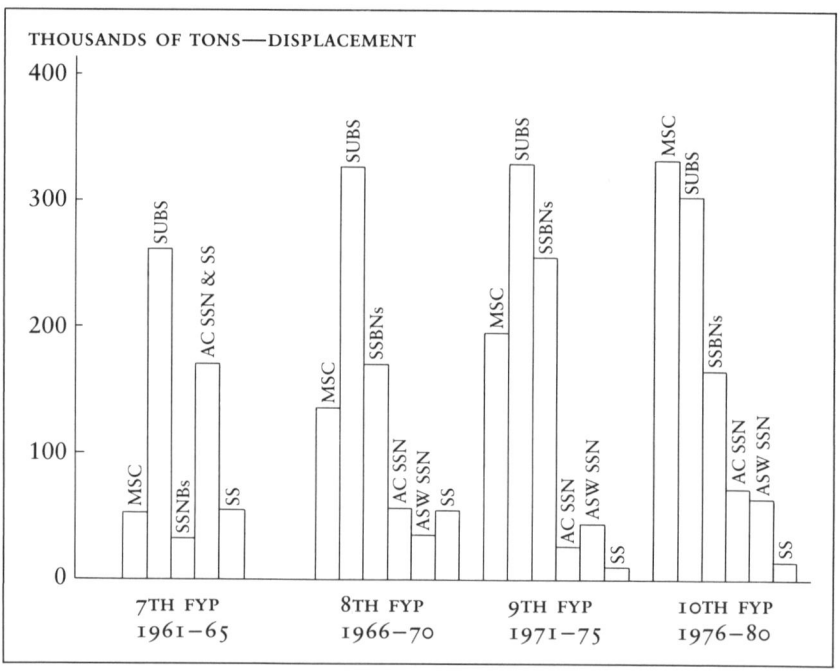

SOURCES: See Figure 4.

NOTE: MSC = major surface combatant (4,000 or more tons), SUBS = submarines, SSBNs = nuclear-powered ballistic missile submarines, AC SSNs & SS = anticarrier/ship nuclear-powered and diesel submarines, ASW SSNs = antisubmarine warfare nuclear-powered submarines, SS = diesel submarines

FIGURE 4 TRENDS IN SOVIET MAJOR NAVAL COMBATANT
CONSTRUCTION BY MAJOR MISSION: STRATEGIC DEFENSIVE
(SDF) AND STRATEGIC OFFENSIVE (SOF) (TONNAGE BY FYP)

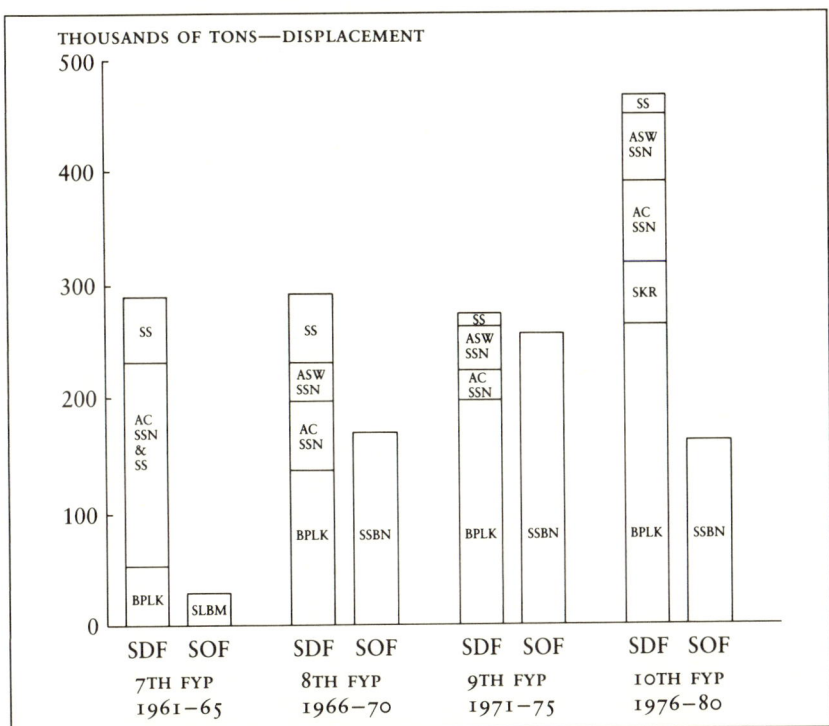

SOURCES: Ship construction data are from Tables 15 and 16 of this work. Individual ship and submarine tonnages are displacement tonnage for each type as reported by *Jane's* (except for Oscar, Typhoon, and Kirov, which are taken from sources previously cited on those programs). The allocation by FYP is necessarily crude, but it is consistent in method. More precise data on dates when keels were laid and hulls launched would probably not change the trends in any significant way.

NOTES: The SKR designation (from the Russian term for "patrol ship, rocket") was given to the Krivak class about 1977. According to *Jane's*, despite its relatively small size (about 4,000 tons displacement) Krivak had previously been designated PLK. This designation, however, apparently did not involve a change in the primary mission (ASW) of the Krivak class ship. Evidently, Soviet shipyards constructed eight SSN attack classes in 1980, plus four diesel-powered boats (Admiral Thomas B. Hayward, USN, "Navy Chief Details Loss of U.S. Edge on Soviets," *Aviation Week and Space Technology* 114, no. 6 [9 February 1981]: 35). Presumably, the eight SSNs include the new Oscar class cruise missile, which, with the first Typhoon class unit and another Delta class boat, would total ten nuclear-powered submarines constructed in the USSR during 1980. This is essentially the average rate established during 1968–70 and subsequently maintained.

Note that the 1980 deliveries include one Typhoon and one Oscar class boat, which were launched but not operational that year. SSBN and attack class SSN totals do not include the first Typhoon and Oscar class boats.

BPLK is an abbreviation of the Russian term for "large antisubmarine warfare ship" (more than 4,000 tons). For other abbreviations, see the note to Figure 3.

Summary of Soviet Force Development
During the 1970s

Trends in the development and procurement of weapons systems designed to fight and win a war by destroying enemy forces and limiting damage to the USSR have been consistent and relatively stable over a period of two decades, before and after SALT. In the 1970s the Soviets procured some fifty-seven to sixty strategic offensive and defensive weapons systems, as compared to about fifty-five during the 1960s. There have been no changes in the pattern since SALT began that cannot be explained (like PVO Strany SAMs) as technological lags that took a long time to overcome. Advances in technology permitted more impressive developments in strategic offensive, as opposed to strategic defensive, systems during the 1970s than during the 1960s. Adverse technological relationships required the Soviets to emphasize R&D for air and missile defense systems in the 1970s much more than in the previous decade. Nevertheless, the USSR procured between thirty-five and forty strategic defensive systems in the 1970s, as compared to some thirty-five systems in the 1960s. Table 18 summarizes the various weapons systems delivered in the 1970s, including both those carried over from the 1960s and the new systems introduced in the next decade. Once again, the total is about 100 systems, including some sixty in the strategic offensive and defensive categories.

As a result of the counterforce priority for their targeting, all Soviet strategic offensive systems have some damage-limiting role. During the 1960s, however, the SS-9 was the only ICBM designated for—and probably targeted exclusively against—U.S. nuclear delivery systems, nuclear weapons stocks, and associated command, control, and communications. In the 1970s the SS-9 was followed by the MIRVed, SS-18 and the SS-19 which carried for counterforce operations some 5,200 ready warheads as compared to the peak SS-9 arsenal of some 300 ready warheads. Hence, USSR investment in the strategic offense for war-fighting objectives has grown, especially fast since the SALT process began.

In addition to these quantitative changes in forces during the 1970s, fundamental qualitative improvements also first appeared in the late 1960s and accelerated over the next decade. Much has been made of ideas that Soviet weapons systems are simple, rugged, relatively inexpensive, evolutionary in design, and use only proven technology. Although overstated, these generalizations were reasonable characterizations of weapons design in the 1950s and 1960s. By the end of the 1970s, however, these ideas had become quite misleading. As has been reported by the undersecretary of defense for research and engineering and other sources, contemporary USSR weapons are complex, and they lag behind their U.S. and NATO counterparts in only a few areas of technology.[33] The latest-model Soviet ICBMs have complex guidance systems and are as accurate as the best American missiles. Both the Alpha and Mike class submarines incorporate technologies that the United States can not presently produce. Major USSR surface combatants are loaded with more electronics and weapons systems than their Western counterparts. The new nuclear-powered Kirov class cruiser "is the most impressively armed surface warship in the world," including three sonar systems and two three-dimensional/two-dimensional early warning radars.[34] USSR aircraft, helicopters, and armored vehicles are increasingly equipped with advanced electronic and optical systems and other high-technology hardware. The Soviet AWACS and the MiG-29, SU-27, and MiG-31 interceptors represent a true technological revolution in air defense aircraft, radar, and air-to-air missile technology. Clearly, these trends will continue throughout the 1980s.

USSR designers no doubt continue to emphasize reliability and to use proven designs where possible, but the day when the Soviets bought their weapons "on the cheap" has long since passed. (The U.S. Navy has not been able to purchase its own smaller nuclear-powered version of the Kirov-class cruiser on the grounds that such a ship is too expensive.)

As noted earlier, by 1973 an authoritative volume had already stated that the USSR must defend its cities, industrial centers, communications, and military establishment from enemy attack. Consequently, "in connection with this, anti-air defense of the country has acquired State significance."[35] (In Soviet parlance, "anti-air" defense of the country includes air, missile, and space defense.) In 1976 Admiral Gorshkov also designated strategic ASW a "State task." In the same year Marshal of Aviation G. V. Zimin published a book in which he reiterated the objective of defending the country from all types of air-space threats.[36] The weapons-development and procurement patterns in the 1970s demonstrates that Soviet decision makers did not allow SALT to change either their weapons-acquisition policies or their national priorities. Evidence for this is presented in the next section, in which USSR economic priorities during the SALT era are examined.

SOVIET MILITARY EXPENDITURES BEFORE AND AFTER SALT

The most rapid growth in USSR military outlays occurred in the years 1959–63 and 1966–70. During the former period expenditures for the military increased from about 13 to approximately 23 billion rubles (in 1955 prices), or nearly 75 percent; in the latter period, outlays nearly doubled, from about 25 to 50 billion rubles per annum (in 1970 prices). The years 1963–65

TABLE 18   SOVIET WEAPONS PROCUREMENT IN THE 1970S

Major mission	Number of systems	System designators
Strategic offensive	17	
ICBMs	6	SS-9, -11, -17, -18, -19
IR/MRBMs	1	SS-20
SLBMs	3	SS-N-6, -8, -18
SSBNs	2	Y, D
Bombers	2	TU-22, -26
ASM	3	AS-4, -5, -6
Strategic defensive	46– 48	
Air defense	15– 16	
SAMs	3	SA-3, -5, -10
Interceptors	3	SU-15, MIG-23, MIG-25
AAM	5	AA-3, -5, -6, -7
EW & GCI radar[a]	4– 5	Tall King, Odd Pair, Thin Skin, Knife Rest, NYSA
Missile and space defense[b]	4– 5	
Interceptors	1	(Galosh)
Radar	2– 3	not available
Antisatellite system	1	
Antisubmarine warfare	21	
Major surface ships	8	Kresta II, Kara, Krivak[c], Moskva, Kiev, Kirov, Udaloi, Slava
Helicopters	2	KA-25, MI-14
Aircraft	4	YAK-36, IL-38, BF-12, TU-142
SSN	3	Viktor I, Viktor II, Alpha
Missiles	4	SS-N-14, -15, -16; FRAS-1
Anticarrier[d]	6 (8)	
SSN/SLCM	3	Charlie, Papa[e], Oscar
SLCMs	3	SS-N-7, -9, -12, -19
Aircraft	(2)[f]	TU-22, -26
Operational-strategic	44– 49	
Ground forces	23– 27	
SSMs[g]	3	SS-12, -21, -22
SAMs	5	SA-6, -7, -8, -9, -11
Tanks[e]	3	T-64, T-72, BMD
APCs	3	BTR-60, BMP, MT-LB
SPs	3	SP-122mm, SP-152mm, ASU-85
ATGMs	4– 5	Swatter, Sagger, Spigot, Spandrel, Spiral
Artillery & mortars	2– 5	
Small arms & munitions[h]	—	

TABLE 18   *(continued)*

Major mission	Number of systems	System designators
Frontal aviation	12– 13	
Interceptors	2	MIG-21, -23
Fighter bombers	3	MIG-27, SU-17/20, SU-19
Reconnaissance	1	MIG-25
Helicopters	2– 3	MI-8, -12, -24
ASMs	2	AS-7, -9
Transports	2	AN-22, IL-76
Navy	9	
Cruisers	1	Sovremennyi
Missile patrol boats	3	Nanuchka, Sarancha, Matka
Logistics support	1	Ivan Rogoff
Landing craft	2	Ropuchka, Polnochniy
Frigates & corvettes	2	Grisha, Petia
Total	107–114	

SOURCES: Compiled from John M. Collins, *American and Soviet Military Trends Since the Cuban Missile Crisis* (Washington, D.C.: The Center for Strategic and International Studies, Georgetown University, 1978); John M. Collins and Patrick N. Cronin, *U.S.-Soviet Military Balance, Statistical Trends, 1970–1983*; Ray Bonds, ed., *The Soviet War Machine* (New York: Chartwell Bros., 1977); Secretary of Defense Harold Brown, *Annual Report FY 1980*; International Institute for Strategic Studies, *The Military Balance, 1971–1972* through *1979–1980*; "U.S. Confirms Soviets Are Building Nuclear-Powered Attack Carrier," *The Washington Star*, 17 December 1979; "More Undisclosed Soviet Strategic Arms Gains," *Armed Forces International* 116, no. 7 (March 1979): 17; Harry E. Eustace, ed., *The International Countermeasures Handbook, 1977–1978*, 3d ed. (Palo Alto, Calif.: EW Communications, 1977); *Aviation Week and Space Technology: SALT I-II* (McGraw-Hill, special issue, 1976); Jack Vorona, deputy director for scientific and technical intelligence, Defense Intelligence Agency, in U.S. Senate, Committee on Armed Services, Subcommittee on General Procurement, *Hearings on Soviet Defense Expenditures*, 96th Cong., 1st and 2d sess., 1 and 8 November 1979, 4 February 1980 (Washington, D.C.: GPO, 1980), p. 70; R. T. Pretty, ed., *Jane's Weapons Systems, 1979 1980* (New York: Franklin Watts, 1979), pp. 67–68; Paul J. Murphy, ed., *Naval Power in Soviet Policy*, USAF Studies in Communist Affairs, no. 2 (Washington, D.C.: GPO, 1978); Admiral Thomas B. Hayward, "Navy Chief Details Loss of U.S. Edge on Soviets," *Aviation Week and Space Technology* 114, no. 6 (9 February 1981): 35; Edgar Ulsamer, "In Focus," *Air Force Magazine* 63, no. 12 (December 1980): 12; Arthur D. Baker III, "Soviet Ship Types," *U.S. Naval Institute Proceedings* 106, no. 11 (November 1980), pp. 111–17.

NOTES: [a]Information on radar systems is limited. Eustace and *Jane's* appear to be the only practical sources. Most of these radars were introduced in the 1960s but procurement evidently continued into the 1970s. Some additional models were probably introduced in the 1970s, although this has not been reported.

[b]Some Galosh production may have extended into the 1970s. Information on large new phased array radars, reportedly suitable for ABM battle management, is sparse.

[c]Redesignated "patrol ships" (*Storozhevoi korabl' raketnyi*, or SKR) in 1977–78, but, like the smaller Petia and Mirka SKR classes, probably still have ASW as the primary mission (see prior discussion).

dThe primary mission of Soviet SLBMs and naval aviation bombers equipped with ASMs is evidently to destroy U.S. or NATO carriers and other naval ships. These systems would be used for the interdiction of NATO sea communication lines (if necessary) after they had performed their primary mission.

eOnly one Papa class SSN, armed with an unspecified type of cruise missile, is reported to have been constructed.

fAlready counted as a strategic offensive system. Parentheses indicate that system also counted under another mission.

gProduction of SCUD missiles undoubtedly continued into the 1970s but procurement of other system components is assumed to have been completed in the 1960s. FROG-7 procurement, however, probably extended well into the 1970s, so the count is conservative on this score.

hBasic infantry weapons (rifles, machine guns, grenade launchers, antitank systems), engineering equipment, communications and ECM, many types of ammunition, trucks, logistic equipment, and all other paraphernalia required by modern military establishments but usually omitted by weapons systems lists. Such weapons and equipment constitute a large part of total procurement.

represented a lull, which may simply have been the result of normal transitional factors as the Soviets moved from one set of deployment programs to another. Alternatively, this lull may have been the consequence of a shift in Khrushchev's priorities from armaments to basic economic investments following the Cuban missile crisis.[37] Whatever the reason, the 1963–65 slowdown in the growth of total USSR military and procurement outlays is one more bit of contradictory evidence against the idea that the October 1962 crisis accelerated the Soviet defense buildup.

Trends in the allocation of GNP during 1955–70 are shown in Table 19.[38] Note the decline in consumption's share and the modest investment increase over this period. Despite the rapid growth of military outlays after 1959, the military share of GNP in 1970 was not much above the 1955 level, owing in large part to the relatively high GNP growth rates during the fifteen years as a whole.

SALT has shown no discernible effect on USSR military expenditure. Its growth rate during the 1970s was less than in the frantic periods 1959–63 and 1966–70. The pace of general economic expansion, however, has slowed much more than that of the military. Consequently, the burden of defense on the economy has increased faster in the 1970s than it did in the 1960s.

Total military outlays and the three major components of defense expenditure for the period 1966–80 are shown on Table 20 in constant 1970 prices (as the USSR defines constant prices). The trend for the military share of Soviet GNP is shown on Table 21.[39] Note that the growth rate since 1970 has averaged more than 8 percent per annum; USSR defense expenditures in constant prices during 1980 were more than double the 1970 level. Note also the rapid rise in military outlays as a share of GNP, from 12–13 percent in 1970 to about 18 percent in 1980. The latter trend is in part a result of the

TABLE 19   TRENDS IN STRUCTURE OF USSR GNP, 1955–70
(1955–69 AND 1969–70 ESTIMATE OF CURRENT PRICES)

Year	CONSUMPTION		INVESTMENT		MILITARY		CIVIL R&D AND BUD-GET ADMINISTRATION		GNP	
	Rubles	Percent	Rubles	Percent	Rubles	Percent	Rubles	Percent	Rubles	Percent
1955	69.8	60.3%	29.9	25.8%	14.0	12.1%	2.1	1.8%	115.8	100%
1958	95.5	62.1	41.6	27.1	14.0	9.1	2.6	1.7	153.7	
1960	107.6	61.6	47.6	27.2	16.5	9.4	3.0	1.7	174.7	
1965	151.0	60.8	65.8	26.5	26.5	10.7	4.9	2.0	248.2	
1968	186.2	56.0	99.0	29.8	41.0	12.3	6.3	1.9	332.5	
1970	215.1	55.6	116.0	29.8	49.0	12.6	7.7	2.0	357.8	

SOURCE: W. T. Lee, "USSR Gross National Product in Established Prices, 1955–1975," *Jahrbuch der Wirtschaft Osteuropas* (Munich: Olzog Verlag, 1979), table 4, p. 412.

TABLE 20   ESTIMATE OF USSR DEFENSE EXPENDITURES IN 1970 PRICES
(BILLIONS OF RUBLES)

Year	Procurement of weaponry	Pay, mainte-nance, opera-tions, and construction	RDT&E and space	Defense expenditures
1966	7.6–8.6	14.7	4.8–7.9	27.1–31.2
1967	10.1–11.2	15.3	5.3–8.8	30.7–35.3
1968	12.6–13.8	17.1	6.2–10.1	35.9–41.0
1969	15.2–16.6	17.9	6.3–10.4	39.4–44.9
1970	17.8–19.5	17.9	7.5–12.4	43.0–50.0
1971	21.2–23.0	19.2	8.0–13.3	48.0–56.0
1972	24.3–26.4	19.9	8.4–14.2	53.0–60.0
1973	28.5–31.0	21.3	9.4–15.8	59.0–68.0
1974	32.2–35.1	22.1	10.2–17.1	64.0–74.0
1975	37.2–41.5	22.9	11.3–18.6	71.0–83.0
1976	41.3–46.1	24.0	11.8–19.4	77.0–90.0
1977	45.1–51.0	25.0	12.4–20.3	82.0–96.0
1978	51.4–57.6	26.0–27.0	12.9–21.3	90.0–106.0
1979	58.5–65.1	27.0–28.0	13.5–22.2	99.0–115.0
1980	66.0–74.0	28.0–29.0	14.1–23.2	108.0–126.0

SOURCE: W. T. Lee, "The Shift in Soviet National Priorities to Military Forces, 1958–1985," *The Annals of the American Academy of Political and Social Sciences* 457 (September 1981), p. 56.

declining growth rates of GNP, which in turn have been largely caused by the rising burden of defense. Several other factors are at work—notably, a decline in the growth of the labor force, an increase in costs for basic materials, and the perennial problems of agriculture—yet the growth in military expenditure is probably the single most important reason that the rate of GNP has declined so much over the last decade.

Obviously, the Politburo must have taken its expectations concerning the content and timing of the SALT II treaty into account when—in 1975—it set the following basic economic priorities for the tenth five-year plan (1976–80):

- Consumption to increase at about the same rate as national income and GNP—about 25 to 30 percent over the five-year period
- Investment to increase by only 16 to 17 percent, with a somewhat larger growth in producer durables—hence, to decline as a share of national income and, correspondingly, of GNP

• Military outlays to increase by about 50 percent—hence, the share of defense in both national income and GNP to increase sharply

For the USSR, the above comprised a relatively unique set of economic priorities. With the possible exception of 1940–41, this was the first time the Politburo planned to cut investment as a share of national income or GNP since Stalin decreed forced industrialization in 1928. The decision not to reduce consumption's share of national income and of GNP also represented a unique feature, particularly in light of the priority assigned to military outlays. Figure 5 places these trends in Soviet national economic priorities in perspective.

During the first two years of the tenth five-year plan (1976 and 1977) and in the annual plan for 1978, the USSR followed its objectives precisely. During the years 1978–80, however, more resources were allocated to investment than originally planned, evidently because of a rise in imports of machinery and equipment—financed by Western credits and by rising prices for oil, gas, and gold—and of a failure to provide the promised growth in consumption. Instead of increasing by only 16 to 17 percent, as originally planned, capital investment over the five-year period 1976–80 expanded by more than 18 percent.[40]

TABLE 21   ESTIMATE OF USSR GNP BY END USE IN ESTIMATED PRICES (BILLIONS OF RUBLES)

Year	Investment	Consumption	Military[a]	Civil R&D and administration	GNP
1966	85.7	161.4	31.2	5.5	284
1967	94.4	172.2	35.3	5.9	308
1968	99.0	186.2	41.0	6.3	332
1969	98.5	200.1	44.9	7.3	351
1970	116.0	215.1	50.0	7.7	389
1971	119.7	227.6	56.0	8.5	412
1972	128.8	240.6	60.0	9.3	439
1973	140.8	251.6	68.0	10.0	470
1974	149.2	265.5	74.0	10.7	499
1975	158.5	282.9	83.0	11.2	536
1980 forecast			126.0		650

SOURCE: W. T. Lee, "USSR Gross National Product in Established Prices, 1955–1975," *Jahrbuch der Wirtschaft Osteuropas* (Munich: Olzog Verlag, 1979), table 5, p. 413.

[a]"Military" estimate represents the high side of the range because the evidence indicates it is the more likely value.

Developments turned out somewhat differently than the tenth five-year plan (shown in Figure 5) projected. Soviet GNP for 1980 was about 23 percent above the 1975 level, instead of the 25 to 30 percent implied by the plan. Investment declined slightly to about 30 to 32 percent of GNP. Military spending, however, probably met the original tenth five-year plan goals. This means that consumption's share of GNP declined instead of remaining a more or less constant, as projected in 1975.

One of the best indicators of the impact of rising military expenditures on the Soviet economy is the rapid growth in the share of weapons procurement from domestic production of machinery and equipment[41]—from about 20 percent to well over 50 percent between 1966 and 1980 (see Figure 6). Allocations of machinery output to civilian uses—producer durables for capital investment and consumer durables for use in households and by individuals—declined correspondingly, from about 80 percent of domestic output in 1966 to approximately 40 percent in 1980. (Exports accounted for 7 to 8 percent of domestic output.)

Particularly over the last few years of the 1970s, the impact of this shift in priorities from civilian production to weaponry had been considerably eased by rapidly rising imports of machinery and equipment. This trend can be illustrated by data for 1978. Net of intermediate products, imports of machinery and equipment in foreign trade prices increased during 1978 by about 2.6 billion rubles.[42] In domestic prices, these imports were prob-

FIGURE 5   STRUCTURE OF USSR GNP, 1960–80 (End of 10th FYP)

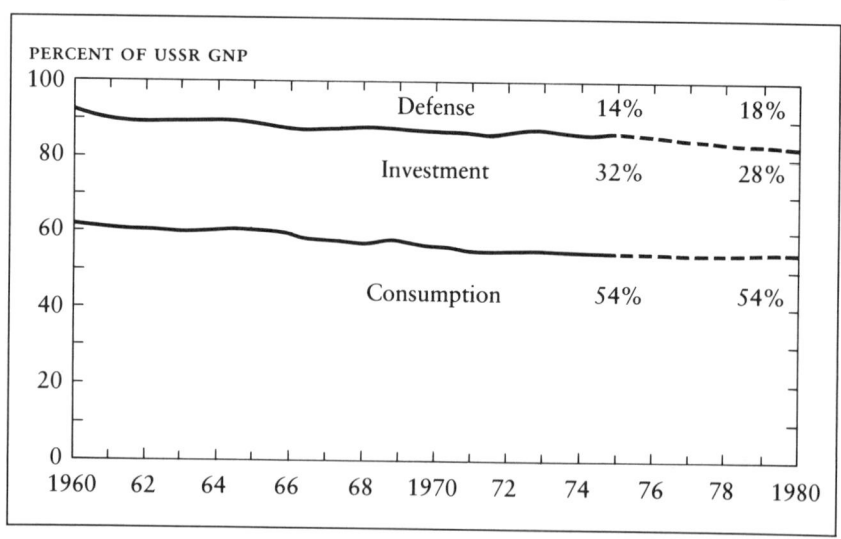

FIGURE 6   MILITARY PROCUREMENT AS A SHARE OF
TOTAL MACHINERY OUTPUT

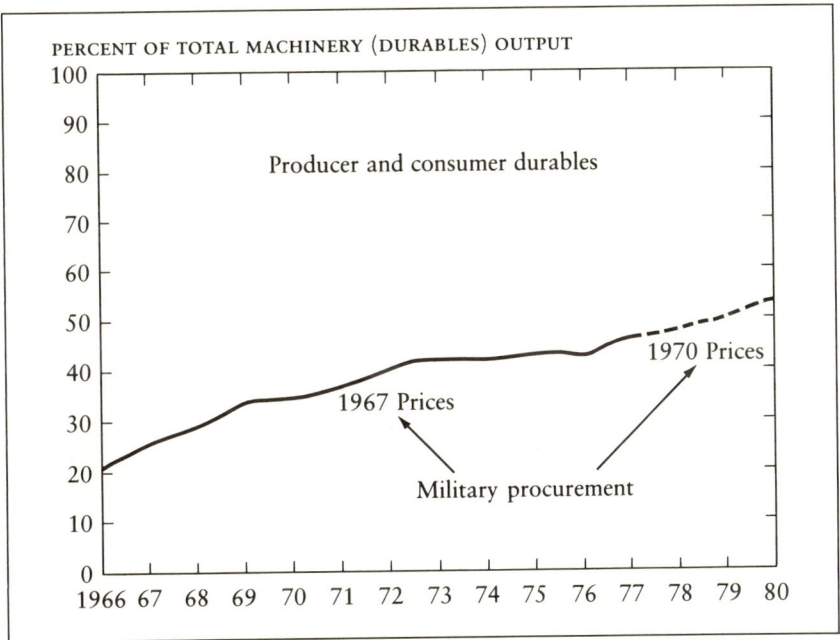

PERCENT OF TOTAL MACHINERY (DURABLES) OUTPUT

ably valued at between 2.8 and 4 billion rubles. Meanwhile, in 1978 allocations of producer durables to capital investment rose by about 3.6 billion rubles, whereas production of consumer durables increased by about 0.8 billion rubles. In other words, imports of machinery and equipment in 1978 probably accounted for the bulk of the increase in allocations to producer durables. Consequently, most of the growth in domestic output of machinery and equipment during that year was in the form of weaponry for the Soviet armed forces. During 1979–1981, the rapid growth in USSR machinery imports slowed but resumed in 1982.[43] The following year, the Soviets imported nearly 50 percent more machinery than in 1980.[44]

Much of this growth in USSR machinery imports involved imports from the United States and its NATO allies. Generally, machinery from these countries incorporates higher technological expertise than the Soviets are themselves capable of or can obtain from Eastern Europe. Throughout the 1970s, increased imports from the West were financed largely by loans and credits, higher prices for USSR petroleum products and natural gas (courtesy of OPEC), and higher gold prices because of U.S. inflation and the decline of the dollar. It is difficult to understand how the Soviets could have maintained their military buildup since the early 1970s without assistance from these external sources. Given both the rise in the value of the dollar and the drop in both oil prices and in the value of gold, it is uncertain how they will be able to continue the buildup through the remainder of the 1980s (as they evidently plan to do) minus the benefits of growing trade with the West. Nevertheless, the rapid growth of machinery imports over the past few years indicates that the Soviets have found at least a temporary solution to this problem.

Allocation of such a large share of USSR machinery output to weapons procurement also has resulted in a rather dramatic increase in procurement's part of military expenditures. Note that in Figure 7 procurement accounted for about 28 percent of the Soviet defense budget in 1966 and approximately 40 percent in 1970. By 1980 procurement's share had risen to almost 60 percent. At the same time, although they rose absolutely, operating costs declined to about 25 percent of Soviet military outlays. Excluding pensions, personnel costs (pay, maintenance, operations, and construction, or PMOC) represented only about one-eighth of Soviet defense expenditures in 1980, as compared to nearly three-fifths of the U.S. budget at that time. These trends in the structure of defense outlays also are shown in Figure 7.

Two factors appear to be driving the share of PMOC costs downward:

FIGURE 7.   STRUCTURE OF USSR MILITARY EXPENDITURES

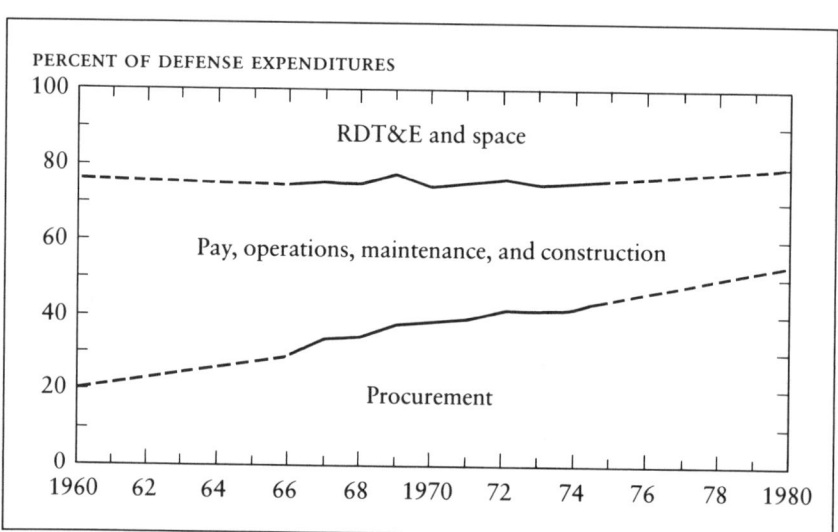

PERCENT OF DEFENSE EXPENDITURES

RDT&E and space

Pay, operations, maintenance, and construction

Procurement

(1) the low pay of conscripts and (2) USSR training and maintenance practices. Enlisted persons are supposed to be well fed and well clothed by Soviet standards, but they receive less pay per month than is needed to buy a bottle of vodka. Recruits probably constitute more than 70 percent of the armed forces. Officers are well paid, and their compensation probably increases at about the same rate as that of civilian workers. Consequently, manpower costs grow steadily but slowly.

Whenever possible, Soviet practices emphasize the use of training vehicles and weapons rather than unit equipment. Military aircraft fly fewer hours and ships cruise fewer miles each year than their U.S. counterparts. These regulations keep operating costs down and make it possible to maintain a high percentage of unit equipment in reliable operating condition. However, it is generally thought that such restrictions result in lower unit combat proficiency.

The decline in direct manpower costs (excluding pensions) has been dramatic—from about 25 percent of defense expenditure in 1960 to approximately 15 percent in 1970 and only 10 percent currently. Adding pension costs would increase the share, although it would not alter the trend significantly. Opportunity costs—that is, the amount the conscripts would have produced if employed in the economy—remain quite high for military manpower. Expenditures for military manpower, however, increase slowly and take a smaller share of total outlays each year.

As noted at the beginning of this chapter, no changes in Soviet military doctrine and strategy appeared during the era of SALT and détente. Similarly, the USSR continued to develop and deploy the same panoply of weapons designed for fighting and winning a nuclear war as before. The only change evidenced was a higher rate of military technological advancement during the 1970s than during the 1960s. The objectives of the party's military-technical policy remained the same: quantitative and qualitative superiority. To pay for all this, Soviet leaders increased the military burden on the economy more rapidly than in the 1960s. Throughout the 1970s the USSR spent at least one-third of its entire annual budget on the military, or about the same proportion as in 1940, on the eve of the German invasion.

To answer the question posed by the title of this chapter, during the era of SALT the Soviets continued to pursue their standing goals of qualitative and quantitative superiority in weaponry and forces. Moreover, because SALT and détente inhibited U.S. strategic weapons programs and gave the USSR access to Western machinery and technology, the Politburo was able to implement its objectives with much more success during the 1970s than previously.

7

Soviet Strategic Force Prospects for the 1980s

From 1969 through the mid-1980s the SALT negotiations and détente had no discernible effect on USSR military policy. In three critical areas—military doctrine and strategy, patterns of force development, and national economic priorities—the SALT process and détente only accentuated prior trends. All indicators point to more of the same for the remaining few years of the 1980s, but with an increased emphasis on strategic defensive systems to close the gaps that still exist between damage-limiting requirements and the capabilities of Soviet strategic forces.

Basic decisions on weapons systems and resource allocation during the first half of the current decade were made by the CPSU leadership prior to the Twenty-sixth Party Congress and were incorporated into the eleventh FYP for the period 1981–85. It is now clear from the scope and composition of the weapons being developed and procured that there has been no change in the pattern (except for an even greater emphasis on strategic defensive systems, for reasons that will be discussed below).

As this book goes to press, yet another round of decisions on weapons system development and procurement is being prepared for the Twenty-seventh CPSU Congress on the twelfth FYP (1986–90), and through the 1990s. Soviet leaders since Brezhnev have not changed their preference for guns over butter. Gorbachev seems to believe he can have both by tightening discipline, making rather modest modifications in economic management, and rearranging investment priorities. At this juncture it appears doubtful that the twelfth FYP will stabilize defense expenditures at their current level of 18 to 21 percent of GNP, let alone reduce them below that level. The only possible indicator to the contrary is the reported Soviet proposal for large reductions in the strategic nuclear arsenals of both sides. It remains to be seen whether this is serious.[1]

The patterns of the 1960s and 1970s and the trends observed in the first half of this decade shed considerable light on the range of major weapons systems the Soviets will procure in the 1980s. The eleventh FYP also provided some insights into resource allocations during the period 1981–85 that are probably indicative of the next five years. The economy was scheduled to grow at an annual rate of about 3.5 percent, consumption at about 3 percent, and investment at 2 percent or less.[2] Total military expenditures were apparently scheduled to increase at 6 to 7 percent per annum, or roughly double the rate of growth planned for other parts of the economy. Outlays for weapons procurement were probably planned to grow by at least 10 percent each year. The Soviets have either met these targets or are close to them.

PROSPECTS FOR STRATEGIC OFFENSIVE FORCES

As in the past, USSR weapons acquisition in the 1980s comprises a mix of programs carried over from the past decade and new programs brought to fruition in the present one. The following trends are summarized from official sources:[3]

• Deployments of SS-17, SS-18, and SS-19 were essentially completed by 1980. Retrofit of the latest, most accurate versions (SS-18 mod 4 and SS-19 mod 3), however, continued through 1984.

• Two new ICBMs, the SS-24 and SS-25, are being flight tested and will become operational during 1985–86. The SS-24 will probably be deployed in both silo and mobile modes; SS-25 deployment may be exclusively mobile.

• Follow-on models to the SS-18 and the SS-24 should begin flight testing in 1986–88.

• SS-20 deployment (400 to 450 launchers) is probably approaching planned levels.[4] These levels may be increased as a result of NATO nuclear modernization, which has somewhat expanded the target base. Meanwhile, a modified SS-20 is being flight tested.

• Deployment of the MIRVed version for the SS-N-18 on Delta III class SSBNs continued through 1982, when the program probably peaked at fourteen submarines. The Delta IV class is equipped with a new MIRVed SLBM, the SS-N-23, which is already operational on two units. As of mid-1985 at least three Typhoon class SSBNs, each carrying 20 MIRVed SS-N-20 missiles, had been built, and two of these were operational. Up to eight Typhoons are expected by the end of the decade.

• All of these new SLBMs have intercontinental range, carry more warheads, and deliver them more accurately than their predecessors.

• Procurement of Backfire medium bombers continues at the rate of about 30 aircraft per year to modernize Supreme High Command (VGK) air armies and Soviet naval aviation for strategic air operations in the Eurasian continental and contiguous oceanic TVDs. Some 25 Bear H heavy bombers, equipped with the AS-15 long-range (1,500 km) cruise missiles, are operational. The new jet-powered heavy bomber, Blackjack, is in advanced stages of development. It, too, is expected to carry the AS-15 air-to-surface missile. Bear H and Blackjack probably will be assigned primarily to attacking targets in the North American TVD.

Although this comprehensive pattern of new system development may resemble that of the early 1970s, it does not necessarily portend an unlimited expansion of the USSR strategic nuclear arsenal. As is argued elsewhere, the SALT II limits of nearly 13,000 (ready) ICBM and SLBM warheads probably satisfy the sufficiency conditions for these components of the Soviet strategic arsenal. The USSR proposal at START for about 12,000 warheads corroborates this judgment.[5] Consequently, the principal objectives of the new strategic offensive delivery systems presently in advanced stages of development and early stages of deployment are probably to reach the SALT II levels by deploying all of the MIRVed systems permitted; reduce the vulnerability of the USSR arsenal to increasingly accurate U.S. systems by replacing silo-based systems with mobile ones; improve accuracy, primarily with hard target systems; and make the overall force more flexible. Tables 22 and 23 show the trends in Soviet strategic missile forces over the first half of the 1980s.

Survivability and flexibility will be enhanced by the introduction of a "triad" element, in the form of the two new heavy bombers (Bear H and Blackjack) equipped with long-range ASMs. The decisions to initiate development of these systems probably date from the early to mid-1970s at the latest. The re-emergence of the intercontinental mission for Soviet heavy bombers and, particularly, the development of the AS-15 ASM (so similar to its American counterpart) represent a major modification of USSR strategic nuclear weapons acquisition policy. This appears to be one case where the simplistic "action-reaction" model of that policy may be the most germane explanation for a Soviet decision.

TABLE 22 EXTRAPOLATION OF SRF TO 1985 UNDER
SALT II CONSTRAINTS
(LAUNCHERS)

Force	1980	1981	1982	1983	1984	1985
SS-4	350	280	260	224	100–150	50–100
SS-5	50	35	15	13		
SS-20	160	240	325	378	390–420	400–450
IR/MRBM total	560	555	600	615	490–570	450–550
SS-11	640	580	550	520	520	500
SS-13	60	60	60	60	60	60
SS-17 (4 MIRV)	150	150	150	150	150	140
SS-18 (10 MIRV)	308	308	308	308	308	308
SS-19 (6 MIRV)	240	300	330	360	360	360
SS-24 (10 MIRV)						20
SS-25						10
ICBM total	1,398	1,398	1,398	1,398	1,398	1,398
MIRVed ICBMs	698	758	788	818	818	818
SRF total (rounded)	1,958	1,870–1,960	1,640–1,820	1,560–1,770	1,510–1,770	1,510–1,820

SOURCES: The 1980 base data came from Table 10. Extrapolations to 1985 based on John M. Collins and Patrick M. Cronin, *U.S.-Soviet Military Balance, Statistical Trends, 1970–1983*, pp. 14–16; U.S. Dept. of Defense, *Soviet Military Power, 1984* (Washington, D.C.: The Pentagon, 1984), p. 51; and ibid., 1985, p. 36. The range of uncertainty for IR/MRBM deployments is designed to bound Soviet reactions to NATO deployments of P-II and GLCM, while also maintaining adequate capabilities to target the PRC and other targets in the Far East.

TABLE 23 Estimates of Soviet SLBM Forces to 1985 under SALT II Constraints (End of Year Data)

Force	1980 Boats	1980 Tubes	1981 Boats	1981 Tubes	1982 Boats	1982 Tubes	1983 Boats	1983 Tubes	1984 Boats	1984 Tubes	1985 Boats	1985 Tubes
Diesel classes												
G	15	45	14	42	14	42	14	42	13	39	12	39
SSBN classes												
H-I & II	3	9	3	9	3	9	2	6	2	6		
Y	29	464	28	448	24	384	23	368	22	352	21	336
D-I	18	216	18	216	18	216	18	216	18	216	18	216
D-II	4	64	4	64	4	64	4	64	4	64	4	64
D-III	10	160	13	208	14	224	14	224	14	224	14	224
Y-II	1	12	1	12	1	12	1	12	1	12	1	12
Typhoon[a]	1	20	1	20	1	20	2	40	2	40	3	60
D-IV											1	16
Totals												
Boats-Tubes	81	990	82	1019	79	971	78	972	76	953	75	967
SSBNs-Tubes	66	945	68	977	65	929	64	930	63	914	62	928
SSBN MIRVs	192		240		244		264		264		300	

Sources: 1980 base data are from Table 11. Note that it is difficult to reconstruct the magic SALT number of 62 accountable boats and 950 tubes from the available data until 1985. One Y-class boat that has been converted to a twelve-tube configuration for the SS-N-17 is included in this table. The projections to 1985 stay as close to the magic numbers of 62 boats and 950 tubes as the arithmetic permits based on John M. Collins and Patrick N. Cronin, *U.S.-Soviet Military Balance, Statistical Trends, 1970–1983*, pp. 17–21; and on U.S. Dept. of Defense, *Soviet Military Power, 1984* (Washington, D.C.: The Pentagon, 1984), pp. 24–26, and ibid., 1985, p. 35. The 1985 numbers are consistent with these Defense Department figures.

[a] The first Typhoon may not have been operational until 1981–82. By 1985 all D-III SS-N-18 SLBMs are assumed to be retrofitted with the seven-MIRV payload specified in the SALT II agreement. Secretary of Defense Harold Brown (*Annual Report, Fiscal Year 1982*, p. 46) lists Typhoon as carrying twenty tubes and says the Typhoon missile, the SS-NX-20, "almost certainly" will be MIRVed. If so, eventually about ten RVs per missile are likely. Collins and Cronin (*Statistical Trends, 1970–1983*, p. 22) lists only six RVs for the SS-N-20; the U.S. Dept. of Defense (*Soviet Military Power, 1984*, p. 26), however, lists six to nine RVs for this missile.

The only factors that might increase the Kremlin's ready ICBM and SLBM arsenal beyond the 12,000 to 13,500 warhead levels negotiated in SALT II and proposed by the Soviets in START would be an expansion of the U.S. target base, the construction of less-vulnerable silos for American missiles, and the imminent prospect of an effective U.S. Strategic Defense Initiative (SDI) against ballistic missiles. Counterforce strikes can only do so much to limit damage to the Soviet Union. An effective SDI would render brute force proliferation of the USSR arsenal more and more impractical as an effective counter. The implications of SDI and of the Soviet strategic arms reduction proposal reported in the United States press during late September and early October 1985 are discussed at the end of Chapter 9.

STRATEGIC DEFENSE

If the USSR is nearing the point at which further expansion of its strategic offensive nuclear arsenal would have little or no payoff for its war-fighting, damage-limiting strategy, then the potential for such returns to improvements in strategic defenses are enormous. There are numerous gaps between the requirements of strategy and the capabilities of Soviet fielded forces, which would have to defend the USSR from the large number of NATO missiles and air weapons that would survive counterforce strikes. It is therefore not surprising to find that the Soviets have a large number of new strategic defensive systems incorporating advanced technologies that provide critical capabilities lacking in prior systems. Some of the principal strategic defensive weapons programs are discussed below.[6]

Deployment of the SA-5 continues. The system has been modified to work with the new SA-10, which has low-altitude capabilities that were largely lacking in the SA-5 and previous models. More than 60 SA-10 launchers are operational. Approximately one-half of these are deployed around Moscow to defend hardened national war-management facilities and other high value military-industrial assets. The remaining SA-10 units are deployed to protect similar battle-management and industrial complexes elsewhere. The SA-10 is the first Soviet surface-to-air missile capable of engaging low-radar cross section cruise missiles. A mobile version of the SA-10 is being developed—probably to facilitate its relocation during wartime to counter SAM-suppression attacks designed to enhance U.S. bomber and cruise missile penetration.

The low-altitude gap in USSR air defenses is being closed by the Soviet AWACS and three new interceptors having true look-down-shoot-down capabilities. Approximately 70 Foxhound and 30 Fulcrum interceptors with these low-altitude capabilities are now operational. The AWACS, designated

"Mainstay," became operational in 1984. At least four of these aircraft are presently flying, and production averages about five per year. Flanker, the third new Soviet interceptor with true look-down-shoot-down capabilities, is nearing deployment. Two new ASMs have been developed for these aircraft—the long-range AS-9 for Foxhound, and the medium-range AS-10 for Flanker and Fulcrum.

The USSR is evidently making a major effort to improve its ground air-defense environment. Some twenty new radar models have been observed at developmental test centers. At least two of these new radars have been deployed during the period 1983–85.

The aggregative effect of Soviet efforts in conventional and advanced ABM and air-defense technologies is indeed impressive. Six second-generation large phased-array radars with ABM battle-management capabilities are now operational or under construction. These new systems, combined with eleven first-generation "Hen House" phased-array radars, provide overlapping coverage against potential ballistic missile attacks from nearly all azimuths.[7]

Ground-, air-, and space-based laser systems for ABM and antisatellite operations are being developed. When these systems could become operational, however, remains highly uncertain. Most forecasts of such capabilities are for the late 1990s or later. Three air-defense laser systems, intended to supplement SAM defenses of high-value targets and to protect naval ships and ground forces, may be deployed much earlier. An airborne laser system is being tested, which could have both antisatellite and air-defense applications. Particle-beam weapons are also being worked on, but it is uncertain how far research and development have proceeded.

Three new space boosters capable of lifting payloads of 15, 30, and 180 thousand kilograms into 180 kilometer orbits are in late stages of development. In addition to orbiting a reusable space plane and a space shuttle, these boosters may be an integral part of Soviet programs for space-based (or combined ground- and space-based) ABM and antisatellite programs.

As emphasized previously, most of the so-called "general purpose" combatants in the Soviet navy are assigned two strategic missions: anticarrier or navy operations and ASW. For the submarine force, these missions are primarily assigned to the Oscar class cruise missile submarine and the other three new nuclear-powered classes (Mike, Sierra, and Akula) that carry ASW missiles. Of the new surface combatants, one cruiser and one destroyer (Slava and Sovremennyi) appear to be designed for the anticarrier or navy mission; the nuclear-powered Kirov class cruiser and the Udaloi class destroyer carry several ASW weapons systems. All of the new submarine and surface classes are much larger. Hence, they have a larger set of weapons systems and more functions than their smaller predecessors, which had limited air defenses and little or no antiship weapons systems.

Soviet naval air forces are being modernized with Backfire bombers for anticarrier or other naval operations. A new helicopter, the Helix, has been added to support both ASW and cruise missile operations. The ASW model of the Bear F, introduced in 1970, has been upgraded.

Passive defenses are being improved by further hardening and dispersal of all elements in the Soviet war-management system. The cumulative cost of this effort, if duplicated in the United States, has been estimated at between $28 and $56 billion. If past experience is any guide, this is probably a conservative estimate.

Tables 24 and 25 depict the changes in size and composition of Soviet strategic defensive forces in the 1980–85 period. Table 26 traces the trends in the Soviet nuclear-powered submarine forces for both strategic offensive and defensive missions. Although the average number of nuclear-powered submarines acquired each year has declined somewhat from the level of the 1970s, total tonnage has increased substantially.

These strategic defensive programs are impressive, not only because of their number and scope but also because of the advanced technologies incorporated in them, particularly in air defense. Unlike the practice of the previous two decades, the Soviets are no longer fielding whatever weapons are available, regardless of their effectiveness. One of the largest and most obvious technological gaps remaining centers on open-ocean search and location of American SSBNs. As pointed out previously, the most likely solution to this problem (if there is one) lies in nonacoustic technologies. Although official U.S. publications seldom mention Soviet activities in this area, there is no reason to doubt that the USSR is making extensive efforts to develop nonacoustic ASW technologies.

The new Moscow ABM defenses and the second generation of large phased-array radars will probably be completed during the period 1986–88. The Soviets would then appear to be in an excellent position to break out of the ABM Treaty by deploying their ABM-X-3 system. Completion of the Moscow defenses will require that most, or perhaps all, of the major components already be in series production. The first- and second-generation large phased-array radars should provide the necessary battle-management capabilities. Soviet reponses to U.S. charges that the Krasnoiarsk radar is a violation of the ABM Treaty are so obviously specious that they merely reinforce suspicions of a planned breakout (if indeed one is not already underway).[8] Past testing of SAMs in an ABM environment, and the ABM potential of the new SA-X-12, heighten concerns of a Soviet breakout. Evident large-scale investment in exotic ABM technologies could result in some

TABLE 24   FORECAST OF MAJOR STRATEGIC AIR DEFENSE WEAPONS SYSTEMS TO THE MID-1980s

	1980	1985[a,b]
Interceptors[b]	2,550	1,100–1,400
MIG-17 Fresco	50	—
MIG-23 Flogger B/G	650	400–500
MIG-25 Foxbat A/E	300	200–250
SU-9/11 Fishpot B/C	300	—
SU-15 Flagon D/E/F	800	200–230
TU-28 Fiddler	150	50–100
YAK-28 Firebar	300	100–120
MIG-31 Foxhound		100–150
SU-27/29		50–100
Look-down-shoot-down radars, up to 8 AAMs		
Air surveillance	9	14–19
TU-126 Moss	9	9
IL-76 Mainstay AWACS[a]		5–10
SAMs[c]	9,250	10,400–14,400
SA-1	3,200	1,000–2,500
SA-2	2,800	2,500–2,800
SA-3 (rails/missiles)	4,500	2,500–4,000
SA-5	1,900	2,000–2,000
SA-10 (missiles)	120	2,400–3,000
SA-12		0–100
ABM defenses		
Radars[d]	2–6	3–4 under construction
Interceptors (at Moscow)	64	100
SA-10, 12[e]	—	

SOURCES: "Soviets Press Production," *Aviation Week and Space Technology*, 16 March 1981, pp. 56–60; *International Defense Review*, no. 7 (1978): 1015–16. *Aviation and Marine International* (71 [1980]: 24) and other sources report that the Soviet AWACS is based on the IL-86 transport rather than the IL-76. *Soviet Military Power, 1983* (Washington, D.C.: The Pentagon, 1983), pp. 28–30; ibid. *1984*, pp. 36–39; John M. Collins and Patrick N. Cronin, *U.S.-Soviet Military Balance, Statistical Trends, 1970–1983.*

[a]The first source cited above expects fifty Soviet AWACS to be deployed; the second source gives a range of thirty to fifty. *Soviet Military Power, 1984* (p. 38) indicates that the first MAINSTAY AWACS aircraft was deployed in 1983–84, that four aircraft have been built, and that "an annual production of about five aircraft is likely."

[b]The 1985 interceptor figures represent only those dedicated to strategic air defense as a result of the major reorganization in the early 1970s when most of the older model, light-altitude air defenses were transferred to units having the dual role of territorial air defense and tactical support of ground force units. See *Soviet Military Power, 1984*, p. 37.

^cIf another SAM is introduced in 1985, it will probably be a version of the SA-12 adapted to national air defense requirements. According to *Soviet Military Power, 1984* (p. 34), the SA-X-12 is both a tactical SAM and an antitactical ballistic missile. *Soviet Military Power, 1985* (p. 48) indicates the 1985 total will be at the low end of the range shown here.

^dTwo large phased array radars were installed in the 1960s and a third is now under construction. Apparently, four more radars have been under construction outside of the Moscow area for some time. According to *Soviet Military Power, 1984* (p. 33), there are a total of six of the new model large phased array radars built or under construction in the USSR. Like the prior Hen House models, all are capable of supporting national ABM deployments. The latest one to be discovered in Siberia is so far removed from the Soviet periphery that it clearly violates the ABM Treaty.

^e*Soviet Military Power, 1984* (p. 34) states that "both the SA-10 and the SA-X-12 may have the potential to intercept some types of U.S. strategic missiles as well." This is repeated in *Soviet Military Power, 1985* (p. 48).

operational capabilities in about the same time that a conventional ABM system could be deployed, or soon thereafter. Finally, hardening of the wartime national management system and relocation of other assets add significantly to the effectiveness of both air and missile defenses.

The emphasis in USSR force development appears to have shifted to strategic defenses, because this is where the largest payoffs will be over the next two decades. Given the long lead times involved in the development of new and exotic strategic defenses, the Soviets probably came to this conclusion at about the time the SALT process and détente began.

Meanwhile, these battle-management radars make possible some degree of national ABM defenses as the SA-10 and SA-X-12 systems are deployed, because both of them "have capabilities to intercept some types of U.S. ballistic strategic missile RVs."[9] Inasmuch as the SA-10 was first deployed around 1980, and the SA-X-12 probably will become operational during 1985–1986, there should be considerable potential to improve the ABM capabilities of one or both of these systems in the course of the next decade. The provisions the United States inserted into the ABM Treaty to prohibit acquisition of ABM capabilities by air defense systems are *de facto* no longer being followed by the Soviet Union.

COMBINED ARMS

USSR combined arms (ground, air, and navy) for operations in the continental Eurasian TVDs are not being neglected either. The pattern of weapons system modernization continues to reflect the balanced emphasis on nuclear and nonnuclear capabilities evident since the mid-1960s, when Soviet doctrine was modified to allow for a conventional phase in a war be-

TABLE 25   PROJECTION OF MAJOR SOVIET NAVAL SURFACE COMBATANTS, 1980–85

	1980	1981	1982	1983	1984	1985
Former large ASW ships (BPK)[a]						
Destroyers and Cruisers						
Kashin	19	19	19	19	19	19
Kanin	8	8	8	8	8	8
Kildin	4	4	4	4	4	4
Krivak	32	32	32	32	32	32
Kretal	4	4	4	4	4	4
Large ASW ships[b]						
Kresta II	10	10	10	10	10	10
Kara	7	7	7	7	7	7
ASW cruisers						
Moskva	2	2	2	2	2	2
Kiev	2	2	3	3	3	3–4
New cruisers						
Kirov	1	1	2	2	3	3–4
Udaloi	2	2	2	3	4–5	5–7
ASW mission subtotal[b]	89	91	93	94	95–96	96–100
Carriers—new nuclear						—
Antiship classes—destroyers and cruisers	5	6	7	8	10–13	12–17
Kynda	4	4	4	4	4	4
Sovremennyi	1	2	2	3	4–5	5–7
Slava			1	1	2–4	3–6
Totals[c]	94	97	100	102	105–109	108–117

Sources: 1980 data from Table 15, projected to 1985. John M. Collins and Patrick N. Cronin, *U.S.-Soviet Military Balance, Statistical Trends, 1970–1983*; *Jane's Fighting Ships, 1982–1983*; *Soviet Military Power, 1984*, pp. 95–96; ibid., 1985, pp. 97–105.

[a]Primary mission probably remains ASW but may possibly be oriented more toward protecting Soviet SSBNs than destroying enemy SSBNs. As noted previously, in the late 1970s the Krivak class was redesignated an "escort" ship.

[b]Despite various changes in designation, strategic ASW probably continues to be the major mission of these classes although they have a much broader spectrum of capabilities than earlier models (see discussion in text).

[c]*Soviet Military Power, 1985* (p. 105) reports forty-seven major Soviet surface combatants constructed in 1980–84, thirty-six of which were constructed in 1981–84. The sources for this table can account for only fourteen to twenty-four major combatants since 1980. The Ivan Rogov amphibious class would add two more, and some may be launched and still fitting out. Nevertheless, there appears to be a major discrepancy in the sources.

TABLE 26   FORECAST OF SOVIET NUCLEAR SUBMARINE
ACQUISITION TO 1985

	1980	1981	1982	1983	1984	1985
Nuclear						
SSBNs	11	14	16	17	18	19
Y-I						
D-I & II						
D-III	10	13	14	14	15	15
Typhoon	1	1	2	3	3	3
D-IV						1
SLCMs	19	19	20	20	21	22
C-I & II	17	17	17	17	17	17
P	1	1	1	1	1	1
O	1	1	2	2	3	4
ASW and Attack	35	40	44	48	53	56
V-I	16	16	16	16	16	16
V-II & III	13	18	21	24	26	26
Alpha	6	6	6	6	6	6
Mike			1	1	2	4
Sierra				1	2	3
Akula					1	1
Total	65	73	80	85	92	97
Annual Nuclear Deliveries		8	7	5	7	5

SOURCES: John M. Collins and Patrick M. Cronin, *U.S.-Soviet Military Balance, Statistical Trends, 1970–1983; Jane's Fighting Ships, 1982–1983; Soviet Military Power, 1984*, pp. 25, 61–63, 95, 96; and ibid., *1985*, pp. 95–97, 105.

tween the two superpowers and their coalitions. Some of the principal programs are described below.[10]

Until the nuclear heavy artillery brigades armed with 203 mm howitzers and 240 mm mortars were introduced during the mid-1970s, the USSR had no nuclear-capable artillery. In the late 1970s it introduced a nuclear-capable 152 mm self-propelled gun; a towed version is now available. In the last decade the number of nuclear-capable artillery tubes has increased from about 800 to nearly 8,000.

In general, artillery units are being modernized with new models, many of which are self-propelled and upgraded with more tubes and rocket launchers at each unit level. As a result, over the last decade there has been a 40 percent increase in the number of artillery tubes in Warsaw Pact units, primarily for those stationed opposite NATO.

Nuclear fire support has been improved by the introduction of the SS-21 and SS-23 missile systems, which have replaced the existing unguided rockets at division levels and older missile models (Scud) at army and front levels. The new missiles have longer ranges and are more accurate. In combination with new conventional munitions, these capabilities make them effective in nonnuclear, as well as nuclear, conflict.

Three new helicopters—one each for ground attack, air superiority, and transport—are entering (or will soon enter) service. The air superiority model has no Western counterpart.

In addition to various other advances in propulsion, fire control, and armor, the T-80 and late model T-64 tanks fire an antitank missile through their main guns. (A decade or so ago the United States dropped a similar antitank missile feature from the project that eventually evolved as the M–1 Abrams.)

Air defenses are being modernized at regiment through division, army, and front levels with three new SAMs and a follow-on to the ZSU-23/4 self-propelled, radar-directed antiaircraft gun. Deployment of the SA-X-12, which has antitactical ballistic missiles and air-defense capabilities, is imminent. Airlift is being improved with the IL-76, and a new transport in the same class as the American C-5 is nearing deployment.

Naval amphibious assault capabilities are being improved. The Soviet navy is the world's largest operator of military air-cushion vehicles. Also, air-assault battalions and brigades have been introduced at army and front levels, respectively.

In the last few years there has been a tendency among certain Western observers to overinterpret these improvements in Soviet capabilities as evidence of a shift to preparations for conventional warfare to the virtual exclusion of nuclear operations, in a war against NATO. Aside from expectations of a longer conventional phase than anticipated in the 1960s, Soviet literature on doctrine, strategy, and operational art does not support such a change. Both the proliferation of nuclear artillery and the deployment of the SS-20 (not to mention the modernization of Soviet air forces) over the past decade have vastly increased USSR capabilities for nuclear war. At the same time, other new weapons systems and organizational modifications have brought Soviet conventional capabilities more or less into balance with their nuclear ones. The existence of more balanced forces does not necessarily mean that the Soviets have ruled out nuclear escalation in a war with NATO.

The new classes of surface combatants discussed under USSR strategic forces also are adding unprecedented dimensions to Soviet naval capabilities for global power projection. As noted previously, this mission was added during the 1970s. Coupled with improvements in amphibious warfare capabilities and the sealift of the merchant marine, with its fleet of modern "roll-on, roll-off" ships, the new classes of surface combatants entering the Soviet

TABLE 27   FORECAST OF SOVIET WEAPONS PROCUREMENT
IN THE 1980S

Major mission	Systems carried over from 1970s	New systems introduced in 1980s	Systems procured in 1980s
Strategic offensive			15–26
ICBMs	1	4–6	
IRBMs	1	0–1	
SLBMs	1	1–2	
SSBNs	1	1–2	
Bombers	1	1–3	
ASMs	1–2	1–3	
Tankers	1	0–1	
Strategic defensive			46–80
Air defenses	6–8	8–18	14–26
SAMs	1	1–2	
Interceptors	2	2–3	
AAM	2–3	1–3	
AWACS	—	1–2	
Radars	0–1	2–6	
C³ systems	1	1–2	
Missile and space defenses	3–4	1–9	4–13
ABM/space radars	2–3	0–4	
ABM interceptors	—	1–3	
Antisatellite systems	1	0–2	
ASW	15–16	7–17	22–23
Major surface ships	5–6	2–3	
Aircraft	1	1–3	
Helicopters	2	1–3	
Submarines (SSNs)	2	1–3	
Naval SAMs	2	1–3	
Missiles	3	1–3	
Anticarrier	3 (4)	3–5	6–8
SSN/SLCM	1	1–2	
SLCM	2	1–2	
Aircraft	(1)	1	
Operational-strategic			44–61
Ground forces	12–14	10–16	22–30
SSMs	2	2–3	
SAMs and AA guns	3–4	3–5	
Tanks	1	1	
APCs	2	1–2	
SP artillery	2	1–2	
ATGMs	2–3	2–3	

TABLE 27   (*continued*)

Major mission	Systems carried over from 1970s	New systems introduced in 1980s	Systems procured in 1980s
Frontal aviation and military transport aviation	9–10	11–17	20–27
Interceptors	1	1–2	
Fighter bombers	3	1–2	
Reconnaissance	1	1	
Helicopters	2	2–3	
TASMs	1–2	2–3	
AAMs	1–2	2–3	
Transports	1	2–3	
Power projection	1	1–3	
Logistic support ships	1	1–3	
Total weapons procured in the 1980s			
Carried over from the 1970s			55–64
Introduced in the 1980s			49–103
Grand total			104–167

SOURCES: Calculations by W. T. Lee.

fleets and under construction can deploy forces by sea to aid insurgencies and client states anywhere in the world. The missile armaments and aircraft of these new combatants also could challenge the most modern Western naval forces in a conventional conflict. The USSR already had done a great deal of mischief through its military aid programs, without any significant naval capabilities outside its home waters. Admiral Gorshkov's new "blue water" navy should be able to do much more, even in the face of hostile opposition.

PROCUREMENT PROSPECTS FOR THE 1980S

Table 27 summarizes developments and projections in numbers of systems to be procured during the 1980s by major mission. The following points should be noted:

• By conservative count, the minimum number of weapons systems to be procured during the 1980s totals 105; the maximum number totals 167. Comparatively, about 100 major systems were identified during the 1960s and 1970s.

• The number of strategic defensive systems that will be deployed in the 1980s is somewhat greater than that delivered during the previous decade. The maximum number predicted for the 1980s is about double the number of strategic defensive weapons systems purchased in the ten preceding years.

• A number of systems procured for air and ASW defenses are based on high technology, which makes them rather expensive.

No matter how one looks at the evidence, the same answer emerges: During the 1980s the USSR will make an enormous investment in strategic defensive weapons systems designed to provide the capabilities required by the Soviet war-fighting, damage-limiting strategy. Strategic offensive capabilities will improve, primarily as a result of more accurate MIRVs on new generations of strategic missiles and of deployment of new cruise missiles for aircraft and other platforms. Passive defense will certainly continue to improve. No revision of the fundamentals of Soviet military doctrine and strategy appears to be under way.

Gorbachev is likely to be in power for some time to come, possibly through the turn of the century. Thus far, the new CPSU general secretary appears to be as committed to military priorities as his predecessors. The real test will be found in how the twelfth FYP (1986–90) is implemented.

In a number of public statements during April–June 1985, Gorbachev appears to have provided some insight into his economic priorities—not only for the twelfth FYP (1986–90) but also through the year 2000. He explicitly linked the twelfth FYP to the fifteen-year plan through the end of the century. The CPSU general secretary set the minimum economic growth requirement at 4 percent per annum, said that defense requirements must be met, and made the usual commitment to the consumer (so often reneged on in the past). He called for greater discipline; restructuring of investments; and a number of changes in planning, management, and incentives that sounded more like modifications than fundamental changes in the Soviet economic system.[11]

Unless the new leader has much more change in mind than his public statements have indicated thus far, or unless events themselves force further change, it appears that the military burden on the Soviet economy will continue to grow in the foreseeable future. The above estimates do not include the cost of the enormous wartime management system (civil defense), military pensions, and other items. These would add up to a significantly larger percentage of GNP than estimated in the foregoing.

8

Capabilities of Soviet Strategic Forces to Perform Their Damage-Limiting Mission

Previous chapters have stressed the war-fighting, damage-limiting objectives of USSR military policy. It should be evident that the Soviets have done their best—technological and resource constraints permitting—to acquire the weapons required to perform the missions assigned to the services by military doctrine and strategy. The USSR entered into the SALT process because its capabilities had fallen far short of its strategic requirements—most specifically in ballistic missile defense. It also feared that the United States was about to acquire the war-fighting, damage-limiting posture that, at the end of the 1960s, the Soviets were far from achieving for themselves. The previous chapters have also demonstrated the continuity of USSR military policy in the SALT-START era: no change in doctrine or strategy; development and deployment of weapons systems to perform the same war-fighting missions as before; and the continued shift in national economic priorities to the military.

This chapter has several theses, the most important of which are that:

• Soviet strategic missiles have been designed to meet the requirements of targeting strategy, and deployments have been sized to the same requirements.

• Whereas the SRF capabilities in the Eurasian TVDs have been commensurate with requirements since the mid-1960s, capabilities in the transoceanic TVD did not match requirements until the early 1980s. Another generation of ICBMs will probably be required to increase Soviet confidence in their capabilities to destroy hard targets, capabilities which are currently sensitive to any unforeseen degradation in missile accuracy.

• USSR targeting strategy is designed to "win" a nuclear war by destroying or neutralizing enemy political, military, and economic assets essential to the enemy's war effort while minimizing damage to nontarget areas by matching yields to target vulnerabilities and damage objectives. The Soviets do not target population as such.

• The capabilities of strategic defensive forces have lagged far behind requirements, primarily because the USSR has not been able to field the requisite weapons technology. The major thrust of military programs during the rest of the 1980s and the 1990s will probably be to narrow the gap between the offensive and defensive capabilities of Soviet forces and the requirements of a war-fighting strategy. Strategic offensive forces will have to be updated, but the real emphasis will be on improvements in strategic defenses.

STRATEGIC OFFENSIVE FORCES

Approach

Many calculations have been made of how much damage USSR strategic missile forces could inflict on the United States. Most of these studies have assumed that the Soviets would attack one or all of three generic sets of targets: the strategic force, the population, and the industrial base. All these analyses have used American estimates of target vulnerabilities and nuclear weapons effects. They have also assumed large yields—for example, nominal one megaton warheads—for attacks on population and industrial targets. A few studies have examined the possibility of attacks on one or more specific industries for illustrative purposes. None of these studies, however, have considered that the Soviets might purposely restrict their attacks to only a few types of industry. Large-yield weapons have also been employed in all studies of the above type known to the coauthors.

This chapter examines how USSR strategic missile forces might attack the United States and its allies, based on available evidence on Soviet objectives in a nuclear war, the types of targets they say they would attack, and the degree of damage they would seek to inflict. Except for estimates of USSR strategic ballistic-missile accuracies, all evidence, factors, and criteria used in this chapter are from Soviet sources. Although the ready arsenal counts are from Western sources, these figures are consistent with the arsenal counts the Soviets acknowledged during the course of SALT I and SALT II. The American estimates of Soviet warhead yields are compared with requirements calculated from USSR data.

The analysis is based on the following premises. First, sufficient evidence is available to construct an approximation of how and for what purposes the USSR would conduct nuclear strikes against the United States and its allies. Second, the evidence is best understood in the general context of Soviet objectives and plans for nuclear warfare in all geographic theaters of operations (Eurasia and the oceanic TVDs as well as North America, the "transoceanic" TVD). Third, developing the analysis historically—showing how USSR capabilities have evolved over the past quarter-century—will provide a better appreciation of likely plans than restricting the analysis to a single point or short period in time.

The essential elements for evaluating trends in Soviet ballistic missile force effectiveness include:

1. Targeting strategy and principles of application
2. Inferred criteria for evaluating force capabilities
3. Estimate of the Soviet view of target arrays in the NATO and "transoceanic" TVDs
4. Technical targeting factors and damage objectives
5. Trends in weapons system effectiveness
6. Trends in the capabilities of USSR strategic missile forces to meet effectiveness criteria

As has been stressed throughout, strategic ballistic-missile forces—ICBMs and SLBMs—will execute strategic nuclear strikes, in coordination with ground, air, and naval forces in all TVDs. Most Soviet ICBMs are assigned to targets in the transoceanic TVD. The majority of SLBMs will probably be withheld from the initial strikes as a reserve for subsequent operations in a multi-TVD war that the USSR expects would last several weeks or even longer.[1]

Although the United States and NATO remain the primary "probable enemies," the USSR has been increasingly concerned about the possibility of having to fight the Chinese at the same time. Because of the American presence in the Western Pacific and U.S. relations with Japan and South Korea, the Soviets have undoubtedly envisaged a "two front" conflict throughout much of the post–World War II period. Until the buildup along the Chinese border commenced in the mid-1960s, however, the Far East theater did not require large USSR ground and tactical air forces. Strategic airpower and missiles were sufficient. During the past twenty-five years, however, Moscow has had to face the prospect of major military operations by strategic, ground, and air forces along almost its entire border from the Kola Peninsula to Sakhalin. The nuclear threat (both strategic and tactical) from the Asian theaters will increase in the future, as Chinese capabilities increase.

Until the early to mid-1960s the Soviets apparently assumed that any nuclear war with NATO would inevitably involve an all-out nuclear exchange with the United States.[2] During the past fifteen years, however, the USSR has probably begun to see possibilities for "decoupling" a nuclear war in the European TVDs from a strategic exchange (homeland-to-homeland) with the United States. Two sources for such a modification in Soviet views are available. First, American declaratory policy in the 1970s evolved toward various operations designed to contain a war by selective use of nuclear weapons that would control escalation and induce the enemy to terminate the conflict by negotiation. This change in U.S. declaratory policy is evidently not taken at face value by Moscow. Rather, the Soviets view it as an attempt to find ways to fight a nuclear war on other nations' territories while avoiding nuclear attacks on the American homeland—in effect, as a nuclear "decoupling" of the United States from NATO.[3] Nevertheless, the USSR probably considers all discussions of "limited options" as a sign of a weakening U.S. resolve to use strategic nuclear forces in defense of its allies.

The second—and closely related—reason that the Soviets may see opportunities to fight a nuclear war with NATO without necessarily conducting a full-scale nuclear exchange with the United States involves the quantitative expansion of and qualitative improvement in USSR strategic forces achieved throughout the 1970s. In the Soviet view, these improvements in strategic forces could prevent the United States from attacking the USSR homeland in a war with NATO as long as the continental United States had not been hit by nuclear weapons.

USSR Nuclear Targeting Strategy

Since it was formulated about 1950 by Long-Range Aviation, Soviet nuclear targeting strategy has remained essentially unchanged. This strategy applies to all services, missions, and TVDs. In thirty-five years the only apparent modification has been the reclassification of enemy air defenses to the same priority as enemy nuclear delivery systems. Although it has been reiterated by many sources, one can do little to improve upon Marshal N. I. Krylov's version of USSR nuclear targeting strategy. He commanded the SRF from 1963 until his death in 1972. According to Krylov, the principal SRF targets would be the enemy's (1) nuclear delivery systems, weapons storage, and production sites; (2) military installations; (3) military industries; and (4) centers of political-military administration, command, and control.[4] Other sources indicate that the first category of targets includes all command-control-communications elements in what the United States calls the "national command authority" down to the individual launcher.

Note that the general population is excluded. The Soviets may attack selected elites if suitable concentrations can be found, but they consider population targeting to be militarily counterproductive and politically immoral. When they describe the American bombing of Hiroshima and Nagasaki as "barbarous,"[5] they are being unfair; apart from representing population centers, those cities included a number of critical military targets. Nevertheless, "barbarous" appears to be the genuine USSR evaluation of U.S. discussion about "maximizing fatalities" among the general population, which has been the core of the American declaratory "assured destruction" concept.[6]

From time to time Soviet leaders and spokesmen at all levels have made statements about how a relatively few large nuclear weapons could take entire countries out of a war and turn large areas into radioactive deserts. Such talk seems to be designed for political effect; it probably does not represent a strategy for targeting. The USSR legitimately uses this sort of discourse to explain to its own people that it is not looking for excuses to start a nuclear war. The Soviets emphasized the destructiveness of nuclear weapons as part of their response to Chairman Mao's statements about the "east wind" prevailing over the "west wind" in such a war. The USSR also discusses the power and horrors of nuclear weapons in its attempts to intimidate Western countries and to encourage domestic political opposition in these countries to strong defense measures.

Nuclear targeting strategy appears to be insensitive to the three basic Soviet scenarios for nuclear war. Whether the USSR succeeds in preempting, launches on tactical warning under attack, or is forced into a second-strike situation after absorbing an enemy attack, its targeting priorities remain essentially the same. Soviet military operations must seize and hold the initiative, independent of the scenario.

USSR military officers have provided some further insight into targeting strategy for industry. Many basic industries, such as metallurgy, are conspicuously absent from lists of targets. The Soviets cite World War II experience, in which basic industries continued to function despite considerable damage. In addition to plants producing military hardware, USSR spokesmen specify petroleum, electrical power, and chemical plants as the industries to be attacked. According to the targeting principles discussed below, in all cases selective attacks on key or "bottleneck" plants and facilities are recommended. The objective appears to be to destroy only what is necessary in order to stop the production of major weapons and redeployment of large military forces.

As described in USSR literature, the Soviets apply their nuclear targeting strategy according to the following operational principles: [7]

- Destroy most threatening forces.
- Select main "links" and nodes in target sets—for example, enemy national command authority.
- Do not destroy large areas or create radioactive deserts.
- Use minimum yields ("explosive power"), depending on target and delivery-system characteristics.
- Do not target population and all industry; it is unnecessarily destructive and not effective.
- Strike simultaneously in several TVDs.
- Hit "most important" targets twice.
- Do not attack and destroy all targets in all TVDs; it is not possible, desirable, or necessary.
- Political leaders will determine the relative weight of strikes.

The principles of nuclear force application are thus consistent with and follow from the general tenets of doctrine and strategy. The enemy is to be defeated by destroying existing military forces and by preventing force reconstitution. The enemy's society, however, is not to be destroyed by attacking the general population or by indiscriminate "cookie cutter" laydowns of maximum-yield weapons on urban areas and industrial plants. To do so would vitiate the USSR political concept of a "socialist" world following the destruction of imperialism in a nuclear war. In the Soviet view, one cannot make the world safe for "socialism" by destroying it.

USSR effectiveness criteria include the probability of destruction for point targets and expected value coverage for area targets. Military area targets usually are composed of several installations of unequal value (in contrast to a petroleum refinery, where the value is more or less equally distributed over the target area). For purposes of the following analysis of overall arsenal effectiveness, however, this distinction is essentially lost in the "noise level" of the calculations. In other words, the total laydown (number of weapons and yields) required to destroy or neutralize a given set of soft targets is not very sensitive to this fine distinction among area target characteristics. Multiple strikes on the same target provide high assurance that effectiveness criteria will be met.

Inferred Sufficiency Criteria for Strategic Missile Forces

Although literature in the Soviet does not refer to "sufficiency criteria" for USSR strategic missile forces, it does enumerate several capabilities that these forces are expected to have:

- Individual weapons systems should be capable of inflicting the required degree of damage—given USSR effectiveness measures, damage criteria, and objectives—on targets of various degrees of vulnerability.
- Sufficient weapons should be available for complete coverage of the target arrays—given individual weapons effectiveness and principles of targeting application—with a high degree of confidence.
- After complete coverage is achieved, large reserve forces must be available.
- Force capabilities should be applicable to any scenario.

It seems reasonable to treat the foregoing as Soviet "sufficiency criteria" that apply to all TVDs—that is, worldwide. It is a demanding set of criteria, because a large number of first priority targets—enemy nuclear delivery systems and associated command-control-communications—have been hardened, and even most soft targets must be struck twice for high assurance.

Target Vulnerabilities in the Various TVDs

Although USSR targeting strategy applies to all TVDs, each of them presents different arrays and vulnerabilities. In general, the important difference is that most of the targets in the Eurasian theaters are soft, whereas the Transoceanic TVD contains a large number of hard as well as soft targets.

Most soft targets in both the Transoceanic and Eurasian theaters require overpressures of 4.5 to 10 psi by Soviet vulnerability definitions and damage objectives. Most soft targets vary in area from less than one to twenty square kilometers. In many cases, they are so located that, by choosing offset aim points, one weapon could inflict the required damage on two or more targets. NATO nuclear forces comprise mostly soft targets: airfields, mobile surface-to-surface missile units, ballistic-missile nuclear submarine bases, and nuclear storage bunkers. Until the French IRBMs became operational in 1970, few hard targets existed in the Eurasian TVDs. Storage bunkers are not likely to rate much more than 30 to 50 psi. In the Transoceanic TVD, however, the Soviets have faced an array of some 1,200 hard targets since the early 1960s. These required about 300 psi overpressure initially, and Minuteman silos were subsequently hardened to withstand around 1,500 to 2,000 psi.[8]

Consequently, the first major challenge for USSR targeting strategy has been to acquire enough warheads with the accuracy and yield combination required to destroy most of the hard targets in the Transoceanic TVD. The second major challenge has been to satisfy soft-target requirements in all TVDs while simultaneously providing a large secure reserve force to support military operations after the initial massive exchange and to dominate the postwar world.

Damage Criteria and Objectives

Soviet technical targeting factors pertinent to an analysis of strategic missile capabilities are (1) nuclear weapons effects, (2) types of targets, (3) target vulnerabilities, (4) height of burst, and (5) use of offset aimpoints when targets are located close together. Damage criteria and objectives pertinent to evaluating the capabilities of Soviet strategic missile forces may be summarized as follows:[9]

• Probability of destruction (*veroiatnost' porazheniia*) applies to hard targets and to all elements of enemy nuclear forces. Most of these are "point" targets. Area coverage is used for most soft targets, which usually occupy an area of less than ten to up to twenty square kilometers.

• Three damage definitions are specified for soft targets like structures and equipment—light, moderate, and heavy. Light damage requires minor repair; moderate, major repair; heavy damage, replacement.

• Damage objectives for area coverage are defined as the percentage of the target area that is covered by the overpressure level required by the damage definitions (light, moderate, heavy). Three damage objectives are specified—neutralization, destruction, and annihilation. Area coverage values are specified for the first and third objectives: 10 to 30 percent for neutralization; 50 to 70 percent for annihilation. Presumably, the value for destruction falls in-between.

• The Soviets require both high probabilities—0.8 and 0.9—and high assurance of achieving their damage objectives. (This is why they specify that targets are to be hit twice.)

Both the damage definitions—light, moderate, heavy—and the area coverage objectives—usually neutralization or annihilation—are presented as options. USSR literature indicates that the VGK, composed of the top political and military leaders, would decide on the damage definitions and the objectives to be applied to various types of soft targets in each TVD.[10] Soviet writings further suggest that the VGK's decisions on these matters might be scenario-dependent.

Trends in Strategic Ballistic-Missile System Effectiveness

The capabilities of individual strategic missile systems and of total deployed arsenals to achieve these objectives against the hard- and soft-target arrays in the various TVDs have varied widely over the past three decades. Table 28 shows the effectiveness of Soviet missiles most likely to be used against hard targets for reported yields and several values for missile accuracy. For example, if the accuracy of the SS-9 were 700 meters or better, it would have been effective against most hard targets in the Transoceanic TVD during the 1960s, but not in the 1970s. With a CEP of 300 meters and a yield of twenty megatons, the single re-entry vehicle of the SS-18 would be effective against any hard target. If the CEP for MIRVed models of the SS-17, SS-18, and SS-19 were 250 meters, one weapon would achieve a single-shot kill probability of 0.9 on a target hardened to 1,000 psi, but two weapons would be required for the same kill probability against a target hardened to 2,000 psi.

TABLE 28   SOVIET STRATEGIC MISSILE CAPABILITIES
           AGAINST HARD TARGETS

System	CEP (m)	Yield (mt)	SINGLE-SHOT PROBABILITY OF KILL (SSPK)		
			500 psi	1,000 psi	2,000 psi
SS-9 (one RV)	700	20	0.98	0.85	0.64
	1,300	20	0.44	0.24	0.13
SS-18 (one RV)	550	20	1.0	0.99	0.84
	300	20	1.0	1.0	0.99
SS-17/18/19	100	0.56	1.0	1.0	1.0
	200	0.56	0.99	0.94	0.79
	300	0.56	0.91	0.72	0.51
	400	0.56	0.75	0.51	0.33
	500	0.56	0.6	0.37	0.23

SOURCE: Calculations by W. T. Lee, based on Soviet algorithms from John Shannon, Science Applications, Inc., in McLean, Virginia.

To take into account system reliability—that is, to assure that the weapons will arrive on target and the target be destroyed—more than one or two weapons must be allocated. For example, three SS-18/19 weapons must be assigned to 2,000-psi targets for high-confidence attacks. That is, for any total weapons system reliability of 0.8 or above, an allocation of three weapons per target gives a 90 percent (or more) assurance that two of them will arrive on each target, thereby assuring a 0.9 kill probability.

Because effectiveness is highly sensitive to actual CEP achieved, it behooves a force planner to pack the highest yield possible into his re-entry vehicles for attacking hard targets—as part compensation for any unforeseen degradation of system CEP under operational conditions. Consequently, SS-18 and SS-19 missiles may carry even higher yields than those reported in Western sources.

Against soft targets, however, the situation is just the reverse. Employing the yield normally ascribed to Soviet missiles against soft targets—as shown in Table 29—far exceeds damage objectives of 10 to 30 percent destruction for neutralization, and 50 to 70 percent coverage for annihilation, of most soft targets. All systems achieve or exceed 100 percent coverage of target areas—96 to 99 percent for the SS-4—up to twenty square kilometers at the 4.5 psi level. Many systems exceed 70 percent coverage of a twenty square kilometer target to 10 psi, and most exceed this criterion for one half that size. These psi levels satisfy moderate USSR damage criteria for soft military targets and typical industrial facilities.

As shown in Table 29, the yields attributed to Soviet missiles produce gross overkill on soft targets with full-range CEPs. In the Eurasian TVDs, most targets are located at less than full range from the USSR strategic-missile launch complexes. For example, the SS-4 and the SS-5 had CEPs of 1,000 meters or less against most of the targets in the Eurasian TVDs.[11] When this factor is taken into account, the overkill shown in Table 29 becomes even more gross.

Such gross overkill of soft targets contradicts not only the tenets of Soviet targeting strategy but also the expectation of USSR military doctrine that there will be a viable postwar world. This raises a basic question: Have Soviet missiles been universally equipped with the large-yield warheads generally ascribed to them by Western sources? This is a much more serious question than the abstract calculations in Tables 29 and 30. The overkill shown in Table 29 implies an immense amount of collateral damage outside the target area. Such unnecessary collateral damage not only contradicts the objective of seizing Western Europe in as intact a condition as possible to aid USSR economic recovery but also the Soviet political objective of dominating a viable universal postwar world. Finally, there are the environmental implications of detonating thousands of megatons when hundreds would be

TABLE 29 SOFT-TARGET EFFECTIVENESS OF SOVIET STRATEGIC MISSILE SYSTEMS (REPORTED CEPS AND YIELDS)

System	CEP (m)	Yield (kt)	EXPECTED VALUE OF TARGET AREA COVERAGE AT 4.5 PSI TARGET AREA (KM²)		
			5	10	20
SS-4	2,000	1,000	0.99	0.98	0.96
SS-5	750	1,000	1.0	1.0	1.0
SS-7	2,000	5,000	1.0	1.0	1.0
SS-11	1,300	1,500	1.0	1.0	1.0
SS-17	550	600	1.0	1.0	1.0
SS-19	450	560	1.0	1.0	1.0
SS-20	450	150	1.0	1.0	1.0
SS-N-6	1,300	600	1.0	1.0	0.96
SS-N-8	1,500	1,500	1.0	1.0	1.0
SS-N-18 (MIRV)	900	150	1.0	1.0	1.0

			EXPECTED VALUE OF TARGET AREA COVERAGE AT 10 PSI TARGET AREA (KM²)		
			5	10	20
SS-4	2,000	1,000	0.69	0.65	0.57
SS-5	750	1,000	1.0	0.98	0.88
SS-7	2,000	5,000	0.97	0.96	0.93
SS-11	1,300	1,500	0.96	0.92	0.84
SS-17	550	600	1.0	0.97	0.78
SS-19	450	560	1.0	0.98	0.78
SS-20	450	150	0.89	0.65	0.35
SS-N-6	1,300	600	0.82	0.74	0.61
SS-N-8	1,500	1,500	0.92	0.88	0.79
SS-N-18	900	150	0.67	0.52	0.33

SOURCE: Calculations by W. T. Lee, based on Soviet algorithms from John Shannon at Science Applications, Inc., in McLean, Virginia.

TABLE 30   EFFECTIVENESS OF SOVIET STRATEGIC MISSILE SYSTEMS
AGAINST SOFT TARGETS (SEMIPARAMETRIC REQUIRED YIELDS
FOR REPRESENTATIVE CEPs)

Yield 50 kt	EXPECTED VALUE OF TARGET AREA COVERAGE AT 4.5 PSI TARGET AREA (KM²)		
CEP (m)	5	10	20
2,000	0.43	0.39	0.33
1,500	0.60	0.53	0.42
1,000	0.81	0.71	0.51
500	0.98	0.88	0.58
350	1.0	0.94	0.60
Yield 150 kt			
2,000	0.70	0.65	0.58
1,500	0.86	0.80	0.70
1,000	0.98	0.94	0.82
500	1.0	1.0	0.94
350	1.0	1.0	0.98
Yield 150 kt	AT 10 PSI		
2,000	0.28	0.25	0.21
1,500	0.41	0.35	0.27
1,000	0.62	0.49	0.32
500	0.86	0.63	0.35
350	0.93	0.67	0.35
Yield 300 kt			
2,000	0.40	0.37	0.31
1,500	0.56	0.50	0.39
1,000	0.78	0.68	0.48
500	0.97	0.85	0.54
Yield 500 kt			
2,000	0.52	0.48	0.41
1,500	0.70	0.63	0.51
1,000	0.89	0.80	0.62
500	1.0	0.96	0.73
Yield 1,500			
2,000	0.69	0.65	0.57
1,500	0.85	0.80	0.70
1,000	0.97	0.93	0.82

SOURCE: Calculations by W. T. Lee, based on Soviet algorithms from John Shannon at Science Applications, Inc., in McLean, Virginia.

sufficient. After all, the dictum of Mao Zedong notwithstanding, the prevailing winds blow from West to East.

The yields required to satisfy Soviet moderate damage criteria are calculated semiparametrically in Table 30 for a range of yields and missile accuracies. As shown here, USSR strategic missiles—like the early generation SS-4 MRBM and the SS-7 ICBM—with full-range CEPs of 2,000 meters could achieve neutralization objectives against 4.5 psi targets with warhead yields of 50 kilotons and annihilation coverage with 150 kiloton warheads. Against 10-psi targets, 500 kiloton warheads exceed the neutralization requirement and could almost achieve annihilation of a ten square kilometer target. At full-range CEPs—2,000 meters—megaton weapons would be required by the SS-4 and the SS-7 only if the damage objective were annihilation, the target area were at least ten square kilometers, and target vulnerability were to exceed 10 psi. Few soft targets have such characteristics, and, as has been pointed out, in Eurasia many of the targets are located at less than full range from the launch points. For contemporary Soviet strategic systems with CEPs in the range of 300 to 1,000 meters even at full range, yield requirements against soft targets drop to between 25 and 150 kilotons, depending on the damage objective and the number of warheads assigned to large-area targets when MIRVed missiles are employed.

What is the rationale for the large yields commonly assigned to USSR missiles? Granted, the Soviets have tested large-yield nuclear weapons, but they have also tested low-yield ones. It is true that they have needed all the yield the missile could deliver against hard targets. But is it necessary to overkill the soft targets with so much collateral damage? Why are most of the reported yields so high?

The yields commonly estimated for USSR missiles are clearly not the result of requirement calculations, as presented in Table 30. It is most likely that conventional estimates of warhead yields represent the maximum that can be packed into the missiles, given the nuclear warhead technology and without regard to (1) damage criteria for soft military and industrial targets, (2) political and economic objectives, and (3) radiation consequences.

Requirement analysis also indicates that the USSR would equip its strategic missiles with warheads having a range of yields in order to approximate its minimum-yield principle. USSR literature provides some evidence to support this analysis. A book on missile employment stated that Soviet ICBMs and IR/MRBMs carried warheads ranging from less than 100 kilotons up to 100 megatons.[12] One test may have been designed to yield 100 megatons, although no evident requirements for such a weapon exist. The USSR has not developed a missile with sufficient payload to carry such a high-yield design. Its strategic ballistic missiles, however, had the capability to carry warheads ranging in yield from less than 100 kilotons to about 25 megatons.

There is no apparent reason why the above-cited book should credit Soviet ICBMs and IR/MRBMs with warheads yielding less than 100 kilotons if, in fact, the missiles did not have such warheads. The stated USSR principle of using the minimum yield required to inflict the desired damage would suggest equipping missiles with a wide range of yields.

Some basic principles stated in a ballistic-missile handbook published in 1969 are consistent with this philosophy.[13]

- Strategic missiles carry various warheads (yields).

- To calculate missile effectiveness, take system accuracy plus yield and calculate the number of missiles needed to ensure that the target is destroyed.

- If guidance-system accuracy were zero, low-yield warheads would be adequate for all point targets. Guidance systems, however, are not error free, so yields must be raised to ensure damage to the target. As guidance accuracy improves, yields may be reduced.

- The optimum yield is the minimum that will ensure destruction of the target—that is, "fulfillment of the military mission."

Estimates of most Soviet strategic-missile warhead yields have declined as full-range accuracy has improved—from 1,000 to 2,000 meters during the 1950s and 1960s to between 200 and 800 meters in the 1970s and 1980s. In many cases the large warheads, which could be carried by the early-model missiles like the SS-9, represented compensation for inadequate accuracy against hard targets. Improvements in SRF missile accuracy appear to have been primarily motivated by the requirement to be able to destroy hard targets—enemy missile silos and the like—because increases in effectiveness against most soft targets are negligible once the CEP is reduced to 500 or 600 meters.

Therefore, the USSR has probably applied its nuclear targeting strategy to coincide with its political and economic objectives in a nuclear war. This means that strategic missiles have been armed with warheads having a variety of yields—ranging from less than 100 kilotons to about 20 megatons—in order to approximate optimal attacks on all classes of targets. MIRVed missiles cannot deliver multimegaton weapons and still remain MIRVed.[14] As previously noted, for shooting at hard targets, the Soviets need all the power they can pack in; much smaller weapons are adequate for soft targets. This is particularly true for large-area soft targets, where two or more small weapons are more effective than a single large-yield warhead.[15] Against such soft targets, the latest models of strategic weapons systems can achieve USSR damage objectives with "optimal" yields in the 25 to 150 kiloton range. Consequently the current Soviet strategic missile arsenal probably consists almost exclusively of yields from 0.05 to 0.5 mt or, perhaps, up to 1.0 mt for hard target weapons.

Attack Design for Strategic Ballistic-Missile Forces in All TVDs

In planning missile attacks on the target arrays in the Eurasian and Transoceanic TVDs, Soviet planners take into account a number of factors. These are recapitulated here.

First, ICBMs and SLBMs are assigned to targets in all TVDs. The entire strategic missile inventory is not assigned to attacks on the continental United States. As many as 100 to 200 ICBMs and a number of SLBMs are likely to be reserved for the Eurasian TVDs.

Second, missiles are assigned fixed targets, whereas aircraft will primarily strike mobile ones. Generally speaking, critical mobile targets are located in the continental Eurasian TVD or in the Oceanic TVDs around the Eurasian periphery. Hence, initial Soviet attacks on the Transoceanic TVD may not include any aircraft. USSR bomber strikes would most likely take place after the initial massive exchange in all TVDs, primarily in support of operations in the Eurasian TVDs.

Third, allocating two missiles (or warheads) for each "most important" target is a relatively simple, if expensive, way of maintaining high confidence that soft targets will be destroyed without extensive retargeting and reprogramming. Most hard targets require three missiles for high-confidence attacks by current SS-18/19 CEP-yield combinations of 250 meters and 500 kilotons. For any total weapon system reliability of 80 percent or above, this multiple-attack practice gives at least a 90 percent assurance that one weapon will arrive on each soft target, and two weapons on each hard target.

Fourth, in assigning missiles to strike each set of targets, system capabilities must be matched with target characteristics and vulnerabilities, given Soviet damage criteria and objectives.

Fifth, the USSR places great emphasis on reserves. Consequently, at least 10 percent of its IR/MRBMs and ICBMs would be held in reserve. In some scenarios, the VGK (Supreme High Command) might withhold a larger percentage of its SRF. Although some SLBMs would be used in the initial strikes, between 50 and 75 percent of the SLBM arsenal would probably be held in reserve.

The basic inventories that the VGK would draw upon to attack fixed targets in all TVDs are presented in Table 31, based on the deployments discussed in Chapters 5, 6, and 7. As already noted, the Soviet Union has

TABLE 31 TRENDS IN SOVIET STRATEGIC MISSILE FORCE INVENTORY FOR SELECTED SNAPSHOT YEARS (NUMBER OF READY WARHEADS)

	1960	1965	1970	1980	1985
Soft-target systems					
SS-4/5	100	1,400	1,300	800	100–200
SS-20[a]				960	2,400–2,700
Subtotal	100	1,400	1,300	1,760	2,500–2,900
SS-6/7/8	10	400	400		
SS-11/25			970	1,280	1,010
SS-13			20	60	
SS-17/24[a]				600	760
Subtotal	10	400	1,390	1,940	1,770
SS-N-4/5	69	96	72	54	39
SS-N-6			208	464	336
SS-N-8				280	280
SS-N-18[a]				480	1,680
SS-N-20[a]				180	540
Subtotal	69	96	280	1,458	2,875
Soft-target total (rounded)	180	1,900	2,970	5,160	7,140–7,540
Hard-target systems					
SS-9			228		
SS-18[a]				3,080	3,080
SS-19[a]				1,440	2,160
Hard target					
Total (rounded)			230	4,520	5,240

SOURCES: Warhead numbers are based on launcher deployments and warhead counts in Tables 3, 4, 8, 10, 12, 22, and 23. Two warheads are counted for each IR/MRBM and most SS-7/8 launchers because soft targets could probably launch a second round in the initial exchange. The 3-MIRV SS-11 payload is counted as two warheads per launcher because with this payload each SS-11 can probably, on the average, destroy at least two targets. With the above exceptions for IR/MRBMs and soft ICBMs, reload missiles are not counted.

^a All MIRV-accountable missiles under the SALT II treaty are assumed to be MIRVed. This is not likely, but no information is available on how many SS-17, SS-13, and SS-19 missiles have been deployed with only one RV. Follow-on ICBMs are counted with of the number of MIRV warheads from Collins as cited in Table 22, p. 16. SS-N-18 SLBMs are assumed to have three MIRVs in 1980 and to have seven in 1985. The SS-N-20 is counted as a 9 MIRV payload, per Soviet Military Power, 1985, p. 32. SS-20s are not counted as hard target systems here, although, as noted in the text, they would be effective when CEP is adjusted for range to target in the Eurasian TVDs.

stocked reload missiles with all types of ICBM launchers. For soft launchers, minimum estimates of the number of reload missiles may be possible. For silo-deployed SRF systems, however, the range of uncertainty cannot be bounded with any confidence. Consequently, the inventories in Table 31 represent ready, on-launcher numbers (except for soft launchers, which are credited with one reload missile each).

Strategic Missile Operations in the Eurasian TVDs.   Given the size and vulnerability of the target arrays, the final step in analyzing the capabilities of USSR strategic missile forces is to match up warhead inventories with target arrays in the various TVDs. This analysis determines whether the Soviets have deployed sufficient forces with the requisite system characteristics to achieve their damage objectives.

Quantifying the number of hard targets for strategic missiles in the various TVDs is relatively easy. The numbers are readily available and reasonably accurate, and any hardened target can be assumed to be a high-priority target. Precisely how many soft targets the USSR would strike in the Transoceanic TVD cannot be determined with precision. Nevertheless, some reasonable inferences can be drawn for the purpose of analyzing the capabilities of strategic missile forces to execute Soviet nuclear targeting strategy.

Out of the original IR/MRBM deployment of more than 700 launchers, some 600 were deployed in the European USSR against NATO targets. From these deployments it may be inferred that the Soviets counted about 700 strategic targets in the Eurasian TVDs, about 600 of which were located in Western Europe. This inference is indirectly supported by some historical evidence.[16] Chief Marshal of Artillery M. I. Nedelin was a member of the supraministerial authority that managed the ballistic missile program in the 1940s and 1950s. He joined the missile authority during the years 1946–48 and became the first commander of the SRF organized at the end of 1959. Sometime in the 1950s (or even earlier) Nedelin formed a staff—probably composed mainly of artillerymen like himself—to plan use of the new weapons. This staff must have sized initial IR/MRBM deployments during the years 1959–64 to the inventory of strategic target arrays inherited from Long-Range Aviation, which had formulated Soviet nuclear-targeting strategy as the Supreme High Command's principal instrument of nuclear weapons delivery until the SRF came into existence.

In those years the guidance systems used in ballistic missiles required that the missile be lined up with the target on the launchers.[17] This was an artilleryman's approach to nuclear fire-planning. (After all, ballistic missiles are a form of long-range artillery.) For time-urgent targets, two missiles per target could be launched almost simultaneously; for nontime-urgent targets, a second (refire) round could be launched some time later—possibly after moving the launcher to an alternative location to reduce its vulnerability to enemy counterstrikes. Either way, the Soviets would have had high confidence that at least one missile would arrive on target.

Deployment of the SS-11 and the SS-4/5 fields in the late 1960s may have been a response to French IRBMs in silos and to actual or anticipated Chinese strategic missiles. The action by France raised the number of hard targets in NATO from a few to about twenty. The SS-4/5s were too inaccurate to be effective against silos, even with the largest yields ascribed to these systems. By the end of the 1970s the Chinese had 90 to 120 strategic missiles deployed, presumably also in hardened installations.[18]

Except for the addition of hardened French and Chinese missiles, the target arrays in the Eurasian TVDs have changed little since the Soviets put those targets on their list (presumably in the late 1960s). The growth in hard targets has been accommodated by the assignment of more ICBMs to cover them and by deployment of the SS-20. With a CEP of 360 meters at full range, the SS-20 is a fairly accurate system.[19] Most of the hard targets in the Eurasian TVDs, however, are located at less than full range from SS-20 bases. Hence, the CEP of the system at actual range to target could be as low as 200 to 250 meters or less, which makes the SS-20 effective against all but the hardest targets. Similarly, the SS-11 ICBM would be considerably more accurate when employed against targets in the Eurasian TVDs than when employed at full range against the Transoceanic TVD.

In sum, during the 1960s about 700 targets probably existed for Soviet strategic missiles in the Eurasian TVDs, approximately 600 of them belonging to NATO. Only a handful of these targets had been hardened. Subsequently, except for the deployment of French IRBMs, there has been little change in the target arrays in Western Europe. There has been considerable growth in the target arrays in the Far Eastern TVD over the past fifteen years, however, principally in the form of hardened Chinese strategic missile launchers. Consequently, the number of hard targets in the Eurasian TVDs has probably grown from virtually none in 1960, to 20 in 1970, to between 130 and 150 by the mid-1980s. The number of soft targets in mainland China and elsewhere in the Far Eastern TVD is more difficult to estimate. If we assume 200 to 300 in the 1970s and early 1980s (as compared to about 100 to 150 in the early 1960s), this gives a total, in round numbers, of 900 to 1,100 strategic targets in the Eurasian TVDs during the mid-1980s—of which about 15 percent are hardened.

Based on the warhead inventories in Table 31, allocations for the initial massive Soviet strategic missile strikes in the Eurasian TVDs are presented in Table 32. ICBM and SLBM allocations are, of course, judgmental. Some

TABLE 32   ALLOCATION OF INITIAL SOVIET BALLISTIC MISSILE STRIKES IN EURASIAN TVDs

	1960	1965	1970	1980	1985
Eurasian TVDs	100	1,400	1,400	2,160	2,900–3,300
IR/MRBMs	100	1,400	1,300	1,760	2,500–2,900
ICBMs (SS/11/19)			100	400	400
Navy SLBMs	55	60	92	156	304
SS-N-4/5	55	60	60	60	48
SS-N-6			32	48	32
SS-N-18				48	224
Eurasian TVD totals (rounded)	55	1,460	1,490	2,320	3,200–3,600

SOURCE: Allocations are drawn from warhead inventory data in Table 31.

portion of these inventories will clearly be employed against targets in the Eurasian TVDs, but there is no direct evidence concerning the scale of such allocations.

In Table 32 these allocations are matched with the estimated target arrays for five snapshot years over the period 1960–85. The requirements column shows the number of warheads needed for high-confidence attacks on all target arrays—two-on-one for soft targets and three-on-one for hard targets—according to the precepts of USSR nuclear-targeting objectives. The net balance column shows the shortfall or excess between the number of warheads allocated and the requirements of high assurance for achieving Soviet objectives in all target arrays.

Several observations follow from the balance sheet on Table 33. First, by 1965 deployments matched requirements; the arsenal fell somewhat short about 1970, as hard targets began to appear and as soft Chinese targets were added to the target base; by 1980 they were back in balance. Second, the 1985 situation is difficult to assess precisely because NATO deployment of Pershing II and ground-launched cruise missiles has increased Soviet targeting requirements, as has the growth of Chinese targets. Deployment of about 500 SS-20s, however, would take care of all these targets, so in 1985 the Soviets probably had 800 to 1,100 more warheads available for use in the Eurasian TVDs than are required to achieve their strategic targeting objectives in these TVDs. Third, the balance sheet shown in Table 33 highlights the importance of refire rounds in USSR strategy for fighting a nuclear war. The first refire—included in the warhead allocations for the IR/MRBM launchers in Tables 31, 32, and 33—provides high assurance of achieving Soviet targeting objectives. Additional rounds hedge against losses to enemy counterforce attacks. For example, if a total of four refires were stocked, targeting objectives in the Eurasian TVDs could still be achieved even if 50 percent of the IR/MRBM launchers were lost to counterforce attacks. The stocking of three to four rounds for each IR/MRBM launcher should therefore not be surprising. This number would approximately represent what the USSR needs to hedge against losses from enemy counterforce strikes and to provide the reserves required to support its offensive operations after the initial exchange.

Strategic Missile Operations in the Transoceanic (North American) TVD.

For the two reasons noted previously, it is not possible to infer the Soviet view of the target arrays in North America from observed deployments. First, in the late 1950s the USSR deliberately decided to give first priority to meeting its objectives in the Eurasian TVDs. Initial ICBM deployments were clearly inadequate. Second, the USSR could not cope with the large number of hard targets in the Transoceanic TVD until it fielded MIRVed missiles on a

TABLE 33   Soviet Target Requirements and Strategic Missile Warhead Allocations in the Eurasian TVDs, 1960–85

Snapshot year	Soft Targets[a]		Hard Targets[b]		Total Requirement	Allocation[b]	Net balance
	Targets	Requirement	Targets	Requirement			
1960	700	1,400			1,400	155	– 1245
1965	700	1,400			1,400	1,460	60
1970	950	1,900	20	60	1,960	1,490	– 470
1980	950	1,900	105	315	2,215	2,320	105
1985	950–1,250	1,900–2,500	130	390	2,290–2,890	3,200–3,600	710–910

Source: Estimates are by W. T. Lee.

[a] As specified in the text, 250 soft PRC targets are assumed for 1970 and 1980. The upper boundary for 1985 allows for Pershing II and cruise missile (GLCM) deployments by NATO.

[b] Warhead allocations are from Table 32.

large scale. Nevertheless, a reasonable approximation of Moscow's view of strategic target arrays in the Transoceanic TVD may be possible by following the principles of its targeting strategy and using data readily available from various sources. The approximate number of hard targets in the Transoceanic TVD is well known. In 1985 the United States had some 1,050 ICBM silos and 100 Minuteman launch control centers. (By 1987 the 37 Titan IIs will have been phased out.) An additional 50 hardened command, control, and communications facilities and nuclear weapons storage depots would make a total of about 1,200 hard targets in the United States.

The U.S. Army, Navy, Air Force, and Marine Corps have fewer than 500 camps, airfields, naval bases, ports, terminals, depots, and other military installations. About 150 industrial facilities are under contract to the Department of Defense and provide one million dollars or more of military hardware end items each year. Most military R&D is located with these military end item suppliers. The Department of Energy lists some 1,700 electric power generating plants and nearly 200 petroleum refineries in the United States. About 325 of the power plants generate approximately 70 percent of the electricity; and 70 to 80 refineries produce about the same percentage of refined petroleum products, plus a large amount of chemicals. This brings the fuel and energy package to some 400 installations. It still leaves the balance of chemicals and some transport, communications, and command centers not already counted among the military installations on the USSR targeting list. The U.S. chemical plant list is long, although not many of these facilities are vital for military production. A large number of the other facilities that the Soviets are likely to target with their strategic missiles have already been counted as military ports, depots, and terminals. Moreover, many of these soft targets are located together, so that one weapon ("aim point") would destroy two or more of them. On the other hand, some large installations may have two aim points.

In sum, the military and economic soft target arrays required to neutralize the United States as a military power probably total 1,000 to 1,200 targets. If correctly estimated, this requirement has been relatively stable over the past twenty-five years. Because this estimate attempts to take into account co-location, it is an estimate for the number of aim points and not installations.

An initial massive Soviet nuclear strike on the Transoceanic TVD would probably:

- Consist entirely of strategic ballistic missiles
- Comprise primarily ICBMs and only a small portion of the navy's SLBMs
- Provide a reserve force of ICBMs for targets in the Eurasian TVDs

- Seek to limit damage to the USSR by destroying American nuclear delivery systems, weapons stocks, nuclear C^3 (command, control, and communications), and senior political and military officials of the U.S. government under all three basic Soviet scenarios—preemption, launch-on-warning, and second strike
- Match missile system capabilities with target sets, depending on target vulnerabilities and the VGK's decision regarding damage objectives

During the 1960s the SS-9s were probably assigned exclusively to hard targets in the Transoceanic TVD because this missile was the only ICBM effective against most hard targets.[20] In the 1970s MIRVed SS-18s and SS-19s replaced the SS-9s. All three systems were designed specifically for the counterforce mission against hard targets. In the 1960s SS-7s, SS-8s, and SS-11s were probably assigned to soft targets. Currently, SS-17s, SS-11s, and SS-13/16s are probably assigned only to soft targets.

Probably no more than 25 to 50 percent of the navy's SLBMs would be used in the initial mass strike in all TVDs (unless SRF losses to an American strike were severe) because SLBMs provide the primary secure reserve force for all TVDs. Because of their relatively poor accuracy, Soviet SLBMs would almost certainly be assigned only to soft targets.

Taking into account these considerations and prior allocations to the Eurasian TVDs (Table 32), ICBM and SLBM inventories available for attacks on hard- and soft-target arrays in the Transoceanic TVD (without allowing for other reserves) are shown on Table 34. The kill probability (PK)

TABLE 34   WARHEADS AVAILABLE FOR INITIAL NUCLEAR STRIKES IN
THE TRANSOCEANIC TVD (READY WARHEADS)

	1960	1965	1970	1980	1985
SRF					
Hard targets[a]			228	4,200	4,900
Soft targets[a]	10	400	1,290	1,840	1,670
SLBMs[b]		15	150	940	1,850
Soft target totals	10	415	1,440	2,780	3,520

SOURCE: Estimates by W. T. Lee.

[a]From Tables 3, 8, 10, 22, 23, and 31, minus allocations to the Eurasian TVDs in Table 32.

[b]"Modern" SLBM inventories (SS-N-6, -8, -18, -20) from Tables 4, 12, 23, and 31, assuming 75 percent of the force generated, minus allocations to Eurasian TVDs in Table 32. The year 1985 assumes the low side of the SS-N-6 and high side of the SS-N-18 projections in Table 32.

required by Soviet planners against hard counterforce targets is about 0.9.[21] The most accurate MIRVed versions of the SS-18 (mod 4) and the SS-19 (mod 3) have a single shot, a reliable PK of about 0.9 against 1,000 psi silos, and a PK of about 0.7 against 2,000 psi silos, given yields of 0.5 to 0.6 megatons and CEPs of 260 meters.[22] Because the rated hardness of Minuteman silos increased from the original average of 300 psi in the 1960s to 2,000 psi in the 1970s, making the SS-18/19 mod 2/1 MIRVs ineffective, the cumulative effect of two SS-18/19 mod 4/3 warheads is required for a PK of 0.9. To maintain high assurance that each hard target would be hit by two warheads—given a weapon system reliability equal to 0.8—the USSR would allocate three warheads per target. Consequently, to achieve their counterforce targeting objectives in the Transoceanic TVD, the Soviets would have to allocate about 3,600 SS-18/19 mod 4/3 warheads for attacks on the hard-target arrays in the United States.

Whereas the hard-target allocations are dominated by stringent accuracy and, to a lesser extent, yield requirements, soft-target allocations are dominated by the number of targets and the confidence desired. One reliable weapon will satisfy damage objectives against most soft targets. Given the estimate of 1,000 to 2,000 soft targets in the Transoceanic TVD, the required allocation is 2,000 to 2,400 weapons for high assurance (greater than 90 percent) that one warhead will arrive on each target. Whether the VGK opts for "neutralization" or "annihilation" damage criteria against the soft-target arrays in the Transoceanic TVD will make a big difference in the average weapon yield and, hence, the extent of collateral damage, although probably not in the number of weapons to be delivered.

Trends in the balance between USSR targeting requirements and ready strategic-missile inventory allocations to the Transoceanic TVD are shown in Table 35. In contrast to the Eurasian TVD, where capabilities have matched requirements since the mid-1960s, capabilities in the Transoceanic TVD have lagged far behind requirements. By 1970 the Soviets had barely sufficient stocks for one warhead per soft-target array in the Transoceanic TVD. It was not until the end of the decade that the ready inventory was sufficient to execute high-confidence (two warheads per target) attacks. Even then, the reserve of some 300 to 700 warheads probably remained inadequate from the USSR point of view. Reserves of 10 to 20 percent of soft-target ICBMs and 50 to 60 percent of SLBMs totaled about 850 to 1,150 warheads in 1980. Currently (1986) reserves are larger, although the soft-target reserve will probably be inadequate until the 380 or so MIRVed SLBMs negotiated in the SALT II agreement have been deployed, carrying as many warheads as can be packed into these missiles.

Trends in USSR capabilities against the first-priority targets in the Transoceanic TVD—American ICBM silos, nuclear weapons stocks, nuclear

TABLE 35   SOVIET TARGET REQUIREMENTS AND STRATEGIC MISSILE WARHEADS AVAILABLE FOR THE TRANSOCEANIC TVD (FIGURES ROUNDED)

Snapshot year	Targets[a]	Requirement[a]	Warheads available	Net balance
Soft targets				
1960	1,000–1,200	2,000–2,400	10	−2,000–2,400
1965	1,000–1,200	2,000–2,400	415	−1,600–2,000
1970	1,000–1,200	2,000–2,400	1,440	−560–960
1980	1,000–1,200	2,000–2,400	2,780	380–780
1985	1,000–1,200	2,000–2,400	3,520	1,120–1,520
Hard targets				
1960				
1965[b]	1,200	2,400	c	−2,400
1970[b]	1,200	2,400	230	−2,170
1980[b]	1,200	> 3,600	4,200	< 600
1985	1,200	3,600	4,900	−1,300

SOURCE: Estimates by W. T. Lee.

[a]As specified in the text.

[b]In 1980 most SS-18/19 operational launchers were of the initial MIRV models. These would have been effective against the original Minuteman silos, rated at about 300 psi, but not against upgraded MM silos, rated at about 2,000 psi. Hence, the targeting requirements in 1980 were well in excess of three-on-one for Soviet counterforce attacks on MM silos. By the mid-1980s, however, three-on-one attacks will satisfy Soviet counterforce objectives because all SS-18/19 launchers will be equipped with mod 4/3 missiles. The minimum requirement for high-confidence attacks is 2,400 warheads, even if the yield and CEP combination of a single warhead gives it greater than or equal to a 0.9 probability of destroying the target.

c Although they would not have been effective against hard targets, many of the 220-odd SS-7/8 ICBMs deployed at this time would probably have been targeted against U.S. Atlas and Titan launchers. Most of these launchers were hardened to some degree but much less so than the Minuteman silos.

command-control from the U.S. president on down—have lagged much further behind requirements. Not until about 1980 did the ICBM ready inventory become sufficiently large to attack all hard targets with missiles designed for that purpose. But even then, Soviet counterforce missiles were marginally effective against the hard-target arrays, because the United States had upgraded 1,000 Minuteman silos from 300 to perhaps 2,000 psi. The first generation SS-18/19 MIRVs were effective against the hard-target arrays, but they were not effective against the upgraded silos, even with three warheads per silo. Only in 1983–84 did sufficient SS-18/19 mod 4/3 ICBMs become operational to achieve Soviet counterforce, damage-limiting targeting objectives in the Transoceanic TVD with both high assurance and adequate reserves.

These trends have three particularly noteworthy implications. First, MIRV technology, which the USSR began to develop in the early 1960s, has been the key to meeting its targeting requirements against both soft and hard targets in the Transoceanic TVD. Second, the Soviets have clearly given first priority to their counterforce objectives, because SS-18/19 ICBMs account for nearly 80 percent of their ready warhead inventory. As usual, it took the USSR relatively longer to develop the technology than it did the United States, but Soviet MIRVs are not an imitative reaction to American ones. And rapid development and deployment of the SS-18/19 mod 4/3 models (to keep pace with increased hardening of Minuteman silos) probably became possible only because of precision machine tools exported from the United States to the USSR in the early 1970s. Third, although the Soviets artfully negotiated the SALT II limits on MIRVs and "heavy" ICBMs to satisfy their targeting requirements in all TVDs, their strategic missile forces are, nevertheless, relatively lean.

Contrary to Western conventional wisdom, Soviet strategic missile forces do not appear to have massive overkill potential. The USSR does not have much to give up, particularly in the large payload SS-18/19 ICBMs and total MIRVed missiles. This accounts for its relative inflexibility in strategic missile negotiations and adherence to the SALT II limits as well as its START proposal for essentially the same arsenal over the next decade. New generations of strategic missiles now under development should provide the Soviets with some negotiating flexibility by the late 1980s or early 1990s, when more accurate ICBMs could reduce the hard-target requirement from three to two warheads per target and when the successor to the SS-20 could carry five or six warheads.

Since the TVD allocations are somewhat arbitrary, Table 36 compares the trends in USSR targeting requirements with available inventories for both hard and soft targets in all TVDs for selected years since 1960. Essentially the same picture emerges. Given the assumptions that have been

TABLE 36   SOVIET TARGET REQUIREMENTS AND STRATEGIC MISSILE READY-WARHEAD INVENTORIES FOR ALL TVDs

Snapshot year	Targets[a]	Requirements[a]	Warheads available[b] (rounded)	Net balance
Soft targets				
1960	1,800	3,600	160	−3,440
1965	1,800	3,600	1,870	−1,730
1970	2,050	4,100	2,900	−1,200
1980	2,050	4,100	4,800	700
1985	2,050–2,350	4,100–4,700	6,430–6,830	2,130–2,330
Hard targets				
1960	100	> 200		
1965	1,200	> 2,400		−2,400
1970	1,220	> 2,440	230	−2,210
1980	1,305	> 3,915[c]	4,520	c
1985	1,330	3,990	5,240	1,250

SOURCE: Estimates by W. T. Lee.

[a]Mid-point of soft targets and requirements in the Transoceanic TVD from Table 34, plus Eurasian TVD targets and requirements from Table 32. Hard targets and requirements from Tables 33 and 35.

[b]Ready warheads from Table 31, with counting rules for soft launchers—IR/MRBMs, SS-11 MRVs, and MIRVed Soviet strategic missiles—as specified in the notes thereunder. Operational availability of Soviet ICBMs is assumed to be 75 percent, inasmuch as the Soviets keep a very small percentage of their SSBNs on station under normal peacetime conditions.

[c]As previously noted, Minuteman silos were upgraded from 300 to 2,000 psi in the 1970s. In 1980 most of the SS-18/19 MIRVs were of the initial models designed in the early to mid-1960s, when MM silos were only 300 psi. In 1980, therefore, about five to six first-generation SS-18/19 MIRV warheads were required for high-confidence attacks on MM silos. This requirement dropped to three warheads per silo for only the SS-18 mod 4 and SS-19 mod 3, which began to be deployed circa 1979.

made about Soviet targeting, inventories did not provide a minimum reserve until about 1980, and the reserve will remain inadequate through 1985 (or even later).

These calculations of the trends in strategic missile capabilities versus targeting requirements do not allow for attrition of Soviet forces by American counterforce strikes or even from U.S. missile defenses. They apply only to USSR pre-emption—the preferred scenario—or to a situation in which prior U.S. attacks did not destroy any significant number of Soviet strategic missile launchers. In fact, American strategic ballistic-missile forces will not be able to destroy more than a fraction of Soviet ICBM silos until the 1990s at best. Nevertheless, many Western observers fail to perceive the deterrent potential of MX to offset Soviet counterforce capabilities and to place USSR silos and other hard targets at risk.[23]

Finally, it is instructive to note what the USSR did not do. During the mid-1960s two mobile IR/MRBMs, mounted on a tank chassis and designated as the SS-14 and SS-15 by NATO, appeared in the annual military parades through Red Square. Evidently, one (or both) of these systems was deployed on a limited scale, even though Western sources do not credit the Soviets with any SS-14/15 deployments. Why did the USSR choose not to produce several hundred of these systems, which would have solved the vulnerability problem of the SS-4s and SS-5s?

The answer to this question may be surmised as follows. The accuracy of these systems probably resembled the SS-13, with a CEP of about 2,000 meters at full range. Therefore, the SS-14 and SS-15 could not have been much more accurate than the SS-4s and SS-5s at comparable ranges. Consequently, deployment of the SS-14 and/or SS-15 would have reduced Soviet vulnerabilities but would not have provided any increase in effectiveness or in reduction of collateral damage. The USSR waited until it had replaced the SS-4s and SS-5s with other systems—ICBMs and the SS-20—that could do both.

Summary and Caveats

The following is a summary of trends in the effectiveness of USSR strategic ballistic-missile forces in the Eurasian TVDs:

   • Strategic strikes in the Eurasian TVDs would be executed by all three families of strategic ballistic missiles—ICBMs, IR/MRBMs, and SLBMs. Since the mid-1960s Soviet forces have been able to satisfy all targeting requirements in the Eurasian TVDs.
   • Deployments of strategic ballistic missiles have been responsive to changes in the size and composition of the target arrays in the Eur-

asian TVDs. Modernization of strategic ballistic-missile forces over the past quarter-century has been designed to increase effectiveness while reducing collateral damage and the vulnerability of Soviet strategic missiles to U.S. or NATO attacks.

• Contrary to Western conventional wisdom, when attacking soft targets the USSR has probably planned to use much smaller warheads than the large yields usually ascribed to its strategic missiles. Given official views of weapons effects and target vulnerabilities, the yields required to achieve targeting objectives are usually much smaller than most estimates of the warheads carried by Soviet strategic ballistic missiles. From 1960 through the late 1970s required yields ranged from 50 to 500 kilotons. During the 1980s required yields dropped to between 50 and 150 kilotons, or even to as low as 25 kilotons, depending on damage objectives.

• Consequently, from the mid-1960s through the late 1970s, massive, initial Soviet strategic-missile attacks on the Eurasian TVDs would probably have laid down 300 to 600 megatons. As a result of SRF modernization with accurate MIRVs (principally the SS-20) initial massive strikes during the early 1980s in the NATO TVDs would probably utilize only 100 to 200 megatons. If Western estimates of USSR missile yields were employed, instead of required yields, the laydown would total several thousand megatons and would not vary from 1960 through 1985.

• Given damage objectives against soft targets and the warhead yields required to achieve these objectives, a Soviet attack on the soft-target arrays in the continental United States would probably be in the range of a few hundred, rather than thousands of, megatons. A strike against American hard targets, however, would total about 2,000 megatons.

• Employing only the yields required, instead of the maximum yields the missiles are capable of carrying, is consistent with USSR objectives to defeat, disarm, and occupy NATO; use Europe's economic assets to assist Soviet recovery; and introduce some version of the USSR politico-economic order into Western Europe.

• By the late 1980s or early 1990s Moscow's strategic ballistic missiles may be able to achieve targeting objectives against many soft targets in the Eurasian TVDs with nonnuclear warheads (including those carrying chemical weapons).

• In the Transoceanic TVD, Soviet capabilities lagged far behind requirements until the late 1970s and the negotiation of SALT II. After three decades of unremitting effort, however, the USSR satisfied most of its targeting requirements by the early 1980s.

• Minimum targeting requirements against soft-target arrays in the Transoceanic TVD were not satisfied until the mid- to late 1970s. The number of reserve warheads needed to support subsequent operations and to dominate the postwar world remained inadequate throughout the 1960s and 1970s.

• Sometime during the late 1980s or early 1990s, the Soviets will probably introduce terminal guidance systems on their ICBMs targeted against U.S. land-based strategic missile launchers to increase their confidence in the effectiveness of these weapons.

• By the mid-1980s, after more than two decades of effort, the USSR finally satisfied its requirement for counterforce targeting of hardened American missiles, weapons, and associated command-control facilities.

• The launcher and MIRV ceilings negotiated in the SALT II agreement and proposed by the USSR in START were designed to satisfy Soviet targeting requirements. By the mid-1980s the USSR had exhausted the damage-limiting potential of strategic ballistic-missile strikes in the Transoceanic TVD and, hence, may have little or no incentive to deploy additional launchers or MIRVed missiles beyond the SALT II limits. The Soviets do have a strong incentive, however, to develop more accurate strategic missiles in order to increase their confidence in counterforce attacks.

• Because USSR strategic-missile force deployments are sized according to targeting and other warfighting requirements, the Soviets do not have much leeway to reduce their forces below SALT II levels. Improvements in accuracy by the end of the 1980s may permit some reduction in their large-payload missiles—currently the SS-18 and SS-19—as the requirement declines from three to two warheads per hard target. Similarly, by the late 1980s a follow-on to the SS-20, carrying five or six warheads, could reduce the number of IR/MRBM launchers required. The West should not expect much more in future agreements to reduce the size of USSR strategic nuclear-missile forces.

This assessment of Soviet strategic-missile force capabilities needs to be qualified by two caveats: (1) confidence in missile accuracy and (2) the limits of counterforce strikes in USSR war-fighting, damage-limiting strategy. There is also the question of the price the Soviets may be willing to pay to stop the American SDI. This will be considered in Chapter 9.

Arthur G. B. Metcalf—who understands the esoteric intricacies of inertial guidance equations and mechanization—has stated that "the earth is a magnetic wart."[24] Consequently, even if, as reported, the Soviets demonstrated a CEP of 200 to 250 meters for the SS-18 and SS-19 on test-range trajectories, they might not be highly confident of maintaining that accuracy when flying northern trajectories from their own launchers to Minuteman silos.[25] Against hard targets, relatively small degradations in accuracy greatly reduce expected effectiveness. One of the reasons the USSR has been developing several new ICBMs is to improve missile accuracy, so that expected effectiveness against hard targets will be less sensitive to degradations in accuracy under operational conditions. A prudent planner, Soviet or American, would be well advised to sufficiently improve the accuracy of inertial guidance systems to make the expected results of an attack insensitive to a CEP twice the value demonstrated in peacetime on the test range. In addition, a prudent planner would develop terminal guidance systems. The USSR is evidently doing both.[26]

For a long time the Soviets have recognized the limitations on counterforce operations to limit damage to their country in the event of a nuclear war. Their statements on this issue are usually intended to convince the United States and NATO that they could not disarm the USSR by a surprise nuclear strike.

General S. Ivanov has argued that the "more sober military men and theoreticians" in the West understand that a surprise attack on the USSR would not save the West from "inevitable defeat" and that "nuclear retaliation from the side of the Soviet Union will inevitably follow." He goes on to state:

> With the existing level of development of nuclear missile weapons and their reliable cover below ground and underwater, it is practically impossible to destroy them completely and consequently it is also impossible to prevent an annihilating retaliatory attack. Along with this, modern means of detection make it possible to reveal the initiation of an enemy nuclear attack and to carry out the necessary retaliatory measures in a timely manner.[27]

These statements by General Ivanov—who was commandant of the General Staff Academy at the time and a senior member of the General Staff itself from 1959 to 1962—are representative of a number of enunciations by military line and political officers who recognize that counterforce operations alone cannot bring "victory" in a nuclear war. But this does not mean that the USSR accepts some sort of mutual balance of forces based on the inability of either side to destroy all of the other's missiles and aircraft on the ground. Rather, it means that counterforce strikes must be employed to limit damage as much as possible and must then be augmented by strategic defenses. General Ivanov continues:

> In regard to the forms of strategic actions of the armed forces in a nuclear war, among their number our military doctrine considers the actions of

strategic nuclear forces and national air defense troops in the repelling of enemy air and outer space attacks, operations in the theaters of military operations, the independent operations of naval forces in the oceanic theaters . . . Tremendous significance is attached to the development of the national air defense troops for the purpose of making them capable to repulse enemy nuclear attacks carried out with the use of air/space defense.

Note that "repelling" enemy nuclear attacks explicitly links strategic offensive and defensive forces and what the West calls "general purpose forces." It is in this context that statements by General Ivanov and others about the limits of counterforce operations to reduce damage should be placed. Such statements do not imply USSR acceptance of a strategic "balance"—a term that Soviet writers almost invariably credit to their Western counterparts—based on the capabilities of strategic nuclear forces of both superpowers to inflict unacceptable damage on the other in a second-strike scenario. Moscow is simply saying that to fight and win a nuclear war it is necessary to have strategic air, missile, space, and civil defenses to limit damage from enemy offensive forces that survive Soviet counterforce strikes.

STRATEGIC DEFENSIVE FORCES

Calculating the effectiveness of nuclear armed ballistic missiles against targets is a relatively straightforward matter, at least in the absence of ABM defenses. The effectiveness of strategic defenses requires far more complicated measures, and the results are subject to a high degree of uncertainty. For example, if the target flies straight and level, SAMs may be highly most effective. Should the target maneuver, SAMs may be quite ineffective. Electronic countermeasures (ECM) usually work well or not at all. Air defense effectiveness varies accordingly.

Nevertheless, some judgments on past trends in Soviet strategic defensive capabilities can be made, and the central issues for the future are readily identifiable. Whereas the development of technology has been on the side of the SRF and the navy's SLBMs in performing their missions, PVO Strany fell far behind in the mid-1960s. This lag occurred despite the deployment of thousands of radars, SAM launchers, and interceptors. Essentially, after two decades of effort, by the late 1950s PVO Strany had fielded a formidable defense against aircraft penetrating at high altitudes. However, it remained vulnerable to ECM and was unable to respond to low-altitude penetration tactics or SRAMs. During the early 1980s the USSR fielded its response to these threats: the SA-10 against cruise missiles, AWACS, and several interceptors with look-down-shoot-down capabilities. Meanwhile, the United States once again raised the technological ante by deploying cruise missiles.

Clearly, the renamed Voiska PVO (which, apparently, has now united both strategic and operational-tactical air defense forces) will be able to perform its mission better in the late 1980s than at any time in the past. Just how much improvement can be achieved will be a matter of much uncertainty for both sides.

Although it is not precluded by the ABM treaty, except for Moscow, ballistic missile defense continues to be a PVO mission. Maintaining and improving air defenses makes no sense—indeed, is a waste—as long as ballistic missile defenses are lacking, because SLBMs constitute more than one-half of the U.S.. arsenal that is likely to survive any Soviet counterforce attack. As was discussed in the previous chapter, advances in Soviet ABM technology since the SALT process began in 1969 indicate that by about the time PVO deploys large numbers of its new interceptors and SAMs in the mid-1980s, the USSR will probably have the capability to install the kind of ABM defenses the United States started to deploy in the late 1960s. These defenses will be supplemented by advanced optical technologies, data processing, and terminal guidance in the late 1980s or 1990s. However, there is no basis for a quantitative analysis of such potential ABM deployments at this time.

Few aspects of USSR defense policy arouse as much controversy and emotion in the United States as Soviet civil defense programs. When even the CIA estimates the cost of replicating USSR civil defense efforts in the United States at two billion dollars annually, it is time to cease denying that the Kremlin has such a program and to try coping with it. As depicted in *Soviet Military Power, 1985*, the USSR has accomplished more in this field than anyone inside or outside of the U.S. government had imagined possible a few years ago.

According to one civil defense manual, by the late 1960s USSR civil defense had the potential of reducing casualties to less than 10 percent of the population.[28] Although credible under certain circumstances, this claim remains subject to many uncertainties. It is one thing to evacuate tens of millions of people and build temporary shelters in summer; it is quite another in winter, even if the Russian people are hardy. It is probable that the Soviets have done much more than is realized to reduce the vulnerability of their leadership and their economy to nuclear attack. Economic exigency demands, on the other hand, have increased concentration of Soviet industry. More and more has been invested in expanding and modernizing existing plants, rather than in building new facilities in dispersed locations and, thus, increasing industrial vulnerability to nuclear attack.

The uncertainties about USSR civil defense performance are probably great enough not to tempt its leaders to rash actions. By the same token, these uncertainties apply both ways. The U.S. declaratory policy of "assured destruction," defined as annihilation of 25 to 30, sometimes even 50, percent of the Soviet population, could not be "assured" even before it was first announced. And the amount of permanent damage the United States could inflict on Soviet industry may be less than is usually assumed, at least in a number of plausible scenarios.

The balance of capabilities versus mission requirements for the Soviet Navy's two strategic defensive missions—defense against enemy carrier aviation and strategic ASW defense against enemy SSBNs—is uneven. The combination of SLBMs, attack submarines, naval air force and Strategic Air Armies' medium bombers equipped with missiles appears to be a match for U.S. and allied carriers. Much would depend on the ECM end game. If the carriers were far enough away from the Eurasian continent, they might be able to defend themselves. On the other hand, Soviet forces could also probably keep them from coming to Western Europe's aid after the SRF— supplemented by the LRA and frontal aviation—had carried out massive strikes on NATO airfields and other nuclear targets.

The navy's strategic ASW mission against U.S. and allied SSBNs, however, suffers from even greater technological deficiencies than Voiska PVO air defenses, despite more than two decades of effort. Thus far, the USSR has made little progress in effective capabilities. Twenty-five years ago Soviet strategic ASW forces could not find American SSBNs and could not destroy them if found. At present they still may not be able to find the SSBNs, but they could destroy some of them if they did.

The USSR has known for two-and-a-half decades that it needs a system or systems which can scan large ocean areas and detect, then track, SSBNs so that Soviet ASW surface, submarine, and air units can be directed into the local area of the SSBN. If the feat is ever performed at all, only non-acoustic sensors are likely to detect and track SSBNs in large ocean areas. To survey ocean areas in which hostile SSBNs may be lurking, the sensors will almost certainly have to be mounted on a spacecraft or some sort of airborne platform of great range and endurance.

Until Moscow fields such a combination of platforms and sensors, its ASW force will be relatively ineffective against American SSBNs in mid-ocean, no matter how many ships and submarines it builds. As has been noted, the continuing investment in ASW suggests that the USSR is convinced it will solve the open-ocean detection and tracking problem. If it does, the strategic relationship between the two superpowers will be profoundly altered. Meanwhile, the Soviets may justify their large ASW investment by the protection it provides to their own SSBNs.

Finally, the USSR ground forces and frontal aviation—supported by military transport aviation, airborne troops, and the navy—must follow up the operations of strategic forces by defeating enemy remnants and occupying their territory. Given the preponderance of USSR strategic forces achieved by the early 1960s in the Eurasian TVDs, the Soviet combined arms forces have not experienced wide gaps between missions and capabilities. The re-equipment programs instituted in the mid-1960s are providing ground and air forces with the capabilities to fight a nuclear and chemical, as well as a conventional, war with NATO.

Although Soviet paranoia would have it otherwise, USSR troops along the Chinese border appear to be adequate—at least for the defense of the homeland's territorial integrity. The Soviets are not likely to have any ambitions to penetrate beyond the Great Wall in a war with the PRC. As long as China is not really a threat, Western Europe remains the focus of USSR ambitions, because control of Europe would change the "correlation of forces" overwhelmingly in favor of the East.

If the USSR were able to decouple nuclear forces in the NATO TVDs from the Transoceanic TVD, it would have overwhelming military superiority over its "probable enemies," thanks largely to strategic missile and air forces. The Soviets should then be able to fight and win a decoupled nuclear war with NATO and to seize Western Europe in a relatively intact condition. They have a conventional edge, although it is probably not enough in their own eyes. U.S. strategic nuclear forces based in the Transoceanic TVD could restore the balance only as long as the threat to use them to defend NATO Europe remained credible.

Consequently, to maximize peacetime political returns from its military posture and to "win" a nuclear war if it occurs, the USSR needs to make major improvements in the capabilities of its strategic defensive forces. Building these required improvements will probably be the principal goal of Soviet military programs through the 1980s.

9 / Summary and Observations

This chapter is designed to summarize the findings on a number of critical issues and to forecast some trends that appear likely to be prominent through the end of the 1980s. The first five sections are essentially summaries. The sixth section attempts to project the principal elements of USSR military policy into the late 1980s. It ends with an assessment of probable Soviet advantages and disadvantages in the strategic arms competition at the beginning of the next decade. The last section points out certain implications for United States policy.

Trends in Doctrine and Strategy

As soon as World War II ended, the USSR began a sustained drive to acquire balanced offensive and defensive forces designed to limit damage to the homeland and to fight and eventually "win" a nuclear war while maintaining superior ground and air power for operations in the Eurasian theaters. Soviet military policy has been remarkably stable over the past quarter-century. Since the early 1960s, military doctrine and strategy have undergone only a few modifications. Nevertheless, there had been considerable turbulence in various weapons programs, particularly during the late 1950s and early 1960s.

Internal debates and disagreements among the politico-military elites contributed to this turbulence, but in most cases external developments and various internal constraints remained the dominant influences. At times,

U.S. or NATO initiatives upset the Kremlin's plans. In other instances, the Soviets were forced by the state of their technology and economy to wait one or two decades before they could develop and produce the weapons required by military doctrine and strategy. Frequently, a combination of all of these factors contributed to gaps between capabilities and requirements. Nevertheless, the USSR has pursued its objectives persistently and at great expense to the peoples of the Soviet empire.

The USSR regime is at its strongest in those areas in which it has blended traditional Russian characteristics, practices, and institutions with Marxism-Leninism. In military affairs, it has not only fused history with ideology but also integrated that amalgamation with modern technology and the productive capacity of the world's second-largest industrial economy.

It is fashionable in some circles to talk about how often Russia has been invaded, beginning with the Mongols. What is frequently overlooked, however, is that the present Union of Soviet Socialist Republics represents a slightly enlarged version of the Russian empire created in the course of some three centuries of military expansion from the principality of Muscovy. Soviet hegemony over Poland, for example, has its tsarist precedents. Elsewhere in Eastern Europe the "socialist camp" consists of countries that were formerly part of the Hapsburg and Turkish empires, with which Russia clashed for two centuries. The tsars also had designs on Afghanistan.

The Soviet strategic nuclear concepts documented in this book are another illustration of this fusion between the traditional and the modern. As it has been in all past wars, the USSR objective in a nuclear war is victory: The enemy must be conquered and his territory occupied. Now, however, the entire country must be defended from attacks by the opponent's long-range bombers and missiles at the same time that his armies are being defeated. The party-state apparatus must continue to function during nuclear attacks; maintain control over the population; direct repair and rehabilitation of the economy; prosecute the war to a victorious conclusion; and organize recovery. Both offensive and defensive forces must not only defeat the enemy but also limit damage to the entire country so that continuity of control can be ensured and recovery achieved. As described in Chapter 8, nuclear attacks must be designed so that most of the peoples in enemy countries will survive and join the "socialist camp" after they have been "liberated" from the "imperialist" yoke by the victory of Soviet arms.

WEAPONS ACQUISITION IN THE USSR

As described by official sources, weapons acquisition is a rational process guided by party policy, which is designed to satisfy the requirements of military doctrine and strategy. Doctrine is formulated by the party, and it establishes Soviet objectives in a future war. Strategy is formulated by the military establishment and approved by the party. It specifies the military forces, missions, and operational concepts required to achieve the objectives specified by doctrine. Doctrine and strategy overlap in the area of weapons acquisition.

Over the past quarter-century, the stability of military doctrine and strategy has been matched by the continuity and long service records of many key individuals involved in weapons acquisition policy. Between them, the late civilian marshals Brezhnev and Ustinov had a total of seventy-six years of experience in weapons development and production. Ustinov was the Soviet Union's third defense minister since 1956; he died in December 1984. Admiral Gorshkov headed the Navy from 1956 to late 1985. Some thirty-four of the top military leaders are members or candidate members of the Central Committee.[1] Gorbachev, however, has no known close ties with the Soviet military. Marshal Sokolov, presently the defense minister, is only a candidate member on the Politburo.

Although party leaders make the final decisions on weapons acquisition, the professional military establishment plays a large and critical role in policy formulation; it does a great deal of the thinking and staff work that goes into Soviet military policy. Most of the research and analysis that is performed by U.S. civilian "think tanks" is conducted in the USSR by intellectuals at senior academies and higher military schools, as well as in defense ministry research institutes. The Soviet General Staff is a modern version of the Prussian model. As a matter of policy, the United States has nothing similar, and no place exists in the American defense establishment for career military intellectuals. Having the higher-ranking military officers do their own thinking may not maximize innovation, but it does avoid political fads and leads to consistency between theory and practice.

Western analysts who stress the political factors in USSR decisions on weapons acquisition start off in the right direction but often end up with the wrong conclusions. The Soviets are the first to admit that politics dominate the process; that the process is guided by the party's "military-technical policy"; and that weapons acquisition policy is formulated and promulgated by the Central Committee (read Defense Council or Politburo). What analysts who stress the political factors miss, however, is that top USSR political leaders take their own processes very seriously. Senior politicians do not formulate military doctrine as a declaratory policy to which they intend to pay little, if any, attention in practice. The Defense Council or Politburo adopts a doctrine as the policy framework to guide its own subsequent actions—to judge and be judged by. Similarly, when the military establishment translates and expands the party's doctrine into strategy, and the political leaders approve that strategy (with whatever amendments they see fit) the strategy subsequently provides policy guidance for decisions on weapons development, production, and deployment and for organization, training, and command-control.

This is not to deny that certain idiosyncracies of the political leaders may influence the process. In particular, Khrushchev was given to sudden whims and to a penchant for proceeding in several directions at the same time. Except for his test of a 100-megaton device and his proposal to turn the Soviet Army into a territorial militia, however, all of Khrushchev's known programs were within the logical and declaratory framework of the nuclear military doctrine and strategy that was formulated and promulgated during his years of political dominance. Only two of the programs, which went counter to this military doctrine and strategy, were reversed. The ground forces, which Khrushchev had cut back to a cadre army, came back strongly under the Brezhnev-Kosygin regime. And even Khrushchev did not seem to have initiated development of a missile to carry a 100-megaton warhead.

Similarly, certain Western analysts who explain Soviet developments as driven by institutional inertia have a point, but they are mistaking the symptom for the cause. Weapons design bureaus do not go out of business in the USSR. They keep grinding out successive generations of weapons systems. In this sense, there exists enormous bureaucratic inertia. What the argument overlooks, however, is that the party created these design bureaus and continues to support them for precisely this purpose: to develop successive generations of weapons systems that meet the demands of CPSU "military-technical policy," the objective of which is to achieve "qualitative and quantitative superiority" over the forces of the implacably hostile and ever-threatening "imperialists." What the party has created, the party can destroy the moment the instrument no longer serves its needs. Various arguments—that the Soviets do not know what else to do with the design bureaus and factories which develop and produce the weapons, or that their continuing existence is the USSR method of avoiding unemployment—have no basis in fact whatsoever. These explanations of Politburo behavior are simply U.S. mirror-imaging at its worst.

Factors like "history, culture, and values" play a role, although it is difficult to relate these elements to specific decisions on weapons system development and force structure. Perhaps one can use these factors to explain 190 USSR divisions.[2] But one cannot extrapolate the pattern of Soviet ICBM and SLBM development, the redesign of frontal aviation weapons systems since the mid-1960s, the proliferation of new strategic and tactical air defense systems in the same period, and individual weapons such as an Akula class nuclear attack submarine or Sukhoi-27 and MiG-29 all-weather superiority interceptors equipped with radar and missiles for look-down-shoot-down engagements from "history, culture, and values."

However, if one looks at the patterns of USSR weapons development and deployment, the characteristics of the systems, the numbers procured, and the concept of operations and asks what kind of politico-military principles would generate such forces, one will arrive at a fair approximation of official military doctrine and strategy. Similarly, if one examines military doctrine and strategy and asks what the Soviets would require in the way of military forces—taking into account their perceptions of the existing threat, the capabilities and limitations of their resources and technology, institutional structure, and modus operandi—their forces in the field are about what one would expect. Whether viewed inductively or deductively, USSR force development is consistent with military doctrine and strategy and the declared objectives of the party's "military-technical policy." When faced with what the Soviets say and how they act, and the high degree of consistency between the two, other explanations fail.

SALT AND SOVIET MILITARY POLICY

Soviet Objectives in SALT

In 1969 the USSR agreed to strategic arms limitation talks, because it perceived that the combination of American ABM defenses and MIRV deployments would place it in a dangerously inferior position over the next decade or two.[3] The Soviets feared ABM most, because they were about fifteen years behind the United States in ABM technology at the end of the 1960s. In contrast, they lagged only about one-third that much in MIRV technology.

Traditionally, the USSR had not regarded ABM and other types of strategic defenses as posing any threat. By 1969, however, articles in *Military Thought* recognized that a drastic and dangerous shift in the strategic military balance favoring the United States would result from American ABM deployments (which had first been announced two years earlier). These writers apparently perceived that a combination of ABM and MIRVs could provide the U.S. with the war-fighting, damage-limiting capabilities that the Soviets were seeking for themselves. In their view, unilateral deployment of both ABM defenses and MIRVs would have put the United States into a much stronger military position vis-à-vis the USSR and would have increased the danger of a U.S. or NATO attack on the Soviet Union and its allies.

The probable USSR view of its strategic military prospects for the 1970s can be simulated by using Soviet analytical techniques and by taking into account the status of their strategic weapons development and deployment programs at that time. This simulation indicates that in 1968–69 Moscow expected the prospective U.S. strategic advantage (1) to frustrate the design objectives of all USSR strategic weapons scheduled or expected to be deployed in the 1970s and (2) to keep the Soviets in a dangerously inferior strategic position until at least the mid-1980s. The Kremlin probably saw the American proposal to engage in SALT as an opportunity to avoid this extension of U.S. strategic superiority. Consequently, in 1970 the USSR eagerly accepted American proposals to virtually ban ABM deployments.

Only four Soviet organizations would have had access to the necessary classified information on their own weapons and programs and possessed the requisite analytical capabilities to have played a significant role in formulating SALT policy. These were the Ministry of Defense, the Military Industrial Commission (VPK), the Defense Industry Department of the Central Committee's Secretariat, and the Defense Council or Politburo. These are the same bureaucratic actors who formulate and execute USSR military policy—its objectives, weapons acquisition programs, and resource allocations.

Although career diplomat V. S. Semenov served as titular head of the SALT delegation, there is no evidence that the Ministry of Foreign Affairs had any significant role in performing the staff work and analysis that went into the decisions on Soviet objectives or that supported the daily negotiations. Other organizations—such as the USA and Canada Institute—may have played an advisory role in some relatively unimportant aspects of the SALT negotiations. These research organizations, however, had neither the skills nor, as far as can be determined, the requisite access to classified information on weapons systems and programs for staff support in the SALT process. Most of this work was performed by the Ministry of Defense, the VPK, and the Defense Industry Department of the Secretariat. As usual, the Defense Council or Politburo made the final decisions. While foreign affairs' ministry officials have been much more prominent in the negotiations during recent years and evidently have been cleared for information on Soviet forces, the locus of staff work and decisionmaking has not changed.

All negotiation on strategic arms has been, and remains, an instrument of USSR military policy. The general objectives have been (1) to avoid a shift in the strategic military balance toward the United States that Soviet analysts feared in 1968–69; and (2) instead to move the "correlation of forces" in favor of the USSR. The Ministry of Defense has probably been the strongest bureaucratic proponent of the SALT process, regarding it as the indispensable means of achieving Soviet policy objectives in the 1970s and early 1980s.

Clearly, the USSR did not enter into the SALT process because it had been converted to the U.S. declaratory policy of "mutual assured destruction" or to any other concept of mutual deterrence. The Soviets achieved most, if not all, of their objectives in SALT but made few, if any, concessions that would detract from their damage-limiting capabilities in the event of a nuclear war. All the limits on strategic offensive forces accepted by Moscow in SALT were consistent with its strategic nuclear targeting requirements to fight and "win" a nuclear war. SALT limited neither the growth in the number of strategic nuclear warheads in the Soviet arsenal nor improvements in their characteristics.

SALT and Soviet Force Development

Table 37 summarizes the continuity of USSR force development patterns in number of weapons systems procured for each major mission during the 1960s and 1970s and lists prospects for the 1980s. Note the following facts:

- About 100 major weapons systems were procured for all missions in the 1960s and 1970s; during the 1980s procurement will exceed 100 major systems (and may easily exceed 150).
- More weapons systems were procured for strategic defensive missions than for strategic offensive missions in both the 1960s and the 1970s.
- More strategic defensive systems were procured during the SALT era than during the 1960s.
- Procurement of weapons systems for strategic defensive missions will evidently dominate the 1980s.

Obviously, SALT has not changed Soviet military policy. If anything, the process only accentuated the USSR drive to acquire damage-limiting, warfighting capabilities.

Economic Priorities in the SALT Era

When the negotiations began in 1969 the Soviet military establishment was receiving about 12 percent of total GNP. The conventional wisdom at the time, promulgated by the CIA, placed the USSR military's share at only 6 percent of GNP (and assumed that it was declining). American SALT advocates expected these military expenditures (at least for strategic forces) to decline if agreements were negotiated. In 1976 the CIA was forced by new evidence to double its estimates of Soviet defense expenditures and to increase those for procurement outlays by a factor of four. Toward the end of 1984 the agency went on record as saying that 13 to 14 percent of Soviet GNP was devoted to the military.[4]

TABLE 37 QUANTITATIVE TRENDS IN SOVIET WEAPONS PROCURED, 1960–90

Major mission	1960s	1970s	1980s		
			1[a]	2[b]	3[c]
Strategic offensive—ICBMs, IR/MRBMs, SLBMs, SSBNs, bombers, ASMs, tankers	20	17	7–8	18	15–26
Strategic defensive	35–36	40–42	27–31	19–49	46–70
Air defense—SAMs, AWACs, interceptors, AAMs, ES&CGI radars, C³ systems	18–19	14–151	6–8	8–18	14–26
Missile and space defense, early warning—interceptors (missiles) and radars	5	3–4	3–4	1–9	4–13
ASW—surface ships, SSNs, aircraft, missiles	8	17	15–16	7–17	22–23
Anticarrier—SSNs, SLCMs, Aircraft, ASMs	4	6	3	3–5	6–8
Operational-strategic	41–42	43–48	22–25	22–36	44–61
Ground forces—tanks, APCs, SP artillery, towed artillery and mortars, SAMs, AA guns, ATGMs	23–24	23–27	12–14	10–16	22–30
Frontal and military transport aviation—aircraft and TASMs	8	12–13	9–10	11–17	20–27
Naval ships	10	8	1	1–3	2–4
Totals	96–98	100–107	56–64	59–103	105–157

SOURCES: Data from Tables 18 and 27.

[a]Carried over from the 1970s

[b]To be introduced in the 1980s

[c]To be procured in the 1980s

Soviet military outlays grew from about 50 billion rubles in 1970 to about 154 billion in 1983, and probably will reach over 170 billion in 1985, for an annual average growth rate of about 8.5 percent. In 1970–76, military outlays grew at the rate of about 10.7 percent per annum but dropped to about 7.6 percent per annum in 1976–83. From 1970 through 1983, Soviet procurement of weaponry rose from about 18 billion to about 86 billion rubles, and probably will reach nearly 100 billion rubles in 1985. In 1976, Soviet procurement outlays were about 45 billion rubles, hence have more than doubled in the last nine years. The corresponding annual growth rates in Soviet weapons procurement are:

1970–76: 16.5	1976–83: 96
1970–83: 12.7	1976–85: about 9
1970–85: 11.9	

Except for the RDT&E component, all data are in 1970 prices, as the Soviets reckon constant ("comparable") prices. Figure 8 shows the trends in the growth and composition of Soviet outlays in the 1970–1985 period.

In terms of the burden on the economy, figured as a share of GNP, Soviet military outlays rose from over 12 percent in 1970 to about 18 percent in 1980, as the Soviets reckon constant ("comparable") 1970 prices. In current 1980 prices, the burden was about 16 percent of Soviet GNP. In 1985, the military burden probably will reach or exceed 21 percent of Soviet GNP in 1970 prices but may not be over about 17 percent in current (1985) prices. This difference is due to price reductions resulting from learning curve economies for weapons, and as a result of price increases in many basic industries since 1980.

From the late 1960s through 1981, military outlays (as measured here) accounted for about one-third of the Soviet State budget each year. Since 1982, the military's share of the budget has risen to at least 36–38 percent in 1984–85.

As was pointed out in coauthor Lee's article in the March–April 1985 issue of *Problems of Communism*, all of the independent checkpoints from Soviet sources have confirmed these estimates. While other estimates were revised upward by factors of two to four by the initial checkpoints, Lee's estimates have not changed because all of the independent checkpoints from Soviet sources have fallen at the mid- to high side thereof. Therefore these are high confidence, if minimum, estimates of Soviet military outlays and of the military burden on the Soviet economy. The checkpoints span nearly two decades, and major items such as Soviet civil defense are not included.

Most of the increase in the USSR military's share of GNP has come at

FIGURE 8   SOVIET MILITARY OUTLAYS, 1970–1985

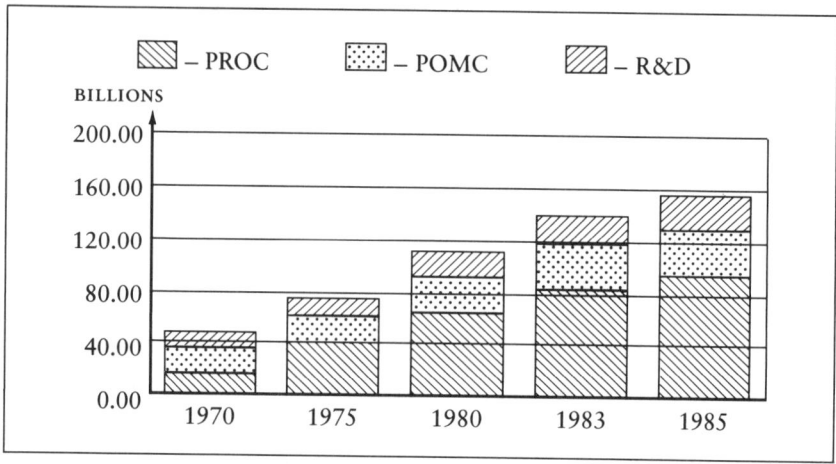

NOTE: ª1970 "Comparable" Ruble Prices

the expense of the consumer, and capital investment has also been severely constrained by the rapid growth of military expenditures. In 1985 Soviet consumers received at best about one-half of GNP, as compared to about 57 percent when SALT began. The slow growth of USSR capital investment in recent years and the slow pace in modernization of machinery and equipment are two of the principal reasons for the sharp decline in the rate of economic growth.

Access to the West's markets and credits, facilitated by SALT, contributed substantially to financing the Soviet military buildup. Since about 1970 the USSR has not been able to balance its books without a surplus from foreign trade. Rapid growth in machinery imports, particularly since 1975, has made it possible to shift domestic resources to weapons production while still maintaining much more growth than planned in outlays for capital investment. During the 1980s, as in the 1970s, the steady shift in national priorities to the military establishment has again been facilitated by Western trade and credits.

The willingness of the Soviet leadership to place such a burden on the economy—foregoing not only consumption but also economic growth—to satisfy the requirements of a warfighting military doctrine and strategy is the best evidence that these decisionmakers are devoted to acquiring the military capabilities they consider necessary for winning a nuclear war. One must await publication of the twelfth five-year plan for firm evidence of Gorbachev's economic priorities. As this book goes to press, the indications are that the new leader believes he can improve Soviet economic performance without reducing the military's claim on the USSR economy.

SALT as Arms Control

Given the historical record, it is difficult to understand why anyone in the West considers the SALT/START process as a means toward genuine arms control. The only arms control achieved during the entire process has been the halting of American ABM deployment and the delaying of U.S. strategic missiles and aircraft modernization—in part because of the illusion that the two treaties have restrained both superpowers.

Three basic facts about these negotiations should be remembered. First, SALT has been applicable to only a part of the strategic forces on either side and, particularly, to only a small portion of Soviet strategic forces. Second, SALT has provided no effective curb on the development of strategic weapons technology and no limitation whatsoever on strategic weapons budgets. Third, between 1970 and 1984, under terms of so-called arms control agreements, both sides have added more than 7,000 warheads to their ready inventories of those strategic missiles and bombers included in SALT. Including refires, the increment to the total USSR inventory may well have been close to 10,000 warheads during the SALT period.[5]

Many would claim that, without SALT, Soviet strategic missile forces would be even larger. No evidence to support this argument exists. On the contrary, the USSR has sized its strategic forces to meet targeting requirements. Once those requirements are met and a sufficient reserve is provided, the Soviets will have enough weapons. SALT or no SALT, the USSR strategic-missile warhead inventory in the mid-1980s would have been about the same. This judgment has been corroborated by the fact that the Soviet START proposal called for a slightly smaller arsenal than permitted by the SALT II agreement.

By Western arms control standards, everything the Soviets have done since the late 1950s has been "destabilizing." Their policy has never been to strike *only* after riding out an enemy nuclear attack. Pre-emption on strategic warning has always been the preferred USSR option. In the mid-1960s the Soviets adopted "launch on tactical warning"—a hair-trigger destabilizing strategy according to any Western definition of stability. During 1984–85 the SS-18 and SS-19 counterforce missiles carried nearly 80 percent of the ready ICBM warhead inventory, another violation (by Western criteria) of strategic stability. USSR air defenses are designed to cancel out one leg of the U.S. retaliatory triad, the leg that, given contemporary air defense and warning technologies, cannot really be used in other than a second-strike mode. ASW is designed to check the third leg of the American triad while protecting Moscow's own SLBM secure reserve force. Finally, Soviet "civil defense" protects the leadership through a vast network of hardened exurban command posts, denies the population as a retaliatory target by evacuation, and relocates all other critical assets that can be readily moved from peacetime locations. The USSR cannot move its cities, but plans to reduce as much as possible their target value to a U.S. second strike. Soviet military policy, before and during SALT, has thus been "destabilizing" on all counts by the criteria of traditional Western deterrence and arms control theology.

Whatever may be destabilizing to the West, however, is the opposite for the Soviets, because—as pointed out in Chapter 3—the USSR concept of deterrence is one-sided: They have the right and duty to deter the West, but the West has no right to deter them. This means that the USSR must do everything in its power to nullify American deterrent forces at every point, which is precisely what it has done or tried to do—except in the case of national ABM deployments—thus far.

It is wishful thinking to expect the Soviets to negotiate limits on strategic missile forces that would be inconsistent with their own strategic targeting requirements, unless forced to do so by President Reagan's SDI program. It is equally illusory to attempt to induce the USSR not to take "destabilizing" measures by exhibiting Western examples of forbearance. The kind of strategic nuclear relationship that would conform to Western notions of mutual interest and stability could be negotiated only under one of two circumstances. First, there would have to be a revolutionary transformation in the Soviet political leadership. Second, the military burden on the USSR economy would have to create such adverse conditions that the current leaders would conclude that they must either change their military policies or risk loss of party control over the country. Unless one or both of these conditions were to occur, strategic arms control negotiations with the Soviet Union will continue to be an exercise in futility and delusion.

Gorbachev may institute some major innovations, although, based on his record to date, abandoning the USSR war-fighting strategy or reducing the military's share of GNP are not among those he has in mind. Since the demise of the SALT II agreement in the U.S. Senate and the advent of the Reagan administration, there has been considerable talk about a renewed arms race and about how concessions to the Soviets might avoid such a race. Until a broader consensus exists on the futility of it all, domestic and alliance politics will compel the United States to continue to negotiate arms control agreements. Under these circumstances, the United States should at least conduct these talks armed with a realistic appraisal of what the USSR is up to. The bottom line for any negotiations with the Soviets must be whether the results strengthen or weaken the security of the United States and its allies. The January 1986 proposal by the USSR for substantial reductions in nuclear arsenals deserves consideration. However, it must be carefully scrutinized for the "hidden agenda" that is characteristic of the Kremlin.

PROSPECTS FOR SUPERPOWER STRATEGIC BALANCE IN THE 1980S

Strategic Offensive and Defensive Forces

Predicting the future is always an uncertain business. Nevertheless, barring drastic political and economic upheavals, a number of trends are evident, and some future events appear likely.

Throughout the remainder of the 1980s the Soviets will probably maintain the overwhelming advantage in strategic offensive forces vis-à-vis the Eurasian theaters that they have enjoyed since the initial IR/MRBM deployments were completed in the mid-1960s. The USSR carefully kept these forces out of the SALT process. They are subject to the new talks, however, which started on 12 March 1985 in Geneva. Although both sides met between 1981 and 1983 at the Intermediate-Range Nuclear Force (INF) negotiations and the Strategic Arms Reduction Talks (START), modernization of the SRF with the SS-20 and with highly accurate versions of the SS-18 and SS-19, of long-range aviation with Backfire, and of the navy's SLBMs with the SS-N-18 and SS-N-20 all proceeded on schedule. Meanwhile, the Soviets did not negotiate away their strategic nuclear advantage over NATO.

The new generation of Soviet ICBMs (the SS-18 follow-on, the SS-X-24, and SS-X-25) will be deployed over the next five years. These systems should provide both the improved accuracy required for more effective, higher-confidence targeting of Minuteman silos, and mobility for survivability.[6] If there is no significant expansion of the U.S. hard-target base, Soviet ICBM hard target force requirements could be reduced by about one-third through the early 1990s. This, in turn, should provide the USSR some flexibility in future strategic force levels. Or it could just maintain a larger reserve, particularly if the United States modernizes its forces with strategic missiles that are effective against hard targets.

Late-model strategic ballistic missiles would achieve Soviet damage objectives against soft targets in all TVDs with relatively low-yield weapons (50 to 150 kilotons). These smaller yields should make Western Europe a much more valuable prize for USSR occupation and reduce collateral damage elsewhere, in accordance with the political objective of a viable postwar world organized on the Soviet politico-economic model. According to the USSR view of weapons effects, the collateral damage radii for these smaller-yield weapons are less than the area of many soft military and industrial

TABLE 38   EXPECTED DAMAGE RADII AT LOW OVERPRESSURES
(RADIUS OF DAMAGE—KILOMETERS)

Yield (mt)	4 psi	2 psi
1.00	5.8	10.0
0.75	5.3	9.1
0.50	4.6	7.9
0.30	3.9	6.7
0.15	3.1	5.3
0.10	2.7	4.6
0.05	2.1	3.7
0.02	1.6	2.7

SOURCE: These radii have been calculated on the basis of John Shannon's research at Science Applications, Inc., on Soviet nuclear weapons effects. Specifically, they are based on USSR data on blast wave propagation on a nonideal surface; U.S. height-of-burst gives damage radii to these psi levels that are 15 to 20 percent or more in excess of Soviet expectations. Western studies commonly use these overpressure levels as the cut-off point for collateral damage to structures outside the target area.

targets, most of which cover areas of five to twenty square kilometers (see Table 38).

Short of persuading Moscow completely to change its military doctrine and strategy, the United States can maintain the triad—ICBMS, SLBMs, and bombers—through the 1980s and 1990s only by adopting new basing modes. The best way to confound Soviet targeters would be to place a large portion of American ICBMs in multiple, closely spaced, very hard silos defended by an ABM system. Mobility is another option, although it involves high costs and various operational constraints.

Whereas, for the first time in the nuclear era, USSR strategic offensive forces now are able to perform their missions in all theaters of operations, the capabilities of Soviet strategic defensive forces fall far short of requirements. As the USSR attempts to close these large gaps in its damage-limiting capabilities, the 1980s promise to be the decade of Soviet strategic defenses. In contrast, the United States offers little competition in this endeavor. The one American ABM site permitted by treaty was dismantled years ago. Strategic ASW is not a specified United States Navy mission. Nevertheless, the U.S. Navy has many individual capabilities, which, if assembled to perform strategic ASW in the open oceans, would probably be effective.[7] Few of the Soviet SSBNs, however, are likely to venture out of protected home waters and other havens.

This book has concentrated on active USSR strategic weapons systems and has relatively neglected passive measures like civil defense. Unfortunately, all aspects of this problem cannot be given detailed coverage. Contrary to the views of professional skeptics in the West, the Soviet civil defense organization has enormous damage-limiting potential to ensure the survival of the political, military, and economic elites; the continuity of the system; the repair and rehabilitation of the economy; and the survival of a large portion of the general population even after massive U.S. nuclear strikes.[8] This judgment is strongly supported by recent editions of *Soviet Military Power* which have outlined USSR leadership protection and the war management system for the first time in the public domain.

In summary, the strategic defensive balance will probably favor the USSR in the 1980s. How much the balance swings in its favor will primarily depend on the following three factors: (1) improvements in Soviet air defenses, particularly against cruise missiles; (2) the ability of ASW forces to detect, track, and locate American SSBNs in the open oceans; and (3) whether or not the USSR breaks out of the ABM Treaty (which they can legally do after giving six months notice).[9]

There are many indications that the Soviets will break out before the end of the 1980s. First, the USSR did not enter into this treaty because it considered ABM defenses (for the Soviet Union) unnecessary or undesirable for political, strategic, or military reasons. Rather, it was fear of the military and political advantages that the United States would gain from ABM deployments that led the Soviets to make the ABM Treaty their top objective in SALT I.

Second, the USSR recognized long ago that counterforce can only prevent so much damage to the homeland. Not all of the enemy's bombers will be caught on the ground; some land-based missiles will survive. The United States may launch on tactical warning or during an attack (as the USSR will try to do). Many of the enemy SLBMs will be at sea. Consequently, to "win" a nuclear war, strategic defenses are required for limiting damage.

Third, even with a breakthrough in detection and tracking, some American SSBNs will survive Soviet ASW operations.

Fourth, deployment of the MX and D-5 missiles will provide the United States with formidable counterforce capabilities it does not now possess, thus increasing USSR incentives to defend its own launchers.

Fifth, the Chinese, French, and British capabilities to destroy Soviet soft targets will increase significantly during the 1980s. Moscow will probably not be able to defend itself against the ballistic missile forces of one or more of these three countries for another decade if its defenses are held to current ABM Treaty limits.

Sixth, the USSR's military policy during the SALT-START era followed the same war-fighting, damage-limiting strategy as before—and at much greater expense to the economy. If the Soviet Union has no defenses against surviving American SSBNs, this strategy will have been wasted.

Seventh, the USSR already has high-acceleration, low-altitude interceptor technology, small phased-array radar, and computer technology that is comparable to or better than similar U.S. technology of a decade ago; it had none of these technologies when it entered into the 1972 ABM Treaty. Antiballistic missile defenses around Moscow are being rebuilt, incorporating this new technology. The Soviets will soon have sufficiently large ABM battle-management radars in operation to make nationwide deployments a reality.

Finally, it should be remembered that the USSR does not require defensive systems that are 100 percent effective. The Russians have a proverb: "The good is the enemy of the best." The demand for total effectiveness of ABM systems is a peculiarly American syndrome. It is not necessary for either air defenses or conventional forces in the United States or elsewhere. To the Soviets, an ABM system that would achieve even 50 percent effectiveness against surviving U.S. strategic missiles might be worth the cost, particularly since hardened military and political assets are easier to protect than "soft" targets. Such ABM defenses would be nearly 100 percent effective against Chinese, French, and British strategic nuclear missiles for another decade or more. In addition, by the late 1980s or 1990s, the USSR could probably supplement a traditional ABM system—high-acceleration missile with a nuclear warhead, terminal and peripheral phased-array radars, computers, and data processors—with more exotic optical systems.

According to Secretary of Defense Caspar Weinberger, "The Soviets currently have the world's only deployed antisatellite weapons system that can attack satellites in near-earth orbit." [10] It is indicative of the thrust and potential of R&D in advanced technologies for the 1990s in the USSR.

There are at least four reasons, however, why the Soviet Union might not exercise its option to break out of the ABM Treaty with its nationwide deployment of conventional ABM defenses in the next few years. First, the United States could respond with a better ABM system. Although conventional antiballistic missile defense R&D had been funded at far lower levels (in constant dollars) than when SALT began, American technology did not stand still in this area. Second, if the Soviets broke out of the treaty, the shock to Washington would be severe and might trigger a real arms race. Third, the USSR economy may not be able to afford to develop a nationwide ABM system on top of everything else. With the military's share of GNP now more than 20 percent (in 1970 Soviet prices), the USSR may be approaching the peacetime limit of what it can spend for the military and still maintain a politically tolerable economic growth rate. Fourth, the fear of President Reagan's SDI may have changed Soviet attitudes.

The main problem with the first three arguments is that they have a poor track record. Similar ones have been advanced since the early 1960s to support expectations that the Soviets would not acquire all of the weapons systems and forces that they have, in fact, fielded as fast as they could. Should the USSR decide to deploy national ABM defenses in the late 1980s, it will probably do so semi-openly rather than clandestinely. Negotiating the change might ease the shock to the United States, and by this time all of the institutional actors in Soviet military policy formulation and force development probably think they can accomplish a great deal by negotiating. Thus far, the pace of ABM research and development, deployment of large radars with battle-management potential, and modernization of the Moscow defenses—which could provide the USSR with some operational experience and the production base for the major hardware items—are following a breakout scenario.[11] Recent intelligence assessments of ABM capabilities for the SA-10 and the SA-X-12 also could mean that nationwide deployment of at least limited ABM defenses may be underway.

In the meantime, President Reagan's Strategic Defense Initiative (SDI) has transformed the above prospects. The USSR has complained that, by proposing to defend both itself and its allies, the United States is really attempting to acquire "first strike" capabilities.[12] This reaction, of course, should not be surprising. It is consistent with the argument in Chapter 3 that the USSR has a one-sided view of deterrence. It is also consistent with the analysis in Chapter 6 (expanded upon in the Appendix) of the reasons why Moscow made the ABM treaty the top priority in SALT.

The Impact of the U.S. Strategic Defense Initiative (SDI)

This book has noted a number of instances in which American initiatives upset Soviet weapons acquisition and force planning, particularly for strategic offensive forces. The Strategic Defense Initiative has the potential of undermining the basis for Soviet strategic force planning embodied in the SALT II agreement and the Soviet START proposal in the same way that the 1967 United States decision to begin ABM deployments threatened to negate the counterforce objectives of the SS-18/19 programs. Not surprisingly, the USSR has responded in a similar manner: stop SDI.

By launching a major R&D program to demonstrate the feasibility of space-based ABM defenses, employing technologies that are presently beyond the state-of-the-art, President Reagan has countered the Soviets in several ways. First, any type or degree of American ABM defenses upsets the targeting calculus that has determined the size and composition of Soviet strategic nuclear forces. Even a limited United States defense destroys the assumption about the probability of ballistic missile penetration to the target, once the missile has been successfully launched and completed its powered flight. Second, despite Soviet technological advances over the past two decades, an all out race with the United States to develop exotic ABM technologies is an extremely expensive and questionable prospect for the USSR. Third, the U.S. Strategic Defense Initiative may have preempted Soviet plans to secretly develop their own version of SDI, as much as they had tried albeit unsuccessfully, to leapfrog the United States in ballistic missile development some three decades ago.

As noted in the previous chapter, it is now evident that the ready ICBM and SLBM arsenal level that the Soviets proposed in START was within less than 10 percent of the arsenal they were permitted under SALT II. This corroborates the analysis in the previous chapter that a ready arsenal of 12,000 to 13,000 warheads (carried by ICBMs, SLBMs, and heavy bombers) satisfies USSR strategic targeting sufficiency conditions, given its requirements for high confidence attacks, large reserves, and relative insensitivity to the scenario. Anticipated improvements in the accuracy of the follow-on to the SS-18 could reduce this arsenal requirement by some 1,500 warheads. Large reductions in the number of ICBM and SLBM launchers would offer the cosmetic appearance of arms reduction without decreasing the size of the arsenal, if the number of MIRVed missiles were not affected. Beyond these possibilities, however, there is little or no room for warhead arsenal reductions.

All this, of course, is predicated on no American ABM defenses. If there is any significant degree of attrition through defense, the balance between the arsenal and targeting requirements changes drastically. Critics of SDI in the United States argue that defenses would be unacceptable if they were only 98 percent effective. To the Soviet planner even 90 percent effectiveness would require a tenfold increase in his arsenal to maintain the targeting status quo.

Of course, there are other ways to offset defenses other than by proliferating the offensive arsenal. However countermeasures to the exotic technologies envisaged for SDI, and for conventional ABM defenses as well, are far more expensive and will take much longer to develop and deploy than U.S. critics are willing to admit. Moreover, it is difficult to estimate the confidence levels for countermeasures and penetration aids. As has been demonstrated, in the absence of defenses, the Soviets can mount very high confidence attacks. On the other hand, if the estimates of countermeasure and penetration aid confidence turn out to be wrong, the whole attack could fail catastrophically.

Another alternative for the USSR is to compete by means of their own SDI. President Reagan's proposal to share mature SDI technology with the Soviets undoubtedly was made in good faith, but the Kremlin politburocrats probably regard it as the most devious of tricks. The USSR has come a long way technologically from the late 1960s, when it made the ABM Treaty its first priority in the arms negotiations. However, the Soviets are still loathe to engage in an all out technological race with the United States. They will run when we run, if they must, but they would prefer to run while we walk. The USSR still has healthy respect for United States technological potential. Kremlin decision makers remember the accelerated pace of American strategic weapons development in the 1950s and 1960s.

Closely related to this argument is the possibility that President Reagan preempted Soviet ambitions to be the first to demonstrate SDI technologies. It is evident from official United States government statements and publications that the USSR has been developing all types of directed energy technologies for many years, perhaps over a longer period of time and on a larger scale than the United States.[13] The new space boosters discussed in the previous chapter should provide adequate lift to deploy space-based, or some combination of land- and spaced-based, ABM defenses employing exotic technologies in the course of the next ten to fifteen years. Consequently, the Soviets may have been planning a technological coup in the next decade or so that now is in jeopardy as a result of the American SDI program.

If recent press reports about new USSR proposals on strategic arsenals are correct, the Soviets may be willing to pay a high price to stop SDI. They are allegedly offering to reduce their arsenal from the 12,000 to 13,000 ceiling of SALT II and their START proposal to between 6,500 and 8,000 warheads.[14] No details on sublimits are available as of this writing. The Soviet proposal, of course, is conditioned on preventing American deployment of any effective defense against ballistic missiles, although some degree of research in exotic defense technologies presumably would be permitted.

When the sub-limits and other unpublished provisions of the Soviet proposal become available, it is likely that the USSR would be able to keep at least 3,500 hard target warheads in its arsenal, or enough to insure high confidence attacks on American ICBM silos and other hard targets as the follow-on to the SS-18 is deployed. With total arsenal limits in the 6,500 to 8,000 warhead range, however, the Soviets would have to forego their traditional requirements for both high confidence attacks on all soft targets and large reserves. Depending on the size and mix of the proposed arsenal, the USSR might be able to satisfy one of these criteria but not both.

In SALT I the Soviets were able to stop American ABM deployments, without imposing any real limits on their own strategic offensive missile arsenal. To block SDI, they just might be willing to pay a price. On the other hand, there evidently exist "Catch-22" provisions that have not been fully reported.[15]

Eurasian Theater Balance in the 1980s

As previously noted, despite the renewal of negotiations on theater nuclear forces in March 1985, the Soviets will probably maintain a clear margin of strategic nuclear-force superiority in the Eurasian TVDs. Barring violent disintegration of their East European empire, USSR ground forces will also maintain superiority over comparable NATO troops through the 1980s. Soviet frontal aviation is no longer an inferior force. Technological lags are disappearing rapidly, and Warsaw Pact tactical air forces have a substantial quantitative margin.

Soviet and Warsaw Pact air defenses for support of ground force operations against NATO are much larger than their counterparts, and the USSR has a great deal of R&D and production momentum in advanced tactical air defenses. Its air-defense interceptor technology is not as good as NATO's best, although advanced USSR models are well along in testing. Late-model SAMs are probably as good as anything developed by NATO (except for Patriot and, perhaps, Roland), and, again, the USSR has several new systems in development such as the SA-X-12 low-to-high-altitude missile that can intercept tactical ballistic missiles. NATO has no counterpart to the SA-X-12. Soviet tactical nuclear inferiority is also a thing of the past. With the deployment of the SS-21, SS-22, and SS-23 battlefield missile systems, the acquisition of nuclear artillery, and continued improvements in frontal aviation, the balance has shifted to the East. Moreover, these new tactical missile systems are now accurate enough to be effective with conventional, as well as nuclear, munitions. USSR chemical-warfare capabilities are so far superior to those of the United States or NATO—thanks in no small part to the equipping and training of Soviet troops for survival in a chemical-warfare environment—that any discussion of the subject is superfluous.

Summary of Soviet Advantages and Disadvantages in Strategic Competition with the United States and NATO in the 1980s

USSR Advantages.   The Soviets will be able to maintain effective strategic counterforce capabilities in all TVDs unless the U.S. protects its ICBMs with multiple silos and ballistic missile defenses. If the government had proceeded with President Carter's mobile MX deployment scheme, the country would have run out of desert in which to build shelters long before the Soviets ran out of warheads with which to target them.

Except for SDI, currently programmed American strategic defensive forces present no challenge to USSR objectives. At the same time, the Soviets are making a major effort to acquire strategic defenses to negate U.S. strategic offensive forces. The margin of USSR advantage in strategic defenses will depend on development of four factors: (1) the USSR's capability to detect and track American SSBNs; (2) the capability to defend its airspace against U.S. cruise missiles; (3) whether or not it breaks out of the ABM Treaty in the late 1980s; and (4) how far along the Soviets are in developing their own SDI. Development and production-momentum appears to place the USSR in a much better position to deploy ground-based ABM defenses nationwide than the United States, which no longer has the R&D and production infrastructure to support national deployment of such defenses before the end of this decade. On the other hand, SDI poses a major challenge to the Soviets for the reasons already stated.

The USSR will maintain and improve its capabilities to defeat and disarm NATO forces and occupy Western Europe relatively intact. Soviet prospects for decoupling a nuclear war with NATO Europe from an intercontinental exchange with the United States will probably continue to improve. USSR military superiority will continue to strengthen the centrifugal forces in Western Europe and to encourage the disintegration of domestic political support for adequate military forces in NATO countries.

Trade with the West and access to loans and credits were essential factors in the financing of the Soviet military buildup during the 1970s. West European dependence on the trade that continues to finance USSR defense programs makes this part of NATO more susceptible to pressures by Moscow. If economic relations with Europe and the United States continue to expand during the last half of the 1980s, as they did in the SALT era, the crisis stemming from the growing military burden on the Soviet economy will be postponed.

Although it is unusually expensive, the USSR has a comprehensive, well-conceived military strategy. Soviet decisionmaking on weapons acquisition remains orderly, consistent, increasingly prescient, and rational. The military-economic infrastructure is relatively efficient, although it is enormous and well organized. In R&D production-momentum over the short term, USSR advantages almost preclude comparison because of the deterioration of the American military-industrial infrastructure since the Vietnam war.

Soviet Disadvantages.   The USSR will also have a number of comparative strategic disadvantages vis-à-vis the United States and NATO during the late

1980s. Coupled with other problems, the growing military burden on the Soviet economy could bring growth to a halt in the 1990s. USSR access to Western markets, loans, and credits is critical to the timing of the impending Soviet economic crisis, unless Moscow reverses the long-term emphasis in its economic priorities from military to civilian uses. No one in the West can predict with any confidence the political consequences of a zero economic growth in the USSR.

In addition to the military burden, the Soviets face a number of persistent and relatively intractable socioeconomic problems. Despite the increasing share of domestic capital investment allocated to agriculture since the early 1960s, farming remains a periodic disaster area. Growth in the USSR labor force, which fueled much of the country's rise to its position as the second-ranking economic power in the world, has virtually ceased. Ethnic Russians will soon become a minority in the Soviet domestic empire. The cost of maintaining relative self-sufficiency in most basic industrial materials is rising rapidly. Since at least the late 1950s centralized planning has ceased to be an economic stimulus.

Barring revolutionary changes in the communist leadership, the USSR faces a two-front military threat and has, in China, a potent ideological competitor for the allegiance of Third World leftists and revolutionary movements. Moreover, keeping Eastern Europe in line will not be easy. In addition to the political and military problems throughout the "socialist camp," the Soviets are ill prepared to assume the hard-currency debts of Poland or any other client state.

The military fields in which the USSR will be least able to compete with the United States and NATO during the 1980s (if the latter choose to compete) are those in which the Soviets are placing most of their efforts and the United States and NATO the least: strategic defenses—air, missile, space, and ASW. This generalization appears to be particularly applicable to space-based ABM defenses. The Strategic Defense Initiative threatens to upset the USSR's game plan; hence, the accusations that it is a "first strike" weapon, and the current attempt to bargain SDI away at the negotiations in Geneva.

WESTERN PERCEPTIONS OF SOVIET MOTIVATIONS

This book opened with a quotation from former Vice-President Walter Mondale on his puzzlement over USSR behavior. The perennial difficulties that U.S. defense intellectuals also have had in understanding this problem is well illustrated by the following excerpt from former Secretary of Defense Harold Brown's last posture statement: [16]

The Soviets, regrettably, do not make it entirely clear to what extent they share the limitations we have set on the goals of our strategic programs. On the other hand, they accept the Anti-Ballistic Missile Treaty and negotiated SALT II—with all the restrictions imposed by these agreements—which assist our maintenance of a balanced, second-strike offensive capability that has a high probability of reaching its targets. On the other hand, the improvements they have made in their ICBMs, their continued emphasis on anti-bomber, anti-missile, and strategic anti-submarine defenses, together with their ongoing civil defense program, can be seen as a concerted effort to take away the effectiveness of our second-strike forces.

In the view of the coauthors of this volume, the USSR always made it clear that it never shared (and does not currently share) the "limitations we have set on the goals of our strategic programs"—both before and since the SALT-START process. Moreover, the contradiction posed by Secretary Brown is only part of the total "contradiction" that, from Moscow's point of view, is not a contradiction at all but simply prudent policy. To understand that the Soviets do not share our goals, one only has to read what they have said, look at what they have done, and observe the trend in their national priorities.

The statements that the Soviets have repeatedly made about their military doctrine, strategy, and objectives in a nuclear war constitute the opposite from official U.S. views on these issues. About the only areas of agreement between the United States and the USSR are (1) that nuclear war is not "totally inevitable" and (2) that neither superpower wants to initiate such a war, although neither side trusts the other on this point. Beyond this, the differences between Soviet and American strategic force goals and objectives could not be more starkly clear. There is nothing murky about what the USSR has said. Even though Soviet writings contain code words for certain objectives, such as pre-emption, and the USSR engages in deception at the highest levels, when assessed in the context of all Soviet literature on nuclear war, both the code words and the deception are relatively rare and quite obvious.

The objectives toward which the Soviets are striving also seem clear. USSR forces have been designed—before and after SALT—to "take away the effectiveness" of American "second strike forces." This is what the SS-9; the SS-18; the SS-19; the interceptors, radars, and SAMs of the air defenses; the navy's ASW forces; and the civil defense program are all about. These forces are all designed to limit damage to the USSR so that it may survive and "win" a nuclear war, which means that the "effectiveness" of U.S "second strike forces" must be reduced to zero if possible. Within the limits of Soviet economic and technological constraints, and subject to perceptions of U.S. and NATO military capabilities, the USSR has consistently fielded forces designed to thwart Western objectives (that is, to inflict "unacceptable levels of damage") and to achieve its own objectives (that is, to defeat the enemy and occupy Western Europe while limiting damage to facilitate survival and recovery). As Secretary Brown noted, USSR armies, air forces, strategic missiles, and aircraft have been built up to levels far beyond what is required to defend the Warsaw Pact against NATO or to enforce traditional American concepts of nuclear deterrence.[17]

The slow but steady shift in Soviet national priorities to the military since the late 1950s is in many ways the ultimate proof of the seriousness with which the USSR pursues its war-fighting, war-winning, and damage-limiting objectives. High rates of economic growth have been priority objectives of the Soviet leadership for decades. Relinquishing these goals to finance the military buildup should be the loudest and clearest message of what the USSR is up to.

Perhaps the objectives of weapons system development and deployment—like Soviet concepts of military doctrine and strategy—are difficult for certain U.S. policymakers to understand because they are so obviously different from their American counterparts. Given the traditional Russian penchant for secrecy, however, it is difficult to specify what more the USSR could have done to make its objectives clear to the West.

Clearly, the arms race continues unabated on the Soviet side—even when the United States tries to pull out. In the expectation that the USSR would follow suit, beginning in the late 1960s the United States tried to moderate the arms competition for more than a decade by practicing unilateral restraint and by designing forces to fit our own strategic concepts. This approach simply did not work. American MIRVs were deliberately designed to be ineffective against Soviet silos. On the other hand, SS-18 and SS-19 MIRVs were produced for maximum effectiveness against American silos. With the help of U.S. precision machine tools, the USSR achieved the design objectives for these ICBMs. After the ABM Treaty had been signed, the United States dismantled most of its air defenses. The Soviets have been working feverishly to improve their own air defenses and to acquire the technology required for an effective ABM system.

It is commonplace in the West to draw a historical analogy between the USSR and Nazi Germany—as totalitarian regimes bent on aggression. This is a favorite comparison, used by many "hawks" (in all seasons) and by some "doves" on those occasions—like the invasion of Afghanistan—when Soviet conduct does not conform to the expectations of their conventional wisdom. Such analogies are justified in some respects but remain, on the whole, dangerously fallacious.

Both the USSR and Nazi Germany have represented expansionist dictatorial systems. Hitler's "rotten democracies" and the Soviets' "imperialist beasts" both refer to the United States[18] and its principal allies. In the use of military power, however, these two mainstream examples of twentieth-century industrialized totalitarianism—as distinct from the more traditional forms of authoritarianism that prevail in most Third World countries—are radically different. Hitler wanted war—at least on some occasions—to the consternation of most of his professional military advisors. The men in the Kremlin have a more patient and subtle approach. As the invasion of Afghanistan has demonstrated, the Soviet Union is willing to "defend the conquests of socialism" before they are lost. Afghanistan, however, is a small-scale military operation that carries virtually no risk of a Western military response. The international penalties have been minimal: partial boycott of the 1980 Moscow Olympics and a brief U.S. grain trade embargo, followed by record American grain sales to the USSR. In most cases, however, the Soviets prefer to let others fight their battles for them. An abundance of volunteers exists: militant interventionists and fomenters of anti-Western revolutions (such as Castro's followers in Latin America); blatant aggressors set on creating their own regional empires (such as the rulers in Hanoi and Qaddafi supporters in the Middle East); and leaders of numerous other revolutionary movements, some of which are based on understandable grievances. Beyond these actors, most of whom are diplomatically recognized, stand the ever-increasing number of groups that learned from Hanoi's complete conquest of the territory formerly known as Indochina that international terrorism does pay.

Overt military aggression against the United States and NATO is the least likely Soviet course of action. The USSR has achieved a margin of military superiority over the West and will try to improve this advantage. However, its objective will not be to meet some timetable for a future war. Unlike those in the U.S. who consider superiority a meaningless concept in the nuclear age, the Soviets perceive three great advantages in having what they call "quantitative and qualitative superiority in forces and weapons." First, military superiority makes the USSR feel more secure and less threatened by a possible United States or NATO attack or an intervention in the internal affairs of the "socialist camp." Second, military superiority strengthens Soviet foreign policy in its endless campaigns to break up the North Atlantic Alliance. Third, strategic superiority constitutes a safe-conduct pass for doing what the USSR considers its duty—that is, aiding and abetting "national liberation" and other revolutionary movements throughout the Third World. Thus, there is no need for a Hitler-type timetable.

In the Soviet view, the "worldwide correlation of forces"—political, military, and economic—has steadily shifted in favor of the USSR since World War II. Moscow expects this trend to continue. Consequently, it has

great expectations of exploiting the "internal contradictions" in the "imperialist camp" by the political use of Soviet military superiority. Economic
relations with the "imperialists," like gas pipeline deals that are financed
and equipped by NATO countries, will make Western Europe even more de-
pendent on Moscow's energy supplies and provide the hard-currency earn-
ings needed to finance an even greater margin of USSR military superiority.

According to the Soviets, deterrence will become more stable as Moscow improves its capabilities to fight, survive, and recover from a nuclear
war. The risk of an unprovoked surprise attack on the United States or
NATO will probably remain low. Continued growth of USSR deterrent capabilities (as the Soviets define them) may increase other risks, however. Historically, the more Moscow has perceived the United States or NATO to be
deterred by its power, the more it has felt free to provide diplomatic support
and material aid to "wars of national liberation" and other armed revolutionary movements. This could increase the incidence and intensity of con-
frontations between the two superpowers and their allies in many areas of
the world. Miscalculations in such circumstances might lead to the nuclear
war that both sides seek to avoid.

Two other foreseeable conditions exist that might lead the USSR to
precipitate a nuclear showdown with the United States and NATO. First,
should the balance of forces move too far in the USSR's favor, the Soviets
might be tempted to accelerate history along its appointed course by military action. Second, the day may come when Moscow perceives the "correlation of forces" to be shifting away from itself. In the 1990s the military
burden, coupled with other endemic problems, might slow economic
growth to zero. If the USSR foresaw that its relative position vis-à-vis the
United States or NATO might deteriorate for some time, it could be tempted
to take military action.

At the beginning of the second half of the 1980s the Soviets have not
only achieved a margin of nuclear superiority after three decades of inferiority but also possess a superior military establishment that is fully integrated with their foreign policy and their arms-control negotiations. In the
near future the United States will be forced to devise an equally good or
better strategy to counter the USSR effectively. Too many policymakers, and
those influencing policy, in the West are still carrying around the intellectual
baggage of the "mutual assured destruction" concept, which has been de-
funct for a decade or more. Given the relative neglect of American weapons
procurement during the 1970s, it would be desirable to buy more of almost
everything for several years to come. In the long run, however, throwing
money at the problem is no solution. To ensure U.S. security and, equally
important, the security of our allies, the United States must have a strategy
to deny USSR war-fighting objectives. Arms-control negotiations must be-

come instrumental, rather than adversarial, to American national security policy. The Strategic Defense Initiative could be a step in the direction of a new, coherent Western strategy, although sharing SDI research findings with the USSR would be foolhardy indeed. Finally, the United States and its principal allies must recognize that, in effect, the Soviets are waging a new kind of economic warfare against the West.

Appendix:
SALT in Soviet Military Policy—Narrowing the Widening Gap

Some observers have argued that the USSR military was forced into SALT by its political leadership.[1] When Secretary of State Cyrus Vance took new American proposals to Moscow in early 1977, the press reported that he had attempted to present them directly to Brezhnev and to circumvent the Ministry of Defense—the putative bureaucratic opponent of SALT agreements. Other analysts have contended that without the U.S. decision to deploy ABM defenses in the late 1960s, there would have been no first agreement.[2]

"Let us not forget that it was only after the Senate had voted, by a majority of one, for the Nixon ABM program that the Russians agreed to the opening of SALT. Indeed there might have been no SALT if America had unilaterally decided against ballistic missile defenses."[3] This statement suggests that some Soviet leader(s) or interest group(s) believed that the USSR had to enter SALT to stop U.S. ABM deployments and that their arguments carried the day. If so, were these leader(s) or group(s) in the political or military establishment (or both), and what was the nature of their arguments?

This Appendix has two basic theses. First, the Soviet military establishment supported SALT II to stop American ABM deployments, which were viewed as a major potential shift in the "correlation of forces" against the USSR. Second, the SALT I agreements not only stopped American ABM deployments but also gave diplomatic cover to MIRV programs designed to provide the damage-limiting capabilities the Soviets had not been able to achieve in the 1980s.

WHY THE TURNABOUT ON ABM DEFENSES?

Basic changes in policies and positions are not made casually in the USSR. When there is a turning point (*povorot*) in the party line, weighty considerations have been involved. The reversal in official Soviet views on ABM defenses between 1967 and the SALT I negotiations can be compared in significance to the one that brought about the Nazi-Soviet pact some three decades earlier.

Prior to SALT the USSR took the position that limiting defensive weapons in general, and ABM in particular, could not represent a legitimate subject for strategic arms control negotiations. Offensive weapons kill and destroy; defensive weapons protect people and property. It was as simple as that. Therefore, the problem centered on offensive weapons.

During a visit to Great Britain in February 1967, then Prime Minister Aleksei Kosygin stated the Soviet position on ABM as follows: [4]

> Which weapons should be regarded as a tension factor—offensive or defensive weapons? I think that a defensive system, which prevents attack, is not a cause of the arms race but represents a factor preventing the death of people. Some persons reason thus: Which is cheaper, to have offensive weapons that can destroy cities and entire states or to have defensive weapons that can prevent this destruction? At present the theory is current in some places that one should develop whichever system is cheaper. Such "theoreticians" argue also about how much it costs to kill a person, $500,000 or $100,000. An anti-missile system may cost more than an offensive one, but it is intended not for killing people but for saving human lives. I understand that I am not answering the question that was put to me [on the possibility of an ABM moratorium—M.D.] but you can draw appropriate conclusions yourselves.

The Soviet prime minister remained unpersuaded about the "destabilizing" nature of ABM by Defense Secretary Robert S. McNamara's lectures at the June 1967 meeting with President Lyndon B. Johnson at Glassboro, New Jersey. In a subsequent television interview, Kosygin essentially repeated what he had said in February: [5]

> As regards an anti-missile system, our position is well known. We believe that the discussions should center not on merely the problem of an anti-missile system. Because, after all, the anti-missile system is not a weapon of aggression, of attack; it is a defensive system. And we feel therefore that what should be considered is the entire complex of armaments and disarmament questions.

Because, otherwise, if—instead of building and deploying an anti-ballistic missile system—the money is used to build up offensive missile systems, mankind will not stand to gain anything. It will, on the contrary, face a still greater menace and will come still closer to war. And we therefore are in favor of considering the whole range of questions relating to arms and disarmament, and we're ready to discuss that question—the general question of disarmament.

Yet when the SALT I talks began two years later, the USSR showed little interest in limiting offensive weapons. The Soviet objective was to ban the ABM. Understanding the reasons for this *povorot* is crucial to comprehending the relationship between the SALT process and USSR military policy. It also represents an explanation for the Soviet reaction to the U.S. Strategic Defense Initiative at the present time.

To understand the Soviet approach to SALT, it is necessary to recall what was said about concepts of deterrence in Chapter 3. Kremlin political and military leaders have a one-dimensional view of deterrence: The USSR and its allies must deter the United States and NATO from a nuclear attack. By definition, however, the latter have no need to deter the USSR. Consequently, the Soviets do not view deterrence as a mutual condition that is stable under conditions of approximate parity in strategic forces. They seek superiority to deter the "imperialists" and to achieve "victory" if deterrence fails. Conversely, any change in the military balance of forces in favor of the United States and NATO weakens deterrence and increases the risk of war. As will be shown, in the late 1960s the Soviet military perceived American ABM deployments as a potential major shift in the strategic balance in favor of the United States. This is the key to the *povorot* in policy on ABM defenses—from Kosygin's statements in 1967 to the USSR position at the beginning of the SALT I negotiations.

INSTITUTIONAL ACTORS IN SALT POLICY FORMATION

In this section a brief look at Soviet actors in the SALT process will be followed by an examination of how USSR military leaders in 1968–69 viewed the prospective balance of forces and what conclusions they may have drawn about their own interests in SALT. A comprehensive survey of the institutions involved in the SALT process has appeared in print.[6] Information is limited, of course, because the Soviets have not revealed much about the individuals or government agencies involved. In trying to establish who does what on SALT issues in the USSR, one must keep in mind two facts.

First, decisionmaking on weapons acquisition is highly centralized in a few organizations—the Defense Council, the Politburo, the Central Committee Secretariat, and the Military Industrial Commission—even if other organizations (the Ministry of Defense, the military-industrial agencies, and their design bureaus) participate in the process.

Second, compartmentalization of information is extremely strict in the USSR. Ministry of Foreign Affairs personnel, who ostensibly headed the Soviet delegation during the SALT negotiations, were not cleared for information on their own weapons programs (data that is available to any American citizen willing to take the time to read the open literature on this subject in the United States).[7] Gromyko did not become a member of the Politburo until 1973, so it is difficult to believe that his foreign ministry played any significant role in formulating Soviet objectives before entering into the SALT process during 1968–69. In fact, probably no one in the foreign ministry at that time knew enough about USSR armed forces to participate in policy formulation. Indeed, it has been reported that the four or five foreign ministry officials in the disarmament group "occup[ied] themselves more with Arabian fairy tales" than with serious matters.[8]

In the SALT II negotiations, Gromyko did play an active role, especially during the latter part. Since becoming a Politburo member, he has probably had access to the detailed information on Soviet missiles needed to negotiate. It is unlikely, however, that this type of access is widespread in the foreign ministry even now. If this is so, it illustrates the point that neither the ministry staff nor Gromyko had much to do with the USSR decision to enter into SALT negotiations and probably had nothing to do with formulating Soviet negotiating objectives.

Most of the functions performed by "think tanks" in formulating defense policy in the United States are performed in the USSR by the professors at the General Staff, Frunze, and other senior service academies. These faculties are composed of military officers; some seem to spend most of their careers in teaching and research; others rotate—usually at relatively long intervals—between the Ministry of Defense and the academies. Presumably, the defense ministry, supported by the academy faculties, does a great deal of the initial staff work that eventually becomes the party's military policy. And presumably the Central Committee's defense industry department performs similar staff work.

Bureaucratic and personal politics play a large role in the process of preparing the staff work and transmitting it to the top leaders, who have ideas of their own on major issues. Nevertheless, for access to the necessary information, trained analysts, and bureaucratic functions, the Ministry of Defense and the Central Committee's defense industry department appear to be the organizations that the Defense Council and Politburo primarily depend upon in making policy on issues affecting Soviet military forces.

People like General Major Anureev, Colonel General Lomov, and their collaborators—not to mention more senior officers, such as the late Marshals Sokolovskii and Zakharov or former chief-of-staff Ogarkov—would have no trouble holding their own, intellectually and analytically, with the best and brightest analysts in the United States. The Ministry of Defense also probably has research institutes staffed in whole or in part by civilians, but little or nothing is known about such organizations.

It is unlikely that the other institutions involved have carried much weight in formulating SALT policy. Vladimir S. Semenov, a deputy minister of foreign affairs, headed the delegation, but his lack of background and information on the weapons systems limited him to "political cues" (although he was evidently privy to "back channel" negotiations kept from the American delegation).[9] Virtually the only members of the USSR Council of Ministers who have access to the information required for participating in policy formulation are those who are also members of the Politburo, the Defense Council, or the Military Industrial Commission (VPK). Academician A. N. Shchukin was a member of the SALT delegation because of his personal position and activities—not because the Academy of Sciences per se plays an important role in formulating strategic arms control policy.[10]

Therefore, Soviet policy and objectives in SALT were decided upon by the same individuals and institutions in the Politburo, Defense Council, Central Committee, and VPK who formulate USSR military doctrine and strategy, make the decisions on which weapons are to be developed and what quantities are to be produced, manage and monitor the programs after the decisions have been made, and insure that the necessary resources are provided by the economy. It would not be surprising if these persons designed their SALT policy objectives to achieve the military capabilities and the kind of strategic relationship with the United States that they had been trying to attain for many years before SALT.

Brezhnev's personal role in SALT and his understanding of strategic weaponry should not be underestimated for two reasons. First, as noted earlier, command of Soviet strategic missiles and aircraft is vested in the top political leadership. In wartime, Brezhnev would have been commander in chief. The military establishment advises and implements, although the political leaders decide the objectives of strategic operations.[11] In a very real sense, SALT represented the Politburo's, not the defense ministry's, strategic forces. Second, as discussed earlier, both Brezhnev and Ustinov were present at the creation of Soviet missile forces during the late 1940s and the 1950s.[12] In 1969 Brezhnev and the other senior party civilians on the Defense Council knew that the capabilities of their forces fell short of the missions assigned them and that it would take at least two more five-year plans before capabilities could begin to catch up with requirements.

Although immediate agreement may not have been achieved among all the concerned parties in Moscow, the Soviets perceived SALT as a means of furthering most of the policies they had been pursuing for some time. The probable basic bureaucratic procedures for formulating and executing USSR military policy objectives in the negotiations are outlined below:

- Within the Ministry of Defense, the General Staff, the faculties of senior academies, and the staffs of the service branches did most of the analysis and staff work and wrote the drafts of recommended policies and options.

- The Ministry of Defense reached an internal consensus and forwarded its position to the Central Committee's Secretariat (most likely to the defense industry department).

- The Secretariat reviewed the Ministry of Defense paper and, after making its own comments or recommendations, forwarded it to the Defense Council.

- The Defense Council debated and decided, but its decisions were probably subject to a Politburo consensus. If serious dissent existed among the military, the Defense Council made the final decisions.

- When the Politburo reached a consensus, the VPK probably served as the principal executive organ directing the Soviet delegation and performed necessary coordination on a daily basis.

- At critical points, major issues went back to the Defense Council for compromises or alternative proposals. Again, decisions were probably subject to a Politburo consensus.

John Newhouse has provided some insight into the role of the VPK and the competence of its chairman. At the May 1972 summit meeting in Moscow—in which the final issues of the ABM Treaty and the Interim Agreement were negotiated—L. V. Smirnov, the VPK chairman, "did most of the talking from his side of the table." Newhouse also provides additional information on how the U.S. and USSR approaches differed. United States delegates were surprised to find themselves negotiating with Smirnov, "a man whom the Americans had never seen and didn't expect to see . . . He came right out of the blue . . . Unlike anyone else on either side of the table, Smirnov had a technician's grasp of the issue. Kissinger, Sonnenfeldt, and Hyland, while fully familiar with the ins and outs of SLBMs, were political animals."[13] Why the Americans did not expect to see the top manager of the Soviet strategic weapons programs, whose future they were negotiating, is a minor mystery that explains a great deal about SALT. Clearly, the unexpected USSR negotiator knew what he was doing.

SOVIET ESTIMATE OF THE "CORRELATION" OF STRATEGIC FORCES IN 1968–69

To better appreciate the way in which the Ministry of Defense may have viewed the military "correlation of forces" between the two superpowers, we will examine (1) a Soviet method for measuring the military "correlation of forces" between the two superpowers at the time; (2) some statements published in mid-1969 that appear to provide unique insight into the defense ministry's approach to SALT; and (3) the status of USSR strategic offensive and defensive forces when SALT began and the prospects for those forces to compete with the United States during the 1970s.

Methodology for a Soviet Net Assessment

In 1967 a senior faculty member at the General Staff Academy, I. I. Anureev, published a methodology for analyzing strategic force relationships. His approach may be summarized as follows:[14]

- Quantitative comparisons of strategic nuclear forces should be made in terms of the combat capabilities of comparable weapons systems.
- Since the performance effectiveness of systems and forces depends on C^3 (command, control, communications) and a number of qualitative factors, these should be quantified as well.
- The essential parameters of the analysis for both sides include:
  1. quantities of weapons of comparable types,
  2. capabilities to inflict damage on counterpart enemy systems and other targets,
  3. system vulnerabilities (a) at launch and (b) to enemy defenses after launch,
  4. capability and reliability of C^3 systems,
  5. capabilities of electronic countermeasures, and
  6. contribution of support systems and activities.
- For any given set of strategic force postures (numbers and characteristics) time and the effectiveness of enemy defenses are critical fac-

tors in determining force capabilities and the correlation of forces as the outcome of an exchange.

- The objective of strategic nuclear operations is to change the correlation of forces in one's own favor by destroying as many of the enemy's delivery systems as possible before they are launched and by maintaining a successful defense against the remainder. Optimal attacks are those that achieve this objective with an economy of means, that is, forces.

- Equivalent megatonnage is used as the common denominator for measuring surviving forces, but it is recognized that this measure has meaning only when the qualitative factors and characteristics of the delivery systems are taken into account.

The bottom line of Anureev's methodology was to limit damage to the USSR. That is, it sought to determine how much of the enemy's strategic forces could survive attacks and penetrate Soviet defenses and how much damage the penetrators could inflict on the USSR. If these military analysts in Moscow applied this two-sided, offensive-defensive damage-limiting model, which recognized the importance of time and qualitative factors to the superpower balance during the late 1960s, they would have foreseen a drastic shift in favor of the United States in the 1970s. The chief defect of this approach involved the measurement of equivalent megatonnage, which has little or no relevance to USSR measures of strategic missile effectiveness.

Anureev's article appears to contain the only mention of equivalent megatonnage ever to appear in *Military Thought*, and it is rarely mentioned in other Soviet literature. Moreover, the translated version of Anureev's equation contains an error that, in effect, leads to the conclusion that MIRVs do not increase the effectiveness of strategic ballistic missiles. Whatever the source of the error in the translated equation, USSR planners obviously reached the correct conclusions about the advantages of MIRVs.[15]

Capabilities and Prospects for Soviet Strategic Offensive Forces in the Late 1960s

No elaborate computerized quantitative analysis is needed to reconstruct the current and prospective balance between USSR and U.S. strategic ballistic missile forces as it probably appeared to Anureev or to any other military analyst who examined the strategic "correlation of forces" in the late 1960s according to a similar methodology. Even without American deployment of ABM defenses, an effective Soviet counterforce capability was a decade in the future.

In the absence of ABM defenses, the new family of MIRVed ICBMs that had been under development since the mid-1960s would provide the capability to attack all the Minuteman silos and to complete coverage of soft targets in the Transoceanic TVD. At the same time, the Soviets probably realized that effectiveness against these silos would be limited until the late 1970s or early 1980s, when CEPs could be reduced to between 200 and 300 meters. By 1968 General Colonel Zheltov, commandant of the Lenin Political-Military Academy, believed that the United States had decided to protect its ICBM silos with the Nike-X ABM. He did not report any quantitative estimates for the effectiveness of these defenses against Soviet missiles, but his remarks about the drastic consequences of removing the "invulnerability" from ballistic missiles attacking enemy missile launchers indicate that the USSR thought Nike-X would be effective.[16]

If the United States were able to defend its silos, Soviet ICBM deployments scheduled for the 1970s would not ensure SRF capabilities to perform their primary damage-limiting mission in the Transoceanic TVD. Some combination of additional missiles and another generation or two of MIRVs would be required. Achieving USSR counterforce capabilities against American ICBMs would require at least two more decades instead of one and might not be consummated at all.

If the United States had deployed a national ABM system, the same problems would have applied to Soviet soft-target objectives. As demonstrated in Chapter 8, the USSR was unable to satisfy its soft-target requirements in the Transoceanic TVD until 1980, and it still does not possess sufficient ready reserves. Consequently, even at 50 percent effectiveness, American ballistic-missile defense deployments in the late 1960s through the early 1970s would have prevented the Soviets from attaining their strategic nuclear targeting requirements against the continental United States for another two decades or so.

Zheltov also noted the ABM potential of laser technology and the military utility of a "cosmoplane," apparently a reference to the Soviet space plane now being flight tested.[17] He tied the future capabilities of USSR armed forces for defeating any aggressor to the successful development of these advanced technologies. In 1970 the Soviets published a handbook on ballistic missile design that discussed detailed design criteria and procedures at great length.[18] The design criteria represent rational military planning—not bureaucratic happenstance or a pursuit of technology for its own sake. Ballistic missiles are designed to destroy certain types of targets that are specified by assigned military missions. The strategy and tactics of missile employment against these targets are "in accordance with the accepted military doctrine."[19]

This missile design handbook specified penetration of ABM defenses as one factor in estimating missile system effectiveness. Because of their lag in ABM technology, however, the Soviets could not even test their missiles against Nike-X defenses. Consequently, in the late 1960s and early 1970s USSR missile designers, the Ministry of Defense, and the VPK could certify all of the other characteristics of their missiles—payload, accuracy, reliability, range—but could not have certified ABM penetration factors.[20] Moreover, it would be the late 1970s, at best, before the Soviets could provide the requisite ABM technology against which to test the capabilities of their missiles to penetrate such defenses.

In the absence of any ability to conduct realistic tests against Nike-X defenses, the USSR could have relied on the exhaustion of defensive interceptors. If knowledge about the number of defensive missiles is precise, this constitutes the only high-confidence approach. But in 1968–69 exhaustion was not a practical option for Soviet planners, because it would take most of the ICBM force that could be fielded in the 1970s (without losses to U.S. counterforce strikes) to exhaust full-scale Nike-X defenses.[21]

In the absence of American ABM defenses in 1968–69, the USSR view of the current and prospective situation for strategic offensive forces probably looked roughly like this:

> • In the 1970s coverage of all soft targets in the Eurasian TVDs had been completed; it could be modernized by replacing the aging SS-4 and SS-5 MR/IRBMs either with a new mobile IRBM or with hardened ICBMs, or both.
> • The immediate problem posed by French IRBMs and hangarettes constructed at NATO airfields could be solved by deployment of SS-11 ICBMs in MRBM fields.[22]
> • In the absence of defenses, existing and new ICBMs would be able to cover all soft targets in the Transoceanic TVDs by the late 1970s. The growing fleet of SS-N-6 SLBMs and the new SS-N-8 would supplement coverage of soft targets and provide a secure reserve force.
> • Had the United States introduced American ABM defenses, however, all this would have changed. The improvements in effectiveness resulting from deployment of the SS-17, SS-18, and SS-19 would not be realizable for two decades or so—that is, until well into the mid- or late 1980s. The soft-target forces would also have been inadequate.

It is in the context of these lead time and effectiveness calculations that Soviet objectives in SALT were formulated.

Strategic Defenses

Strategic defenses, essential for limiting damage to the USSR and which constituted the bottom line of Anureev's method, were in relatively poor condition when SALT began. As noted, Soviet air defense was a decade or more from developing anything to cope with SRAM armed bombers penetrating at low altitude. The SA-10, the first strategic surface-to-air missile since the SA-5, would not be ready for deployment until the late 1970s. The same lead time applied to airborne control and interceptor radars having look-down-shoot-down capabilities. ASW forces would be numerically limited for many years, and the technology for locating American SSBNs still awaited several scientific "breakthroughs."

By 1968–69 the Soviets had probably lost whatever illusions they may have had about the ABM system deployed around Moscow. At best, this system could handle only a few, well-spaced-out attackers. Although the R&D on advanced antiballistic missiles was underway, the USSR needed ten to fifteen years to equal the United States in three essential components: (1) high-acceleration missiles of the Sprint type for endoatmospheric intercepts; (2) a small, high-performance phased-array radar similar to the American missile site radar (MSR) for local defenses; and (3) computer technology to process the radar signals and manage the battle. Nothing like the Nike-X system could be fielded by the Soviets until the 1980s. Finally, as previously noted, without something approximating Nike-X technology the USSR could not perform realistic tests on the capabilities of its own ICBMs and SLBMs to penetrate these defenses. In the late 1960s the navy's anticarrier forces were about the only component of Soviet strategic defenses whose capabilities were reasonably commensurate with requirements.

Net Assessment

To the USSR in 1968–69, the American MIRV program must have looked threatening, and the combination of ABM with MIRV, frightening. Even if they knew about the low yields of Minuteman and Poseidon warheads, the Soviets probably found it unbelievable that these missiles were not as accurate as U.S. technology could make them. Moscow probably still doubts that the United States deliberately engineered Minuteman III and Poseidon to be ineffective against hard targets.

The United States regarded an ABM that was only 50 percent effective as worthless; the Soviets probably did not share that view. If they had, they would have dismantled their entire air defense forces and stopped trying to build strategic ASW ships and submarines. To the USSR, the Nike-X system probably appeared to be considerably more than 50 percent effective—even against the MIRVs it would be able to deploy in the mid- and late 1970s.

In the Ministry of Defense's view, all of the gains in offensive capabilities against the Transoceanic TVD during the 1960s, and most of the gains expected for the 1970s, would be negated by American ABM defenses—even if these defenses had a high leakage rate. If viewed in terms of Anureev's damage-limiting balance sheet, the combination of MIRVs and ABM would have provided the United States with a great strategic advantage. Given Moscow's one-sided posture on deterrence, the American acquisition of a damage-limiting capability—in combination with the reduction of net USSR second-strike capabilities to the levels of the early 1960s—would have substantially increased the risk of a U.S. or NATO attack on the USSR. In such an event, if the United States had had an effective damage-limiting capability and the Soviets had not, Moscow would have had little or no chance of "victory." This was hardly a position from which Kremlin leaders would be confident of their deterrent, much less of their capability to fight and "win" a nuclear war.

There is evidence to support this analysis. In May 1969 *Military Thought* (a journal restricted to General Staff officers) carried an article by its editor stating that the possibility of war depended on a number of "political and military-technical factors. Of special importance here could be the disruption of the 'nuclear balance of power'" that might result from a sharp increase in the nuclear potential of one side or the other or from the acquisition of a "highly-effective means of protection from a nuclear attack of the enemy in conditions when the other side lags considerably in resolution of these missions." The author then asserted that if the nuclear balance were to change in favor of imperialism, "the danger of a nuclear war will increase many fold." [23]

Three principal inferences seem justified. First, like other Soviet writers, General Major Zemskov sees nuclear deterrence as one-sided rather than mutual; he stated as much earlier in the article. "Imperialism is counting mainly at the present time on a sudden nuclear strike" that could be carried out simultaneously against the USSR and other Warsaw Pact countries. (In other words, the danger of nuclear war lies entirely in actions that the United States or NATO may initiate.) Second, the ABM system that the Americans started to deploy in the late 1960s was, or had the potential to become, an effective defense. Third, deployment of an ABM would increase the danger of a nuclear attack on the Soviet Union. In the context of discussion, Zemskov stated: "Actually, as already has been noted, in modern conditions any variant of attack does not exclude destructive retaliatory operations of the other side. Therefore, in any conditions, measures must be taken which would exclude such an attack."[24] This same thesis—that is, that a prudent aggressor would be prepared to defend his country against the missiles that would survive his attack—had appeared in *Military Thought* a year earlier.[25] In other words, Zemskov's statements appear to be a cryptic summary of the implications of a prospective shift in the balance of forces against the USSR in 1968–69, as reconstructed in prior sections of this chapter.

Zemskov's article was published one year after the Soviets had agreed to participate in SALT I and about six months before the first formal session. To fully appreciate the change in the traditional USSR attitude about antiballistic missile defenses, it is necessary to go back some two years for Prime Minister Kosygin's previously cited statements. ABM defenses are not weapons of aggression; offensive weapons pose the threat to mankind. In 1967 this attitude toward antiballistic missile defenses was still prevalent. Zemskov's statements two years later were quite out of character. Something must have happened to cause such a basic change. Why did banning ABM deployments become the first Soviet priority as soon as the SALT I negotiations started?

Clearly, it was not conversion to the U.S. declaratory policy of mutual assured destruction (MAD) that caused the USSR to view American ABM defenses as intolerably dangerous. The most likely explanation is that sometime in 1967–68 Moscow conducted an appraisal of its own strategic prospects for the 1970s along the lines outlined above. Using Anureev's method, or a similar one, the USSR concluded that the future would be grim indeed if the United States were to continue on its course. Only the defense ministry (or some combination with the VPK and the defense apparatus in the Central Committee) had access to both the necessary classified information on Soviet forces and the analytical tools to conduct this appraisal. Once the appraisal had been made, these were the only organizations that could draft the policy options. And only the Defense Council or Politburo could decide which policy to follow so that SALT might be used to extricate the USSR from its extremely unfavorable position.[26]

PROBABLE SOVIET OBJECTIVES IN SALT I

If this is a reasonable explanation for Zemskov's statements on the danger of American ABM deployments, then the USSR military could not have been more hostile to SALT than the Pentagon. It is more likely that, among the various bureaucracies, the Soviet military was most vociferous in urging the political leaders to enter negotiations to avert an impending adverse shift in the correlation of military forces. If so, the Ministry of Defense probably urged the Politburo to pursue the following objectives in the strategic arms limitation talks:

- Prohibit ABM defenses (or limit these defenses) so that, during either a pre-emptive or a second strike, the effect on Soviet strategic offensive force capabilities would be negligible.
- Place a limit on the number of U.S. MIRVed ICBM and SLBM launchers and Strategic Air Command bombers so that the Ministry of Defense would have a stable threat to plan against.
- Since the USSR would have to accept the same general constraints on the scope of ABM deployments—as well as on the number of strategic offensive missiles and bombers—as the United States, negotiate the launcher limits in such a manner that the development and deployment of the four MIRVed ICBMs, the SS-N-8, SLBMs, and the Backfire bomber could proceed as scheduled.
- Ensure that the USSR be permitted to deploy the large throw-weight missiles necessary to achieve an effective counterforce capability against American ICBMs.
- As a hedge against future U.S. counterforce capabilities, negotiate a large and secure reserve SLBM force.
- Make certain that most USSR Eurasian strategic forces are excluded from SALT but try to include U.S. and NATO tactical nuclear systems.
- Except for ABM defenses, exclude all other strategic defensive systems from consideration.
- Place no limits on R&D or funding of Soviet strategic systems.

To many readers, this may impute too much rationality to Soviet military planners. Actually, it only suggests prudent awareness of a far superior technology in the hands of the enemy; a propensity to believe in the effectiveness of defenses; due consideration for the long lead times necessary for advanced weapons system development; and straightforward calculations of force capabilities.

In retrospect, evidence of USSR interest in several of the postulated objectives appeared early in the negotiations. Specifically:

- Moscow wanted ABM defenses limited to low levels or to none at all. Henry Kissinger put it succinctly: "By 1970, when we had an

ABM program, however inadequate, it was the only subject the Soviet Union was willing to discuss with us in SALT." [27]

• Although both sides were willing to discuss numbers of weapons, the Soviets were much less willing to talk about MIRVs, improved support systems, and potential innovations.

• The USSR agreed that "strategic" systems included those that could strike the respective homelands of the two superpowers which had nothing to do with the operative Soviet definition of "strategic" missiles. [28] The USSR also pressed the United States to include U.S. tactical systems deployed abroad on the basis of this agreement. Although this approach was anticipated by a few observers, it took the American delegation by surprise. [29]

• As Newhouse notes, "the Soviets didn't negotiate seriously until they had established a big lead in the number of offensive missiles they possessed." [30] The United States made little effort to inhibit development of the SS-16, SS-17, SS-18, and SS-19 until late in the SALT I negotiations. The USSR, however, disregarded both the letter and the spirit of the U.S. unilateral declaration on the size of new "light" ICBMs.

Several years after the foregoing assessment of Soviet objectives in SALT I had been written, more issues of the General Staff's restricted monthly journal became available. The July 1971 number contained an article by one V. Dmitriev that seems pertinent to what went on in the USSR during SALT I and SALT II. The writer had made no known prior contributions to this periodical. Also, his article is apparently the only treatment of the relationship between military strategy and diplomacy to have appeared in *Military Thought* since World War II. The following points summarize the message: [31]

• Diplomacy and strategy have much in common. "Success in one area can create the preconditions for success in the other, and vice versa."

• "Since domestic policy is of primary significance for every societal system, *both diplomacy and military strategy constitute a continuation of the state's internal policy*, are organically linked with it, and pursue aims of support and strengthening of the given social system, seeking consolidation of the position of the given state within the system of states" (emphasis in the original).

• "Constituting a continuation of a nation's domestic policy in the area of relations with other countries, *diplomacy and strategy inevitably are of* a clearly expressed class character" (emphasis in the original). This statement is followed by the standard comment that the diplomacy of imperialist states is aimed at subjugating peoples, whereas the diplomacy of socialist states seeks peace and the self-determination of peoples.

• Two pertinent precepts from Lenin are cited. First, do everything possible to keep the imperialists from uniting against the USSR and "attract them to the side of the Soviet Union by the advantages of economic ties or to ensure their neutrality in potential conflicts." Second, strengthen the military power of the USSR and maintain a united military front against the imperialists.

• A historical survey of past Soviet diplomatic successes follows. *"In its foreign policy activities the party was always guided by Lenin's statement that diplomacy and military strategy are correct, powerful and produce positive results only when they are closely interlinked in direction, content, ultimate missions and goals."* (Emphasis added.)

• The roster of past successes used to support the argument included the Treaty of Brest-Litovsk, which ended World War I with Germany, Soviet success in persuading a number of small states not to join the Entente powers during the Russian civil war; the Treaty of Rapallo with Germany in 1922, which ended the united Western front in dealing with the USSR; and the 1939 Nazi-Soviet pact. The following observation is made about this last success: "It took a good deal of courage to explain to the peoples of the Soviet Union and the entire world why the USSR should conclude a nonaggression pact with such a country as Nazi Germany."

• "Military strategy, just as military science as a whole, is strong and correct only when it is built on careful consideration of all objective factors, in strict conformity with the tasks and capabilities of a state's foreign and domestic policy."

• "At certain periods in history diplomacy and military strategy may function as a means of foreign policy, accomplishing missions on the basis of interaction, that is, *diplomacy may settle by peaceful means matters pertaining to military strategy*, and vice versa." (Emphasis added.)

• "In spite of the fact that diplomacy accomplishes specific missions with its own special means, successful attainment of the stated objectives in the final analysis depends on *successful accomplishment of military-strategic missions*" (emphasis in the original). This statement is followed by a discussion of how Soviet military successes in the latter part of World War II caused a number of Germany's allies to defect and deterred Turkey and Japan from attacking the USSR.

• The last paragraph in the article opens with a statement that the socialist countries are taking full advantage of all technological opportunities to strengthen their defenses. It then states that "the increase in the role of political leadership in making decisions of a military-strategic character and in carrying out diplomatic activities in no way reduces the importance of military science and military strategy. Military strategy resolves all matters connected with consideration of all factors of a domestic and external category, planning of future military operations on this basis, and estimates of the capability of potential enemies."

It is often argued that Aesopian language has been used to communicate sensitive policy issues in the USSR. Although the above-cited article does not refer to SALT or to any other Soviet negotiations underway at the time, it does not appear to be Aesopian. When the writer tells his readers not to worry, the message is clear to Soviet readers: They will never be told the details of the SALT negotiations—at least not by their own government. As in the past, the party leaders were using the talks with the United States to help solve problems that strategy alone could not solve. Like previous negotiations and treaties, SALT represented an instrument of policy to strengthen the military power and security of the USSR.

The timing of Dmitriev's article may not have been entirely coincidental. The first half of 1971 happened to be a critical period in the SALT I negotiations (particularly the month of May, when both sides were setting the stage for the subsequent ABM Treaty).[32] The Interim Agreement on offensive forces quickly followed. By late 1970 or early 1971 the Defense Council and the Ministry of Defense had probably become confident of achieving what they wanted from SALT I.

The ABM Treaty and the Interim Agreement:
A Likely Soviet View

If the inferences outlined above represent a reasonable approximation of USSR objectives in SALT I, members of the Politburo, the Defense Council, the Central Committee, and the Ministry of Defense should have been pleased with the results. They had attained their goals at the price of only a few concessions that affected Soviet military programs. Indeed, the only limits conceded appear to have been largely offset by the acquisition of weaponry not constrained by either SALT I or SALT II.

No restraints on the Soviet's own military forces were required to achieve what they wanted most—a virtual ban on antiballistic missile defenses. Even if the Nixon administration had been wholly in favor of the ABM program, it would have been up against a Congress that was becoming increasingly reluctant to fund it. In fact, the U.S. administration was internally divided, and public opinion was shifting against the ABM. The "Safeguard" version of the original "Sentinel" deployment concept was more of a political move—designed to pacify American critics of any ABM deployments—than a technically and fiscally rational option.

The Interim Agreement on strategic offensive systems placed no restrictions upon the development of the SS-16, SS-17, SS-18, SS-19, and successor systems. The Soviets may have made two concessions on deployments: the 1,620-launcher ceiling for all ICBMs and the 308 limit on SS-9s and on their replacements, the SS-18s. The only reason the 1,620-limit on launchers could be considered a concession is that the USSR may have planned to replace most, if not all, of its IR/MRBM force with ICBMs. The first steps in this direction were already underway when SALT began—that is, the deployment of SS-11 ICBM launchers in IR/MRBM fields. Whatever concessions the Soviets made on the total number of ICBM launchers, however, were balanced by the absence of constraints on IR/MRBMs. The USSR may deploy as many SS-20s as it wants, and it evidently plans to deploy up to 500 of these launchers, armed with more than 1,000 missiles carrying 3,000 warheads.[33]

Limiting SS-9/SS-18 launchers to 308 may have represented a concession of some substance. The USSR probably wanted to build some 500 silos for these missiles. About 300 missiles would be adequate, however, as long as the Soviets can MIRV them. The number of American ICBM silos is frozen at 1,054; these silos remain undefended. The USSR could deploy the SS-19 and its successors. No effective limits were placed on either the accuracy or the throw-weight of the SS-17 or the SS-19, which total 6,000 and 7,000 pounds, respectively. Both violate the intent of the U.S. unilateral declaration on missile silo volume that was designed, however ineptly, to limit the throw-weight of SS-11 replacements to roughly the same 2,000 pounds. In fact, about 75 percent of the Soviet ICBMs deployed in 1980 were "heavy" models, as defined by the U.S. unilateral declaration to the Interim Agreement.

USSR tactics in negotiating SLBM limits were remarkably successful. The Soviets may not have entered SALT with precisely the 750 to 950 "modern" SLBM tube-limit in mind, but they almost certainly operated on the principle that they wanted a large SLBM force as a secure reserve. In the absence of defenses, their ICBMs could be vulnerable to American counterforce strikes, even if the USSR had already adopted launch-on-warning to reduce that vulnerability. No constraints were placed on the development of new SLBMs, on throw-weights, or on accuracy. The USSR later developed longer-range SLBMs, like the SS-N-8 and the SS-N-18, that can reach many U.S. targets from Soviet home waters.

During SALT American negotiators apparently thought that large SLBM forces compensated for the USSR's lack of overseas staging bases.[34] Soviet fleets normally maintain only about 10 percent of their nuclear-powered missile-carrying submarines on station, whereas the United States uses facilities in Spain and Britain to keep about half of its SSBNs within striking distance of the USSR in peacetime. Others consider the low on-station factor of Soviet SLBMs to be based on inferior technical performance. The more likely explanation is that these SLBMs are not part of a "triad" in the American sense. Rather, in the USSR SSBNs primarily constitute a secure reserve force, only a small part of which would be committed to the initial exchange.

The bulk of this reserve force would be used to support the war that the Soviets expect to fight after the initial exchange and to deal with any nuclear powers that stay out of the original conflict. This concept explains both the low on-station factor and the emphasis on increasing SLBM range. American negotiators were mirror-imaging and did not know that development of the SS-N-8, with its ICBM range, was proceeding and that three more SLBMs with similar range capabilities—SS-N-18, SS-N-20, and SS-N-23— were being designed or in the early development stages. American intelligence apparently did little, if anything, to counter these misperceptions.[35]

A large part of the Soviet strategic forces—IR/MRBMs and Long-Range Aviation medium bombers—were successfully excluded from the negotiations, while the USSR constantly placed the U.S. on the defensive by trying to include most nuclear-capable American tactical forces—the forward based systems (FBS)—within the ceilings. Although the United States did keep the FBS out of the Interim Agreement, the Soviets evidently made some progress on this issue by influencing the planned level of NATO nuclear modernization finally agreed upon in 1980.

If, as this chapter argues, the Ministry of Defense's priority objective in SALT I was to limit American ABM deployments so that the balance of forces would not shift in favor of the United States, it succeeded. The defense ministry was probably even more satisfied when the United States abandoned its one deployed ABM site at the Minuteman fields in return for a USSR pledge not to exercise its right to deploy at a second site.

Air defense and strategic ASW did not enter into the SALT negotiations. The United States has followed the logic of the ABM Treaty by virtually dismantling air defenses. The Soviets did not follow suit (confounding many expectations) and stepped up investment in air defense development and procurement. Strategic ASW is following a similar pattern.

The funding of research, development, technology, and engineering (RDT&E) for advanced weapons concepts and systems—the essence of any agreement that would really control arms—was either not discussed or specifically left unconstrained. There were no overt Soviet proposals to exclude these issues from SALT I. Because the United States had no intention of raising them, it was unnecessary for the USSR to say anything on the subject.

The ABM Treaty and the Interim Agreement eliminated the threat of a dominant American strategic advantage over the USSR—a situation that would have lasted more than a decade. In addition, the political climate created by SALT facilitated Soviet access to Western markets and credits, which, in turn, supported the continued military buildup designed to vitiate the objectives the United States thought it was pursuing in SALT.

Notes

FOREWORD

1. Testimony of Robert M. Gates and Lawrence K. Gershwin on behalf of the Central Intelligence Agency, U.S. Senate, Committees on Armed Services and on Appropriations, *Soviet Strategic Force Developments* (Washington, D.C., 26 June 1985).

CHAPTER I

1. Arthur J. Alexander, "Decision Making in Soviet Weapons Procurement," *Adelphi Papers*, nos. 147 and 148 (London: The International Institute for Strategic Studies, Winter 1978–79), p. 43.

2. The literal translation of ranks sounds awkward. They are rendered in this manner because they do not always correspond to seemingly equivalent ranks in the United States armed forces. See Appendix B, "Soviet Military Ranks," in Harriet Fast Scott and William F. Scott, *The Armed Forces of the USSR*, 3d rev. ed. (Boulder, Colo.: Westview Press, 1984), pp. 410–11.

3. Harriet Fast Scott's research indicates that Soviet officers who have a degree in philosophical sciences invariably are political officers. In the absence of this guideline, Ms. Scott's files are the principal reliable source of information on institutional affiliations.

4. General of the Army A. A. Epishev, "The CPSU and the Soviet Armed Forces," *Military Thought*, no. 1 (January 1968): 9. This is a restricted General Staff journal (*Voennaia mysl'*), translations of which are employed here.

5. Some of the principal sources from *Military Thought* are Epishev, ibid.; Colonel A. Aleksandrov, "The Bases and Principles of Soviet Military Organization," no. 12 (December 1967); and General Major E. Nikitin and Colonel S. Baranov, "The Revolution in Military Affairs and Measures of the CPSU for Raising the Combat Might of the Armed Forces," no. 6 (June 1967).

In addition, General of the Army E. E. Mal'tsev (*KPSS: Organizator zashchity sotsialisticheskogo otechestva* [Moscow: Voenizdat, 1974]) provides historical information on the origin of the five-year plan for military construction of the armed forces, which began in 1929 with the adoption of this type of planning for the economy as a whole. At least since the beginning of the second plan cycle in 1934, the CPSU objective has been "superiority" (ibid., pp. 163–64) over the capitalist armies in all major weapons systems.

6. The following discussion of the relationship among party policy, military strategy, weapons procurement, and military budgets is based primarily on these articles in *Military Thought*: General Major V. I. Zemskov, "Ideological and Theoretical Bases of Soviet Military Doctrine," no. 1 (January 1972), and "Questions on the History and Theory of Military Science," no. 4 (April 1971): 27–28; Colonel S. Taran, "Leninist Theoretical Principles of Soviet Military Strategy," no. 6 (June 1971): 46–48; General Colonel M. Povalyi, "Military Strategy and Economics," no. 4 (April 1971): 29–43; General Major M. I. Cherednichenko, "Military Strategy and Military Technology," no. 4 (April 1973): 47–60; Lieutenant Colonel V. Ivanov, "Methodological Questions of Scientific Leadership of the Armed Forces of the Land of Socialism," no. 2 (February 1973): 20–25; Colonels B. Trushin and M. Gladkov, "The Economic Foundation of the Military-Technical Policy of a Country," no. 12 (December 1968): 23–31; General Major K. Bochkarev, "The Soviet Army: Offspring of Great October," no. 10 (October 1967): 24–25. See also Colonels M. Gladkov and B. Ivanov, "Economics and Military-Technical Policy," *Kommunist vooruzhennykh sil'*, no. 9 (September 1972): 10–12.

7. Marshal of the Soviet Union A. A. Grechko, *Na strazhe mira i stroitel'stva kommunizma* (Moscow: Voenizdat, 1971), p. 53.

8. Ibid.

9. General Major V. I. Zemskov, "Questions on the History and Theory of Military Science," *Military Thought*, no. 4 (April 1971): 28.

10. Cherednichenko, "Military Strategy and Military Technology," p. 47.

11. Povalyi, "Military Strategy and Economics," pp. 29–30 and 33–36; Taran, "Leninist Principles," pp. 46–48; and Cherednichenko, "Military Strategy and Military Technology," pp. 47–48 and 54–55.

12. Cherednichenko, "Military Strategy and Military Technology," pp. 54–55.

13. Povalyi, "Military Strategy and Economics," p. 36.

14. Chapter 4 discusses the missions and operational concepts of the Soviet armed forces.

CHAPTER 2

1. Michael MccGwire, "The Rationale for the Development of Soviet Seapower," (Paper prepared for presentation at SEA LINK 78, SACLANT's Triannual Symposium, Annapolis, Md., 20–22 June 1978), presents the strongest case for a large conventional navy under Stalin.

2. Harry S. Truman, *Year of Decisions*, vol. 1 (Garden City, N.Y.: Doubleday, 1955), p. 416.

3. General Major E. Nikitin and Colonel S. Baranov, "The Revolution in Military Affairs and Measures of the CPSU for Raising the Combat Might of the Armed Forces," *Military Thought*, no. 6 (June 1968): 3–4.

4. Personal communication to coauthor Lee from Mr. Sergei Sikorski.

5. General of the Army V. F. Tolubko, *Nedelin: pervyi glavkom strategicheskikh* (Moscow: Molodaia gvardiia, 1979), pp. 150–60 and 171–203.

6. Interview with N. S. Khrushchev by Arthur Sulzberger, *New York Times*, 8 September 1961; cited in Thomas W. Wolfe, *Soviet Power and Europe, 1945–1970* (Baltimore, Md.: Johns Hopkins University Press, 1970), p. 186.

7. General of the Army P. F. Batitskii, "Development of the Tactics and Operational Art of the Country's Air Defense (PVO) Troops," *Military Thought*, no. 10 (October 1967): 36 and Nikitin and Baranov, "Combat Might of the Armed Forces," cited in note 3 above, pp. 3–5.

8. General of the Army P. A. Kurochkin, "A Chronicle of Heroism and Victories," *Military Thought*, no. 5 (May 1968): 87 and Harriet Fast Scott and William F. Scott, *The Armed Forces of the USSR*, 3d rev. ed. (Boulder, Colo.: Westview Press, 1984), p. 159.

9. R. T. Pretty, ed., *Jane's Weapons Systems, 1979–80* (New York: Franklin Watts, Inc., 1979), pp. 67–68.

10. When one looks at Stalin's decisions to acquire nuclear weapons, delivery systems, and other advanced (for that time) weaponry, one must disagree with those American observers who have concluded that the Soviets did not understand the military utility of nuclear forces. See, for example, George F. Kennan, "The United States and the Soviet Union, 1917–1976," *Foreign Affairs* 54, no. 4 (July 1976): 670–90.

11. Harriet Fast Scott, editor's comments to chap. 3, Marshal V. D. Sokolovskii, ed., *Soviet Military Strategy*, trans. of 3d ed. (New York: Crane, Russak & Co., 1975), p. 118. The article quoted appeared in General Major N. Pavlenko, "Nekotorye voprosy razvitiia teorii strategii v 20-kh godakh," *Voenno-istoricheskii zhurnal* 8, no. 5 (May 1966): 12 n. 9.

12. Stalin's "permanently operating factors which decide the course and fate of wars" included the following: (1) stability of the rear, (2) morale of the army, (3) quantity and quality of divisions, (4) armament of the army, and (5) organizing abil-

ity of the command personnel (Raymond L. Garthoff, *The Soviet Image of Future War* [Washington, D.C.: Public Affairs Press, 1959], pp. 24–25).

13. "K itogam diskussii o kharaktere zakonov voennoi nauki," *Voennaia mysl'*, no. 4 (1955): 21.

14. Herbert S. Dinerstein, *War and the Soviet Union* (New York: Praeger, 1959): 28–64.

15. Kurochkin, "Chronicle of Heroism and Victories," p. 91. See also General of the Army V. Ivanov, "The Development of Soviet Operational Art," *Military Thought*, no. 3 (March 1967): 11–13.

16. Cited in General Major S. Kozlov, "The Development of Soviet Military Science After World War II," *Military Thought*, no. 2 (February 1964): 46.

17. N. S. Khrushchev, *Disarmament: The Road to Consolidating the Peace and Insuring Friendship Between Peoples* (Moscow: Foreign Languages Publishing House, 1960). The coauthors are indebted to Harriet F. Scott for the January 1960 *Pravda* reference.

18. John W. R. Taylor, ed., *Jane's All the World's Aircraft, 1974–75* (London: Jane's Publishing Co., 1974), pp. 499–502 and 510.

19. Pretty, *Jane's Weapons Systems, 1979–80*, p. 68.

20. International Institute for Strategic Studies, *The Military Balance, 1985–1986* (London, 1985), p. 23.

21. Harry F. Eustace, ed., *The International Countermeasures Handbook, 1977–1978*, 3d rev. ed. (Palo Alto, Calif.: E. W. Communications, 1977), pp. 245–60.

22. Norman Friedman, "Soviet Responses to U.S. Naval Initiatives," H1-2901/4RR (Croton-on-Hudson, N.Y.: Hudson Institute, April 1979).

23. The basic data on USSR defense expenditures and GNP in this section are taken from W. T. Lee, *The Estimation of Soviet Defense Expenditures, 1955–75* (New York: Praeger, 1977); W. T. Lee, *Soviet Defense Expenditures in an Era of SALT* (Washington, D.C.: United States Strategic Institute, 1979); and W. T. Lee, "USSR Gross National Product in Established Prices, 1955–1975," in Hans Raupach, ed., *Jahrbuch der Wirtschaft Osteuropas*, vol. 8 (Munich/Vienna: Guenter Olzog Verlag, 1979), pp. 399–429. See also U.S. Senate, Armed Services Committee, Subcommittee on General Procurement, *Hearings on Soviet Defense Expenditures and Related Programs*, 96th Cong., 1st & 2d sess. (Washington, D. C.: GPO, 1980); and U.S. House of Representatives, Permanent Select Committee on Intelligence, Subcommittee on Oversight, *Hearings on CIA Estimates of Soviet Defense Spending*, 96th Cong., 2d sess. (Washington, D.C.: GPO, 1980).

CHAPTER 3

1. For an excellent guide to Soviet literature on military doctrine and strategy, see the National Strategy Information Center publication by William F. Scott (*Soviet Sources of Military Doctrine and Strategy* [New York: Crane, Russak & Co., 1975]).

2. Colonels V. Morozov and S. Tiushkevich, "On the System of Laws of Military Science and Principles of Military Art," *Military Thought*, no. 3 (March 1967): 17, 23 and 28; Colonel S. Il'in, "The Moral-Political Factor in Modern War," ibid., no. 8 (August 1965): 41–53; Marshal V. D. Sokolovskii, ed., *Voennaia strategiia*, 3d ed. (Moscow: Voenizdat, 1968), pp. 221–28, esp. p. 223 for the conditions of deterrence. The essential passages concerning Soviet views on possibilities and conditions for USSR deterrence of a U.S. or NATO nuclear attack are unchanged in all three editions. (The first edition was published in 1962.)

3. Marshal R. Ia. Malinovskii, "Terrible Lesson of History," *Military Thought*, no. 6 (1966): 1–4; Marshal S. S. Biriuzov, "The Lessons of the Beginning Period of the Great Patriotic War," ibid., no. 8 (August 1964): 1–4; Marshal R. Ia. Malinovskii, "Historical Exploits of the Soviet People and Their Armed Forces in the Great Patriotic War," ibid., no. 5 (May 1965): 2.

Biriuzov says the West rejected Soviet collective security proposals before World War II, because the "ruling classes" were blinded by hatred for a "socialist country." For the Soviet argument that the allies deliberately delayed opening the second front in Europe, see Colonel V. M. Kulish, *Raskrytaia taina: Predistoriia vtorogo fronta v evrope* (Moscow: Voenizdat, 1960) and the review of this book by Colonel A. Strokov and Lieutenant Colonel V. Sakistov in *Military Thought*, no. 3 (March 1966): 98–106.

For a statement describing the United States as continuing Hitler's policies, see Gorbachev's speech on the fortieth anniversary of VE Day in *Pravda*, 9 May 1985.

4. Editorial, "A Great Half Century," *Military Thought*, no. 10 (October 1967): 8.

5. Ibid.

6. For some examples of these standard arguments from *Military Thought*, see General Colonel A. Radzievskii, "Thirty Years of the Military Academy of the General Staff," ibid., no. 10 (October 1966): 6; Editorial, "A Great Half Century" pp. 1–16; Editorial, "The 51st Anniversary of the Soviet Armed Forces," ibid., no. 2 (February 1969): 1–9; Malinovskii, "Terrible Lesson of History," pp. 1–4 and 22; and Colonel V. Morozov, "The Third Edition of 'Marxism-Leninism on War and the Army,'" ibid., no. 7 (July 1963): 77–78. The arguments are essentially the same as those in chapter 4 of the third edition of Sokolovskii's *Voennaia strategiia*.

7. Editorial, "The 51st Anniversary," p. 3.

8. General Major S. A. Tiushkevich, *Sovetskie vooruzhennye sily* (Moscow: Voenizdat, 1978), p. 378. The coauthors are indebted to Harriet and William Scott for this reference.

9. General of the Army S. Ivanov, "Soviet Military Doctrine and Strategy," *Military Thought*, no. 5 (May 1969): 47. The author was commandant of the General Staff Academy from 1968 to 1973.

10. Editorial, "The 51st Anniversary," p. 2.

11. Ibid., p. 3.

12. Ibid., p. 4. In the CPSU journal *Kommunist* no. 3 (February 1979): 122, the Soviets placed their invasion of Estonia, Latvia, and Lithuania in 1940 into the proper (that is, Soviet) historical context: "Soviet forces did not interfere in the do-

mestic affairs of the Baltic countries, strictly observing the stipulations of the mutual aid pacts concluded between them and the USSR. Meanwhile, the presence of Soviet troops on Lithuanian, Latvian, and Estonian territory protected the Baltic nations from the interference of foreign imperialists. This demoralized the forces of the bourgeoisie and inspired the revolutionary masses to this struggle for the overthrow of the fascist dictatorship." Translation taken from Mose L. Harvey and Foy D. Kohler, eds., *Soviet World Outlook* 4, no. 36 (15 June 1979): 6.

13. General Major K. Bochkarev, "An Evaluation of the Results of the June Plenum of the Central Committee of the Communist Party of the Soviet Union," *Military Thought*, no. 7 (July 1968): 13–14.

14. N. S. Khrushchev, *Disarmament for Durable Peace and Friendship* (Moscow: Foreign Languages Publishing House, 1960); Defense Minister Marshal R. Ia. Malinovskii, "Speech to the Twenty-second CPSU Congress," in *XXII s"ezd KPSS (17–31 oktiabria 1961 g.): stenograficheskii otchet*, vol. 2 (Moscow: Politizdat, 1962), pp. 108–21; Colonel G. A. Fedorov, ed., *Marksizm-Leninizm o voine i armii*, 2d rev. ed. (Moscow: Voenizdat, 1961); and Marshal V. D. Sokolovskii, ed., *Voennaia strategiia*, 1st ed. (Moscow: Voenizdat, 1962).

For a bibliography of major monographs published between 1960 and 1975, see Scott, *Soviet Sources*. An extensive selection from many of the most important articles published in open USSR literature prior to 1967 appeared in William R. Kintner and Harriet Fast Scott, *The Nuclear Revolution in Soviet Military Affairs* (Norman: University of Oklahoma Press, 1968).

15. Of the many definitions of CPSU military doctrine, perhaps the best is that provided by the late Marshal A. A. Grechko, *Vooruzhennye sily sovetskogo gosudarstva*, 2d ed. (Moscow: Voenizdat, 1975), pp. 340–41.

16. For a fairly standard definition of Soviet military strategy, see Sokolovskii, *Voennaia strategiia*, pp. 16–17. For a more ambitious definition, clearly labeled as the personal opinion of the authors, see Marshal V. D. Sokolovskii and General Major M. Cherednichenko, "Military Strategy and Its Problems," *Military Thought*, no. 10 (October 1968): 32–43. In determining the share of national income for defense, Sokolovskii and Cherednichenko (p. 39) appear to be expanding the boundaries of military strategy (although they explicitly state in a footnote [p. 43] that the political leaders make the final decision on all such matters).

17. Others also have offered ambitious definitions of strategy that seem to encroach on doctrine. See, for example, A. A. Grechko, *Na strazhe mira i stroitel'stva kommunizma* (Moscow: Voenizdat, 1971), p. 53 and Sokolovskii and Cherednichenko, "Military Strategy and Its Problems," pp. 33–35.

18. W. T. Lee, "The 'Politico-Military Industrial Complex' of the USSR," *Journal of International Affairs* 26, no. 1 (1972): 73–86. See footnotes 16, 17, 20, 22, and 23 on pp. 80–82.

19. For a typical statement on the decisiveness of such a war, allowing no room for "compromise" or "political agreements" to terminate it, see General Colonel N. A. Lomov, "Several Problems of Control in Modern Warfare," *Military Thought*, no. 1 (1966): 1–17. A similar statement is made by General Colonel N. A. Lomov, Gen-

eral Major I. I. Anureev, and Colonel M. I. Galkin, eds., *Nauchno-tekhnicheskii progress i revoliutsiia v voennom dele* (Moscow: Voenizdat, 1973), p. 138.

20. General Major K. Stepanov and Lieutenant Colonel E. Rybkin, "The Nature and Types of Wars of the Modern Era," *Military Thought*, no. 2 (February 1968): 74–75 and Grechko, *Na strazhe mira*, p. 53.

21. Contrary to the conventional wisdom, "victory"—as the Soviet objective should deterrence fail—has a long history in both the military establishment and in the statements of USSR political leaders. In the period 1957–60 Khrushchev stated several times that "socialism" would survive a nuclear war and that "capitalism" would not. His pamphlet *Disarmament for Durable Peace and Friendship* (1960) was the one subsequently cited by the military as the political authority for "victory" and complete "defeat of the enemy" in a nuclear war. The origin of these objectives can therefore be traced back to the mid-1950s in both *Military Thought* and in public statements by the incumbent CPSU general secretary. They recur throughout the literature of the 1970s. Three of the most authoritative monograph sources are General Colonel A. S. Zheltov, Lieutenant Colonel T. R. Kondratkov, and Colonel E. A. Khomenko, eds., *Metodologicheskie problemy voennoi teorii i praktiki*, 2d rev. ed. (Moscow: Voenizdat, 1969), pp. 143, 277, 287, and 289; Lomov, Anureev, and Galkin, *Nauchno-tekhnicheskii progress*, pp. 165, 173, 176, and 224; and Grechko, *Vooruzhennye sily sovetskogo gosudarstva*, pp. 208–9. Zheltov was commandant of the Political-Military Academy named after Lenin, and the book was written by political officers. Lomov and Anureev served on the faculty of the General Staff Academy; contributions to their book came from both political and line officers. Grechko was minister of defense from 1967 until his death in 1976.

22. Sokolovskii, *Voennaia strategiia*, 3d ed., p. 359. All three editions state that "protection of the rear area of the country and groups of the Armed Forces from enemy nuclear attacks . . . are achieved mainly by annihilation of the enemy's means of nuclear attack in the regions in which they are based." See also Lomov, Anureev, and Galkin, *Nauchno-tekhnicheskii progress*, pp. 6 and 108. General Major I. Zav'ialov ("An Answer to Opponents," *Military Thought*, no. 10 [October 1965]: 51–53) indicates that the argument on strategic defense did not involve these issues but a rather esoteric question about the distinction between a defensive strategy, which all rejected, and defensive operations to limit damage, which all agreed upon. For positions strongly supportive of Zav'ialov, see General Colonel N. Tsyganov et al., "Types and Forms of Combat Operations," ibid., no. 8 (August 1965): 27–28 and 32–34; General Major V. Kruchinin, "Contemporary Strategic Theory on the Goals and Missions of Armed Conflict," ibid., no. 10 (October 1963): 14, 17, and 18–20; and General Major N. Vasendin and Colonel N. Kuznetsov, "Modern Warfare and Surprise Attack," ibid., no. 6 (June 1968): 47–48.

23. Lomov, Anureev, and Galkin, *Nauchno-tekhnicheskii progress*, p. 139.

24. Like "victory" and war fighting, pre-emption was one of the earliest tenets of Soviet military strategy. It had been formulated in the first stage of the post-Stalin debate (1953–55) on USSR military doctrine and strategy in the nuclear age. In strategy, pre-emption is only to be implemented on notice of the warning that the

Soviets expect to receive in a crisis; it is not to be confused with preventive war and unprovoked surprise attack "out of the blue." Because the literal term for preemption is subject to such misinterpretation, however, since the late 1950s the USSR has seldom used it. Instead, it uses the terms "frustrate," "disrupt," and "repel" (a surprise attack by the West) and stresses the importance of surprise and of seizing the initiative. An excellent treatment of this issue appears in chapter 6 of Herbert S. Dinerstein, *War and the Soviet Union* (New York: Praeger, 1959). For another representative open source, see W. T. Lee, "The 'Politico-Military Industrial Complex.'" During the 1960s several Soviet writers defined the meaning of "frustrating" and "repelling" an attack on the USSR as combined offensive counterforce and defensive—air, missile, space, and civil defense—operations. See Zav'ialov, "An Answer to Opponents," pp. 51 and 53; Vasendin and Kuznetsov, "Modern Warfare and Surprise Attack," p. 47; General Colonel M. Povalyi, "Development of Soviet Military Strategy," ibid., no. 2 (February 1967): 71; and Morozov, "The Third Edition of 'Marxism-Leninism,'" p. 83. Launch under attack (on tactical warning of incoming enemy missiles and aircraft) was added to the third edition of Sokolovskii (p. 337), although the formulation is somewhat vaguely stated. It had been given unambiguously the previous year by Marshal N. Krylov, "The Nuclear-Missile Shield of the Soviet State," *Military Thought*, no. 11 (November 1967): 18. Krylov commanded the Strategic Rocket Forces from 1963 until his death in 1972.

25. Colonel M. Skovordkin, "Some Questions on Coordination of Branches of Armed Forces in Major Operations," ibid., no. 2 (February 1967): 36 and 39; General Major Kh. Dzhelaukhov, "The Infliction of Deep Strikes," ibid., no. 2 (February 1967): 42–47; General Major N. Komkov and Colonel P. Shemanskii, "Certain Historic Trends in the Development of Troop Control," ibid., no. 10 (October 1964): 13; General Lieutenant G. Semenov, "The Content of the Concept of an Operation," ibid., no. 1 (January 1968): 91–94; General Major S. Begunov, "The Maneuver of Forces and Matériel in an Offensive," ibid., no. 5 (May 1968): 46 and 47; and Captain First Rank N. V'yunenko, "Naval Support of Ground Forces," ibid., no. 7 (July 1963): 64–66 and 74.

26. For a discussion of Soviet nuclear targeting strategy and additional source citations, see Chapter 8. Perhaps the most politically authoritative source on selective targeting of industry is Zheltov et al., *Problemy*, pp. 120–21. The earliest available USSR statement on using minimum yield weapons—"minimum expenditure of explosive power"—is from Kruchinin, "Contemporary Strategic Theory," p. 17. Kruchinin was on the strategic studies faculty at the General Staff Academy during the 1960s, probably as early as 1963. See General of the Army V. G. Kulikov, ed., *Akademiia General'nogo Shtaba* (Moscow: Voenizdat, 1976), pp. 185 and 192. Most of the passages about the use of large-yield weapons without concern for collateral damage were removed from Sokolovskii's *Voennaia strategiia*, when the corrected second edition was issued in 1963. See the translation of the third edition, with an analysis and commentary by Harriet Fast Scott (Scott, ed., *Soviet Military Strategy* [New York: Crane, Russak and Co., 1975], pp. 168, 451, and 460), which compares all three editions.

27. Entry "Voenno-tekhnicheskoe prevoskhodstvo," in *Sovietskaia voennaia en-*

tsiklopediia 2: 253, states that strengthening the USSR's defenses "demands" achieving "military-technical superiority over the armed forces of the aggressive imperialist blocs" and goes on to say that Soviet military doctrine "determining the direction of the preparation of the country and the Armed Forces for repulsing aggression, provides the program of action for insuring military-technical superiority of the Armed Forces over their probable adversaries." Military doctrine is the province of the party. See footnotes 15, 16, and 17. The encyclopedia was edited by Marshal A. A. Grechko, chairman of the editorial commission and a Politburo member from 1973 until his death in 1976. He was succeeded as chairman by Marshal N. V. Ogarkov, chief of the General Staff, a candidate member on the Central Committee in 1966, and a full member of the committee since 1971. General Colonel A. A. Epishev, chief of the Main Political Directorate until 1985 and member of the Central Committee since 1964, is one of three deputy chairmen.

For writings by both line and political officers on the superiority objective, see Colonel A. Gurov, "Economics of War," *Military Thought*, no. 7 (July 1965): 7 and General Major A. Kornienko and Captain V. Korolev, "Economic Aspects of Soviet Military Doctrine," ibid., no. 7 (July 1967): 33. Colonel S. Tiushkevich ("The Methodology for the Correlation of Forces in War," ibid., no. 6 [June 1969]: 31–32) discusses the advantages of superiority. Colonel S. Baranov and General Major E. Nikitin ("The Revolution in Military Affairs," ibid., no. 6 [June 1968]: 7) state that "no lags will be allowed in the military field; maintaining reliable military-technical superiority is a task conditioned by the international duties of the Soviet Union." General Major of Engineering and Technical Services A. Parkhomenko ("Problems of Management in the Area of the Development of Armament and Military Matériel," ibid., no. 9 [September 1966]: 67) states that "in order to solve such a serious problem as the ensuring of military superiority over a probable enemy it is first of all necessary to develop weapons which at least do not yield to the armament of an opposing country." General Major K. Bochkarev ("An Evaluation of the Results of the June Plenum," ibid., no. 7 [July 1963]: 3) states that the USSR is "confidently building up a military advantage over its probable foe."

28. For a discussion of CPSU military-technical policy, see the following representative sources (most of whose authors are political officers): Colonels G. Trushin and M. Gladkov, "The Economic Foundation of the Military-Technical Policy of a Country," ibid., no. 12 (December 1968): 23–30; Colonel A. Aleksandrov, "The Bases and Principles of Soviet Military Organization," ibid., no. 12 (December 1967): 25, 27, and 29; Baranov and Nikitin, "The Revolution in Military Affairs," pp. 1 and 2–5; Grechko, *Na strazhe mira*, pp. 52, 53, and 56; Editorial, "The 51st Anniversary," p. 7; General of the Army A. A. Epishev, "The CPSU and the Soviet Armed Forces," ibid., no. 1 (January 1968): 11–18; and General Major K. Bochkarev, "The Soviet Army—Offspring of Great October," ibid., no. 10 (October 1967): 17–27. For party control over the military purse, see Sokolovskii and Cherednichenko, "Military Strategy and Its Problems," p. 39 and n. 5.

29. Lomov, Anureev, and Galkin, *Nauchno-tekhnicheskii progress*, pp. 139–40; Sokolovskii, *Voennaia strategiia*, 3d ed., pp. 387–95.

30. See the comments by Colonel M. Fedulov et al., "Problems of Modern Com-

bined Arms Combat," *Military Thought*, no. 10 (October 1964): 31–32 on an article by General Lieutenant Reznichenko that appeared in ibid., no. 3 (March 1964).

31. Krylov, "The Nuclear Missile Shield," p. 18; Sokolovskii, *Voennaia strategiia*, 3d ed., p. 334.

32. M. M. Kir'ian, *Voenno-tekhnicheskii progress i vooruzhennye sily SSSR* (Moscow: Voenizdat, 1982), p. 312. Similar hints, however, had appeared at least a decade earlier.

33. G. A. Fedorov, chief ed., *Marksizm-Leninizm o voine i armii*, 2d ed. (Moscow: Voenizdat, 1961), p. 57. The coauthors are indebted to Harriet Fast Scott for this reference. The reader should keep in mind that the political officers speak for the CPSU Central Committee, of which the political directorate is a department. On policy matters, the Central Committee is a euphemism for the Politburo and on military policy, for the Defense Council.

34. Sokolovskii, *Voennaia strategiia*, 3d ed., p. 298.

35. Ibid., 2d ed., p. 258.

36. Ibid., 3d ed., pp. 253–54. *Soviet Military Power, 1984*, pp. 40–41.

37. Tiushkevich, "Correlation of Forces in War," p. 32.

38. Entry "Voenno-tekhnicheskoe prevoskhodstvo," in *Sovetskaia voennaia entsiklopediia* 2: 253.

39. Grechko, *Na strazhe mira* (1971) and idem, *Vooruzhennye sily sovetskogo gosudarstva*, 1st ed. (1974) and 2d ed. (1975).

40. Lomov, Anureev, and Galkin, *Nauchno-tekhnicheskii progress*.

41. One of these books is a text on military strategy, completed in 1975 and edited by General of the Army and Commandant of the General Staff Academy I. E. Shavrov. See Kulikov, *Akademiia General'nogo Shtaba*, pp. 205–6. The other was written by Colonel E. I. Rybkin (*Voina i politika v sovremennuiu epokhu* [Moscow, 1974]) and is listed in *Sovetskaia voennaia entsiklopediia* 1: 109 as recommended reading under the entry for "Aggression" by L. L. Kruglov. The coauthors are indebted to William and Harriet Fast Scott for these references.

42. Nora Beloff ("Escape From Boredom: A Defector's Story," *Atlantic Monthly*, December 1980, p. 48) cites Galina Orionova, who worked at the USA and Canada Institute for ten years until she defected in 1979. See also Barbara Dash, *A Defector Reports: The Institute of the USA and Canada* (Falls Church, Va.: Delphic Associates, May 1982).

43. L. I. Brezhnev, "Velikii Oktiabr' i progress chelovechestva," *Kommunist vooruzhennykh sil* 58, no. 22 (November 1977): 14–15.

44. Entry "Doktrina voennaia," *Sovetskaia voennaia entsiklopediia* 3: 225–29.

45. N. V. Ogarkov, "Strategiia voennaia," ibid. 7: 555–65.

46. Marshal N. V. Ogarkov, "Mif o 'sovetskoi voennoi ugroze' i realnost'," *Pravda*, 2 August 1979.

47. Grechko, *Vooruzhennye sily sovetskogo gosudarstva*, 2d ed., pp. 208–9. One of the best definitions for the scope of Soviet military doctrine appears on pp.

340–41, but, beyond reaffirming victory and superiority, not much is said about content.

48. Sokolovskii, *Voennaia strategiia*, 3d ed., pp. 289 and 253.

49. The official USSR defense budget has a distinguished history of being used as a means of disinformation. Most scholars in the United States maintain that Soviet military expenditures included procurement in the 1930s and during World War II. If so, procurement was removed from the official budget at the beginning of the Korean War to camouflage the military buildup during those years. In mid-1961 some missing defense funds were transferred back into official "defense" to accommodate Khrushchev's public statement about increasing USSR military spending by several billion rubles, after his meeting with President John F. Kennedy in Vienna. During the 1950s and 1960s official Soviet defense expenditures probably included most outlays for pay, maintenance, operations, and military construction. Since 1970, however, official "defense" has been reduced by nearly one billion rubles, whereas outlays for pay, maintenance, operations, and military construction have clearly increased. See discussion on "Soviet Defense Spending," *Problems of Communism* 34, no. 2 (March-April 1985): 126–32.

50. Anthony Austin, "Moscow Expert Says U.S. Errs on Soviet War Aims," *New York Times*, 25 August 1980.

51. N. V. Ogarkov, "Strategiia voennaia," pp. 564–65. It is ironic that the candid Soviet literature of the 1960s on military doctrine was given little credibility in the West until the mid-1970s, when the USSR not only ceased to be candid about many aspects of its military doctrine and strategy but also began to engage in skillful disinformation about these subjects.

52. The initial formulation of "victory" as the objective dates from the conclusion of the original debate on Soviet nuclear doctrine and strategy during the period 1953–55. See the editorial, "K itogam diskussi o kharaktere zakonov voiny," *Voennaia mysl'*, no. 4 (April 1955): 22 and Dinerstein, *War and the Soviet Union*. The "victory" objective recurs throughout the literature into the 1970s. See note 21.

53. N. S. Khrushchev, *Disarmament for Durable Peace and Friendship* and L. I. Brezhnev, "Speech at the Celebration of the Fiftieth Anniversary of the October Revolution," *Pravda*, 2 November 1967.

54. The initial definition of what the Soviets envisage as "victory" in a nuclear war appeared in W. T. Lee, "The 'Politico-Military Industrial Complex' of the USSR," *Journal of International Affairs* 26, no. 1 (1972): 81–82. Our definition represents a revision and is based primarily on materials in *Military Thought*, which was not in the public domain at the time. Access to this journal has enabled us to formulate a broader and more refined definition of "victory" than that inferable from the unclassified literature of the 1950s and 1960s. It is now clear that the USSR has no intention of negotiating the settlement of a nuclear war with the Western governments in power at the beginning of such a war. (A negotiated settlement was not discussed as a Soviet objective in the open literature either; the open literature was even less explicit than *Military Thought*.) For additional points on the "victory" objective from recently declassified issues of *Military Thought*, see General Major I. Anureev,

"The Correlation of Military Science with the Natural Sciences," ibid., no. 11 (November 1972): 36; General Lieutenant V. Reznichenko, "Tactics: A Component Part of the Art of Warfare," ibid., no. 12 (December 1973): 38; Editorial, "The Tasks of Soviet Military Science in Light of the Decisions of the Twenty-fourth CPSU Congress," ibid., no. 8 (August 1971): 4–5; and General of the Army V. Kulikov, "The Indestructible Unity of Peoples: The Builders of Communism," ibid., no. 12 (December 1972): 19–20.

55. Malinovskii, "Terrible Lesson of History," pp. 1–4; Marshal S. Biriuzov, "The Lessons," pp. 1–4; Malinovskii, "Historical Exploits," p. 2; and Kulish, *Raskrytaia taina*, reviewed by Strokov and Sakistov. For typical Soviet views of how "imperialist" war-lust leads to attacks on "national liberation movements," see Radzievskii, "Thirty Years," p. 6; Editorial, "A Great Half Century"; Editorial, "The 51st Anniversary" and Colonel V. Morozov, "The Third Edition of 'Marxism-Leninism,'" pp. 77–78. The arguments are essentially the same as those in chapter 4 of Sokolovskii's *Voennaia strategiia*, 3d ed. For an indictment of the "chain of imperialist crimes" from the Korean War through the Hungarian rebellion and the "quiet" counterrevolution in Czechoslovakia, see Captain First Rank N. Shumkhin, "Collective Defense: The Guarantee of Sovereignty of the Countries of the Socialist Commonwealth," *Military Thought*, no. 5 (May 1972): 18–19.

56. General Colonel N. Lomov, "Problems of Control in Modern Warfare," 1–17.

57. Sokolovskii, *Voennaia strategiia*, 3d ed., chap. 7; Grechko, *Vooruzhennye sily sovetskogo gosudarstva*, 2d ed., pp. 108 and 113–15; Gurov, "Economics of War," p. 5; M. Povalyi, "Military Strategy and Economics," ibid., no. 4 (April 1971): 33; and General Major Kh. Dzhelaukhov, "The Augmentation of Strategic Efforts in Modern Armed Conflict," ibid., no. 1 (January 1964): 21 and 24.

58. For a number of sources on this point, see W. T. Lee, "Soviet Nuclear Targeting Strategy and SALT," in Steven Rosefield, ed., *World Communism at the Crossroads* (Boston: Martinus Nijhoff Publishing, 1980), pp. 55–88.

59. See, for example, General Major A. S. Milovidov, "War and the Socialist Revolution," *Military Thought*, no. 11 (November 1971): 1–16. This thesis is developed at some length in the Appendix of the present work.

60. As Colonel V. Khalipov ("The Twenty-fourth CPSU Congress and the Contemporary Stage of Development of the World System of Socialism," ibid., no. 3 [March 1972]: 2) phrased it, the world socialist system "opens up new and favorable prospects for the worldwide triumph of socialism." Milovidov ("War and the Socialist Revolution," p. 15) stated that "the end objective of the socialist revolution is not simply the destruction of capitalism at any price but rather the building of communism."

61. See Editorial, "Party-Political Work on Increased Combat Readiness of the Armed Forces," ibid., no. 7 (July 1973): 6 for quotation.

62. General Major N. Shushko and Lieutenant Colonel V. Kozlov, "The Development of Marxist-Leninist Teaching on War and the Army (a Survey of the Literature)," ibid., no. 4 (April 1968): 95 and 99. The coauthors are indebted to Harriet Fast Scott for this reference.

63. B. Dmitriev, N. M. Nikol'skii, and General Major Talenskii all published their "deviations" toward pacifism during the period 1963–65.

64. Raymond L. Garthoff, "Mutual Deterrence and Strategic Arms Limitations in Soviet Policy," *International Security* 3, no. 1 (Summer 1978): 115.

65. Kulikov (*Akademiia General'nogo Shtaba*) gives a list of deputy commandants and their photographs after pp. 96 and 126. Bochkarev is not among them. This has been confirmed by Harriet Fast Scott, who also provided us the date of his retirement. (Moreover, "general major" is a one-star rank; a deputy commandant has a two- or three-star rank.)

66. Demonstrative use refers to the detonation of one or a few weapons in a location where little or no damage would be done. Limited use refers to striking a select few of the enemy's military or economic assets to convince him that he should cease and desist from some course of action (for example, a conventional attack on one or more NATO countries).

CHAPTER 4

1. Harriet Fast Scott and William F. Scott, *The Armed Forces of the USSR*, 3d rev. ed. (Boulder, Colo.: Westview Press, 1984), pp. 141–82. This basic research study of the Soviet military establishment is the best book on the subject. Recent organizational changes have been reported in the 1983 through 1985 editions of *Soviet Military Power*, issued by the Pentagon.

2. Entry for "Raketnoe oruzhie," *Sovetskaia voennaia entsiklopediia* 7: 47–50; General Major M. I. Cherednichenko, "Military Strategy and Military Technology," *Military Thought*, no. 4 (April 1973): 47–60; A. M. Siniukov and N. I. Morozov, *Konstruktsiia upravliaemykh ballisticheskikh raket* (Moscow: Voenizdat, 1969), pp. 5 and 16–17.

3. Article entitled "Ob"edinenie" in *Sovetskaia voennaia entsiklopediia* 5: 679–80; General Colonel I. Shavrov, "Soviet Operational Art," *Military Thought*, no. 10 (October 1973): 1–16.

4. A. S. Zheltov, T. R. Kondratkov, and E. A. Khomenko, *Metodologicheskie problemy voennoi teorii i praktiki*, 2d rev. ed. (Moscow: Voenizdat, 1969).

5. The discussion of missions assigned to the various branches of the armed forces is taken primarily from four Soviet books: V. D. Sokolovskii, *Voennaia strategiia*, 3d rev. ed. (Moscow: Voenizdat, 1968), pp. 332–68; A. A. Grechko, *Na strazhe mira i stroitel'stva kommunizma* (Moscow: Voenizdat, 1971), pp. 41–49; N. A. Lomov, ed., *Nauchno-tekhnicheskii progress i revoliutsiia v voennom dele* (Moscow: Voenizdat, 1973), pp. 41–49; and S. G. Gorshkov, *Morskaia moshch' gosudarstva* (Moscow: Voenizdat, 1976), pp. 238, 352–54, and 360–61.

The primary Western sources used are John G. Hibbits, "Admiral Gorshkov's Writings: Twenty Years of Naval Thought," in Paul J. Murphy, ed., *Naval Power in Soviet Policy*, USAF Studies in Communist Affairs, no. 2 (Washington, D.C.: GPO,

1978) and chap. 6 in Michael J. Deane, *Strategic Defense in Soviet Strategy*, Monographs in International Affairs (Coral Gables, Fla.: Advanced International Studies Institute, University of Miami, 1980), pp. 77–94.

References to the above and other sources are cited to support the argument on specific issues. Moreover, the missions of the Soviet air force are discussed according to the operational role of the SAF's principal elements.

6. For the "operational-strategic" concept in a TVD, see the entry for "Ob"edinenie" in *Sovetskaia voennaia entsiklopediia* 5: 679–80; and Shavrov, "Soviet Operational Art."

7. Gorshkov, *Morskaia moshch' gosudarstva*, pp. 352 and 361.

8. Sokolovskii, *Voennaia strategiia*, p. 359.

9. Marshal of Aviation S. A. Krasovskii, "Trends in the Use of Aircraft in a Nuclear War," *Military Thought*, no. 3 (March 1967): 25–31; S. A. Krasovskii, chief ed., *Aviatsiia i Kosmonavtika SSSR* (Moscow: Voenizdat, 1968), pp. 351–52; Colonel A. Vereshchagin et al., "Aircraft in Combat Operations at Sea," *Military Thought*, no. 11 (November 1968): 57.

10. General Colonel of Artillery G. Peredel'skii, "Artillery in the Struggle to Attain Fire Superiority," *Military Thought*, no. 10 (October 1973): 57–58.

11. In addition to the previously cited works of Lomov, Grechko, and Gorshkov, on service missions, see Rear Admiral K. Stalbo, "Naval Science: Structure and Tasks," ibid., no. 7 (July 1973): 77–79; and Captain Second Rank V. Bestuzhev, "Combat Actions on the Sea," ibid., no. 7 (July 1971): 76. The latter reference alludes to the views of "foreign experts" that clearly apply to the Soviet navy.

12. Admiral A. Chabanenko, "Combating Rocket-Carrying Atomic Submarines," ibid., no. 12 (December 1967): 45–47 evaluates the capabilities of all three types of ASW platforms and concludes that submarines are the most effective.

13. For the characteristics of the Alpha class SSNs, see Chabanenko, "Combating Rocket-Carrying Atomic Submarines," p. 47; Admiral A. Kharlamov, "Some Trends in the Development of Navies," *Military Thought*, no. 10 (October 1967): 65–66; and Captain First Rank N. Shatrov, "Trends in the Development and Employment of Naval Fleets," ibid., no. 1 (January 1972): 55–56. The last source specifically mentions that titanium hulls are required for deep-diving SSNs. See Department of Defense, *Soviet Military Power, 1985* (Washington, D.C.: The Pentagon, April 1985): p. 96 for tonnage.

14. The evidence for ASW as the primary mission of most, if not all, of the new Soviet cruiser classes is discussed in chap. 3 of Gorshkov, *Morskaia moshch' gosudarstva*. The quotation is from p. 337.

15. Deane, *Strategic Defense in Soviet Strategy*, pp. 78–84. The most explicit enunciations of this objective in the SALT era appeared during 1973–76. In 1976, Gorshkov issued his previously cited statement on the importance of strategic ASW. See also T. K. Jones and W. Scott Thompson, "Central War and Civil Defense," *Orbis* 22, no. 3 (Fall 1978): 681–712.

16. For a review of strategic indicators that the Soviets do not intend to abide by

the ABM treaty forever, see W. T. Lee, *Viability of the ABM Treaty in the 1980s: A Note on the Issue*, DNA-4769T-1, vol. 1 (Washington, D.C.: Center for Planning and Research, 1980), esp. the summary discussion in chap. 9. For the implications of recent Soviet progress in ABM weaponry, see chapters 7 and 8.

17. Sokolovskii, *Voennaia strategiia*, p. 359.

18. Lomov, *Nauchno-tekhnicheskii progress*, p. 272. Note that this is essentially the same as Admiral Gorshkov's statement about strategic ASW published in 1976. Moreover, in Soviet usage the term "air defense" usually means air, missile, and space defense. For antisatellite programs, see 1984 and 1985 editions of *Soviet Military Power*, pp. 34–36 and 43–45, respectively.

19. Sokolovskii, *Voennaia strategiia*, pp. 303, 343, and 359; Lomov, *Nauchno-tekhnicheskii progress*, pp. 108 and 279; Grechko, *Na strazhe mira*, p. 46; entry on "Voiska PVO Strany," in *Sovetskaia voennaia entsiklopediia* 2: 316–21.

20. For a similar appreciation, see Deane, *Strategic Defense in Soviet Strategy*, pp. 84–94.

21. An expanded discussion of this subject appears as an excerpt in U.S. Department of Defense, *Soviet Military Power, 1985*, quoted at the end of section 6.

22. Lomov, *Nauchno-tekhnicheskii progress*, p. 140.

23. William T. Lee, *Inventories in the Soviet Economy: Some Implications for Targeting* (Washington, D.C.: Center for Planning and Research, December 1978), p. 3. Normal inventories rose from about 43 percent of GNP in 1958 to about 47 percent in 1975.

24. Recently, a Soviet writer made what appears to be the only reference to the magnitude of state reserves after the Second World War. A. G. Koriagin (Koriagin, chief ed., *Sotsialisticheskoe vosproizvodstvo: Dinamizm i rezul'tativnost'* [Moscow: Mysl', 1983], p. 20) indicated that expenditures for state reserves amounted to between 5 and 6 percent of USSR gross national product during the period 1946–50.

25. Entry on "Zapasy materialnykh sredstv," in *Sovetskaia voennaia entsiklopediia* 3: 400–402.

26. General Major A. Korniyenko and Captain V. Korolev, "Economic Aspects of Soviet Military Doctrine," *Military Thought*, no. 7 (July 1967): 28. Korniyenko is probably a political officer, since he was previously head of the military economics faculty at the Political Military Academy named after Lenin.

27. General Major A. Korniyenko, "Military Economics as a Science," ibid., no. 7 (July 1969): 35.

28. Lieutenant Colonel E. Galitskiy, "The Coordination of Civil Defense with Units of the Armed Forces," ibid., no. 4 (April 1968): 47–52.

29. According to then General of the Army V. Kulikov ("The Indestructible Unity of Peoples," ibid., no. 12 [December 1972]: 16), "defense of the socialist homeland and of the conquests of socialism effected by the worker and peasant state, constitutes a *general law* of the socialist revolution, the building of socialism and communism." (Emphasis added.) Kulikov is a first deputy minister of defense and a member

of the CPSU Central Committee. He was chief of the General Staff from 1971 to 1977 and has been commanding officer for Warsaw Pact forces since 1977.

For much more on these themes, see Colonel V. Zubarev, "The Defense of the Achievements of Socialism: A General Law of the Building of Communism," ibid., no. 3 (March 1971): 36–52. This article carried an editorial note that it was one of a series, published for the edification of all concerned on the topic of "military problems in the history of scientific communism." For pertinent material on Soviet aid to revolutionary movements and "wars of national liberation," see V. Ivanov, "Methodological Questions of Scientific Leadership," ibid., no. 2 (February 1973): 16–33; and an editorial, "The Leninist Course: Along the Path Marked by the Twenty-fourth CPSU Congress," ibid., no. 4 (April 1973): 1–13.

30. See chap. 6 in Richard F. Staar, *USSR Foreign Policies After Détente* (Stanford: Hoover Institution Press, 1985), pp. 110–30.

31. Colonel M. Shirokov, "Military Geography at the Present Stage," *Military Thought*, no. 11 (November 1966): 59–60.

32. Marshal A. A. Grechko, *Vooruzhennye sily sovetskogo gosudarstva*, 2d rev. ed. (Moscow: Voenizdat, 1975), p. 107.

33. Marshal A. A. Grechko, *The Armed Forces of the Soviet State: A Soviet View*. Soviet Military Thought, no. 12. Translated and published under the auspices of the United States Air Force (Washington, D.C.: GPO, n.d.), p. 90.

34. Grechko, *Vooruzhennye sily sovetskogo gosudarstva*, 2d rev. ed., p. 108. See also U.S. Air Force translation of Grechko's 2d ed., *The Armed Forces of the Soviet State: A Soviet View*, p. 90.

35. Grechko, *Na strazhe mira*.

36. "Passive Measures" in U.S. Department of Defense, *Soviet Military Power, 1985*, pp. 51–53.

37. This section makes no pretense at being an exhaustive treatment of Soviet military operational concepts. It is only intended to outline those few concepts that are pertinent to the treatment of USSR military force development in our book.

38. Scott and Scott, *Armed Forces of the USSR*, 3d rev. ed., pp. 105–40. See also the entries for VGK, GKO, and Stavka in *Sovetskaia voennaia entsiklopediia* 2: 113 and 621–22, 7: 512. For some rather explicit remarks on prior policy planning and the role of the political leadership in a nuclear war, see Colonel General M. Lomov, "Several Problems of Control in Modern Warfare," *Military Thought*, no. 1 (January 1966): 2–4 and 9.

39. See entry, "Stavka (SVGK)," in *Sovetskaia voennaia entsiklopediia* 7: 511–12. During the Second World War there were more than 200 meetings of the Politburo, Orgburo, and the Central Committee to deal with the most important policy issues, according to Colonel K. Spidchenko and Lieutenant Colonel (res.) G. Fedorov, "The Leninist Style for Management of a War Economy," *Military Thought*, no. 5 (May 1971): 25–40.

40. The role of war games in testing the tenets and recommendations of military science and in improving official views about how to conduct nuclear war has been

discussed in an article by Captain First Rank N. Shumichkin, "Collective Defense: The Guarantee of Sovereignty of the Countries of the Socialist Commonwealth," ibid., no. 5 (May 1972): 30. For the advantages of maneuvers in which each side operates according to its own "views on the conduct of military operations," see Rear Admiral V. Andreev, "Methods of Military Science," ibid., no. 8 (August 1971): 40. On the use of experimental exercises to test concepts of military operations, see the editorial, "Development of Military Theory: An Important Factor in Increasing the Fighting Power of the Armed Forces," ibid., no. 2 (February 1973): 11.

Rear Admiral M. Kholodov and Colonel A. Sidorenko ("The Character and Basic Principles of Military Science Research," ibid., no. 8 [August 1971]: 30) note that field exercises are "very beneficial" even if they "involve various conventions and simplifications." According to Rear Admiral V. Andreev, "Of the greatest scientific value are bilateral exercises and war games whereby each side is guided by the views on the conduct of military operations prevailing in the armed forces of the depicted nations and coalitions. In this case, a model is constructed that objectively portrays the actions of the sides."

41. General Major N. Komkov and Colonel P. Shemanskii, "Certain Historic Trends in the Development of Troop Control," ibid., no. 10 (October 1964): 6.

42. Ibid., p. 13.

43. General Major Kh. Dzhelaukhov, "The Infliction of Deep Strikes," ibid., no. 2 (February 1966): 48. The author served on the faculty of the General Staff Academy at the time he wrote this article.

44. Sokolovskii, *Voennaia strategiia*, pp. 297, 346–47, and 434.

45. Ibid., p. 347. For an extensive treatment of the Soviet "operational-strategic" concept, see the entry under "Ob"edinenie" in *Sovetskaia voennaia entsiklopediia 5*: 679–80; General Colonel I. Shavrov, "Soviet Operational Art," *Military Thought*, no. 10 (October 1973): 6, 8, and 9; and General Lieutenant V. Reznichenko, "Tactics: A Component Part of the Art of Warfare," ibid., no. 12 (December 1973): 38.

46. General Major S. Begunov, "The Maneuver of Forces and Matériel in an Offensive," *Military Thought*, no. 5 (May 1968): 42–48. It is likely that initial strategic maneuver of most force components would take place in the crisis period prior to initiation of hostilities.

47. Ibid., pp. 42–43.

48. In September 1980, the Soviets conducted an exercise in which they demonstrated a reload capability for their largest missile, the SS-18; see Clarence A. Robinson, Jr., "Soviet SALT Violations Feared," *Aviation Week and Space Technology* 113, no. 12 (September 22, 1980): 14–15. See also U.S. Department of Defense, *Soviet Military Power, 1985*, pp. 36–39 on theater nuclear weapons.

49. The following citations are a sample of printed material on the subject of reserves and force reconstitution: General Major Kh. Dzhelaukhov, "Combating Strategic Reserves in a Theater of Military Operations," ibid., no. 11 (November 1964): 38; General Major A. Muzychenko, "Comprehensively Develop the Theory of Military Economics," *Military Thought*, no. 8 (August 1971): 63–67; General Lieutenant V. Reznichenko, "Characteristic Features and Methods of Conducting an Of-

fensive," ibid., no. 1 (January 1972): 66–77; and Grechko, *Vooruzhennye sily sovetskogo gosudarstva*, 1974 ed., pp. 106–12.

CHAPTER 5

1. Physically, this base has expanded tremendously over the past twenty-five years. The institutional structure, however—design bureaucracy, experimental plants, series production factories—was in place at the end of the 1960s.

2. Three hundred launchers would ensure that about 250 missiles would arrive on target. This number would be roughly adequate for attacks on 100 MM LCCs, hardened national command-control facilities, nuclear weapons storage sites, and production facilities.

3. U.S. Senate, Committee on Aeronautical and Space Sciences, *Soviet Space Programs, 1966–1970*, Senate Doc. No. 92–51, prepared by Charles S. Sheldon II et al. (Washington, D.C.: GPO, 1971), p. 168. Perhaps significantly, these two shots were the only launches in the "Elektron" series.

4. Secretary of Defense Harold Brown, *Department of Defense Annual Report, Fiscal Year 1980* (Washington, D.C.: The Pentagon, 1981), p. 66. In contrast, Secretary of Defense Caspar W. Weinberger (*Soviet Military Power, 1985* [Washington, D.C.: The Pentagon, 1985]) states on p. 36 that "refire missiles are also available for the SS-20."

5. Major General George J. Keegan, Jr., USAF (ret.) ("New Assessment Put on Soviet Threat," *Aviation Week and Space Technology* 106, no. 13 [March 28, 1977]: 38–48) reported the Soviet IR/MRBM missile inventory to be between 1,000 and 3,000 missiles. Edgar Ulsamer ("Moscow's Goal is Military Superiority," *Air Force Magazine* 63, no. 3 [March 1980]: 42–52) stated that each SS-20 launcher "is reloadable with three missiles plus a reserve contingent." It is likely, therefore, that the Soviet SS-4/5 IR/MRBM missile inventory totaled about four times the number of launchers, and the same factor may also have applied to SS-7 and SS-8 ICBM launchers.

6. Edgar Ulsamer, "The Politburo's Grand Design: Total Military Superiority," *Air Force Magazine* 64, no. 3 (March 1981): 41–49.

7. U.S. Senate, Armed Services Committee, Subcommittee on General Procurement, *Hearings on Soviet Defense Expenditures and Related Programs*, 96th Cong., 1st & 2d sess. (Washington, D.C.: GPO, 1980). (See also Chapter 2, note 23.)

8. On the CIA performance, see W. T. Lee, *The Estimation of Soviet Defense Expenditures, 1955–75* (New York: Praeger, 1977), pp. 4–22, 83–95, and 133–140; U.S. Senate, *Hearings on Soviet Defense Expenditures*; W. T. Lee, *Soviet Defense Expenditures in an Era of SALT* (Washington, D.C.: United States Strategic Institute, 1979); and U.S. House, Permanent Select Committee on Intelligence, Subcommittee on Oversight, *Hearings on CIA Estimates of Soviet Defense Spending*, 96th Cong., 2d sess. (Washington, D.C.: GPO, 1980); and W. T. Lee, *Understanding the Soviet*

Military Threat: How CIA Estimates Went Astray (New York: National Strategy Information Center, 1977), pp. 7–24 and 45–48.

CHAPTER 6

1. United States Arms Control and Disarmament Agency (ACDA), *Arms Control
and Disarmament Agreements* (Washington, D.C.: GPO, 1982), pp. 156–57.

2. The accuracy of ballistic missiles is expressed in terms of the "circular error
probable" (CEP), which means that 50 percent of the missiles launched will deliver
their warheads within a specified distance—for example, within 0.5 nautical miles of
the target. Hard targets are rated at the overpressures they can withstand, expressed
in pounds per square inch, or psi.

3. CEPs, yields, and deployment data are from John M. Collins, *U.S.-Soviet Military Balance* (New York: McGraw-Hill, 1980), pp. 446–47. Collins reports the CEP
of the SS-18 mod 4 as about 260 meters (0.14 nautical miles) and the SS-19 mod 2 as
the same. Because the SS-19 mod 2 and mod 3 are contemporaneous, the CEP of the
mod 3 is assumed to be the same as that of the mod 2.

4. Ibid.

5. The link between U.S. precision machine tools and the accuracy of late-model
Soviet ICBMs is from the testimony of Dr. Jack Vorona, deputy director for scientific
and technical intelligence, Defense Intelligence Agency, in U.S. Senate, Committee on
Armed Services, Subcommittee on General Procurement, *Hearings on Soviet Defense Expenditures and Related Programs*, 96th Cong., 1st & 2d sess., 1 and 8 November 1979, 4 February 1980 (Washington, D.C.: GPO, 1980), 70.

6. U.S. Department of Defense, *Soviet Military Power, 1985* (Washington, D.C.:
GPO, April 1985), pp. 96–97.

7. John W. R. Taylor, ed., *Jane's All the World's Aircraft 1979–80* (London: Jane's
Publishing Co., 1979), p. 194, citing *U.S. Department of Defense Posture Statement,
Fiscal Year 1979*. See also *Jane's* for 1981–82, pp. 202–4, on the MIG-23.

8. Edgar Ulsamer, "Moscow's Goal is Military Superiority," *Air Force Magazine*
63, no. 3 (March 1980): 50 and *Soviet Military Power, 1985*, p. 49.

9. The United States expected the SA-10 to be deployed in early 1978, although
this did not happen. American officials suggest the cruise missile connection as
the reason. See the report based on statements by U.S. Undersecretary of Defense
William Perry in *International Defense Review* 1 (1979): 12. Other published
sources indicate deployment of the SA-10 underway on Soviet naval combatants.
Aviation and Marine International (71 [March 1980]: 23) reported that both the
new Sovetskii Soiuz and Kirov class cruisers were armed with the SA-N-10, which is
evidently the Soviet navy's version of the SA-10.

10. Secretary of Defense Harold Brown, *Department of Defense Annual Report
Fiscal Year 1981* (Washington, D.C.: GPO, 1980), p. 82, and Ulsamer, "Moscow's
Goal is Military Superiority", p. 50. Both sources indicated that deployment of the

SA-10 was imminent. Chairman of the Joint Chiefs of Staff, General David C. Jones, USAF (*United States Military Posture for FY 1982*, p. 101) reported that the SA-10 was being deployed about mid-1980. See also, *Soviet Military Power, 1985*, p. 50.

11. Brown, *Annual Report Fiscal Year 1980*, p. 73; and Jones, *Military Posture for FY 1982*, p. 101.

12. Henry Bradsher, "Soviet ABM Defense Step-up Has Pentagon Concerned," *Washington Star*, 16 February 1978. See also Jones, *Military Posture for FY 1982*; and Clarence A. Robinson, Jr., "SALT 1–2" in *Aviation Week and Space Technology* (1976), special issue, p. 35. This last writer ("Soviet SALT Violations Feared," *Aviation Week and Space Technology*, 22 September 1980, p. 15) reports that one of the new interceptors is designed for high altitude—presumably outside the atmosphere—and the other for terminal phase or atmospheric intercepts. This is the same concept employed in the U.S. Nike system developed during the mid-1960s.

13. *Aviation Week and Space Technology* (1976), special issue, p. 79.

14. Walter Pincus, "Soviets Update Antiballistic Missile Systems With New Radar," *Washington Post*, 14 September 1980; Ulsamer, "Moscow's Goal Is Military Superiority," p. 50; "More Undisclosed Soviet Strategic Arms Gains," *Armed Forces International* 116, no. 7 (March 1979): 17. According to the last source, a team assessment of the battle-management capability of the new radars was headed by Dr. Eugene Fabini, Secretary of Defense Harold Brown's "most trusted consultant on intelligence and technical affairs." On page 69 of the *Department of Defense Annual Report Fiscal Year 1980*, however, Secretary Brown referred to these four new radars as "detection and tracking radars." General Jones (*Military Posture Fiscal Year 1982 Department of Defense Program for Research, Development, and Acquisition*, p. II–18) reports that these radars "are believed to be associated with ballistic missile defense."

15. Robinson, "Soviet SALT Violations Feared," p. 14.

16. Henry S. Bradsher, "Soviet Arms Control View Frustrates U.S. Officials," *Washington Star*, 7 July 1981.

17. Some limited deployment of a Soviet ASAT system seems to have been reflected in the SALT II Treaty. The "Common Understanding" to subparagraph (c) of Article 9 prohibiting the placement of nuclear weapons in space does not require "dismantling or destruction of any existing launchers of either Party." ACDA, *Arms Control and Disarmament Agreements*, p. 264.

18. "Soviets Launch Second Satellite Intercept in Nine Months," *Aviation Week and Space Technology* 114, no. 6 (February 9, 1981), pp. 28–29.

19. Robinson, "Soviet SALT Violations Feared," p. 15.

20. Baker, "Soviet Ship Types," pp. 111–117.

21. Ibid., p. 116.

22. *Aviation and Marine International* 71 (March 1980): 23.

23. Captain John E. Moore RN, FRGS, ed., *Jane's Fighting Ships, 1977–78* (London: Macdonald and Jane's Publishing Co., 1977), p. 680. Apparently, the second

Alpha had just been completed because this issue of *Jane's* reported two units, whereas previous editions carried only one. This should have been a signal that the program was not dead.

24. Admiral N. Kharlamov, "Some Trends in the Development of Navies," *Military Thought*, no. 10 (October 1967): 66.

25. Admiral A. Chabanenko, "Combat Rocket-Carrying Atomic Submarines," ibid., no. 12 (December 1967): 47.

26. Captain First Rank N. Shatrov, "Trends in the Development and Employment of Naval Fleets," ibid., no. 1 (January 1972): 55.

27. George C. Wilson, "Soviet Navy Has Faster, Lighter Sub," *Washington Post*, 18 May 1979; "News in Brief," *International Defense Review* 13, no. 2 (1980): 164.

28. U.S. Department of Defense, *Soviet Military Power, 1985*, p. 95 states that Mike embodies the state-of-the-art in propulsion and pressure-hull design.

29. "Newest Delta Sub Pivotal in Latest SALT Violation," *Aviation Week and Space Technology* 104, no. 21 (May 24, 1976): 20–21; Edgar Ulsamer, "Disquiet for the Silent Service," *Air Force Magazine* 67, no. 10 (October 1984): 25–26.

30. Captain Second Rank V. Bestuzhev, "Combat Actions on the Sea," *Military Thought*, no. 7 (July 1971): 81.

31. Fleet Admiral S. G. Gorshkov, *Morskaia moshch' gosudarstva* (Moscow: Voenizdat, 1976), p. 337.

32. Interview with Admiral Thomas B. Hayward, "Navy Chief Details Loss of U.S. Edge on Soviets," *Aviation Week and Space Technology* 114, no. 6 (February 9, 1981): 35 and Edgar Ulsamer, "In Focus," *Air Force Magazine* 63, no. 12 (December 1980): 26. Hayward states that U.S. navy intelligence was surprised by the appearance of Oscar.

33. William J. Perry, *FY 1982 Research, Development and Acquisition*, chap. 1, pp. 1–5.

34. Captain J. W. Kehoe, USN and K. S. Brewer, "The Kirov," *International Defense Review* 14, no. 2 (1981): 154–58.

35. General Colonel N. A. Lomov, General Colonel I. I. Anureev, and Colonel M. I. Galkin, eds., *Nauchno-tekhnicheskii progress i revoliutsiia v voennom dele* (Moscow: Voenizdat, 1973), pp. 273 and 275.

36. G. V. Zimin, *Razvitie protivovozdushnoi oborony* (Moscow: Voenizdat, 1976), p. 105. Cited by Michael J. Deane, *Strategic Defense in Soviet Strategy*, Monographs in International Affairs (Coral Gables, Fla.: Advanced International Studies Institute, University of Miami, 1980), p. 80.

37. W. T. Lee, *The Estimation of Soviet Defense Expenditures, 1955–75* (New York: Praeger, 1977), p. 65.

38. W. T. Lee, "USSR Gross National Product in Established Prices, 1955–1975," in Hans Raupach, ed., *Jahrbuch der Wirtschaft Osteuropa's*, vol. 8 (Munich: Guenter Olzog Verlag, 1979), pp. 412 and 415.

39. W. T. Lee, *Trends in Soviet Defense Expenditures*, Report No. AAC-TR-10001/79 (Washington, D.C.: Analytical Assessments Co., 1979), pp. 17 and 19.

40. *Narodnoe khoziaistvo SSSR v 1983 g.* (Moscow: Statistika, 1982), p. 355.

41. Lee, *Soviet Defense Expenditures in an Era of SALT*, p. 17. Later data have confirmed this estimate.

42. *Narodnoe khoziaistvo SSSR v 1978 g.* (Moscow: Statistika, 1977), pp. 547 and 551.

43. Ibid. *1979 g.*, pp. 567 and 569.

44. "Vneshnetorgovyi oborot SSSR," *Ekonomicheskaia gazeta*, no. 7 (February 1981): 1; *Narodnoe khoziaistvo SSSR v 1983 g.* (Moscow: Statistika, 1982), pp. 561–563.

CHAPTER 7

1. "U.S. Officials Say Soviet Arms Plan is Not Balanced," *New York Times*, 1 October 1985.

2. *Pravda*, 28 February 1981.

3. Secretary of Defense Harold Brown, *Department of Defense Annual Report, Fiscal Year 1982* (Washington, D.C.: GPO, 1981); Chairman of the Joint Chiefs of Staff General David C. Jones, USAF, *United States Military Posture for FY 1982*; William J. Perry, undersecretary of defense for research and engineering, *The FY 1982 Department of Defense Program for Research, Development, and Acquisition; Report of the Secretary of Defense Caspar W. Weinberger to the Congress*, 99th Cong., 1st sess. (Washington, D.C.: GPO, 4 February 1985), p. 49; U.S. Department of Defense, *Soviet Military Power*, 3d ed. (Washington, D.C.: The Pentagon, 1984), pp. 22–32, 51–53, and 96; ibid., 4th ed. (1985), pp. 23–36.

4. *Soviet Military Power*, 4th ed. (April 1985), p. 36, stated that about 400 SS-20 launchers were deployed, some 270 of them vis-a-vis NATO; *New York Times*, 27 September 1985, gave the total as 441.

5. Gates and Gershwin, *Soviet Strategic Force Developments*, p. 4.

6. Dept. of Defense, *Soviet Military Power*, 3d ed., pp. 32–41, 61–67, and 97–99; ibid., 4th ed., pp. 43–59, and 91–109.

7. Ibid., 3d ed., pp. 32–33; ibid., 4th ed., pp. 45–48.

8. "The President's Unclassified Report to the Congress on Soviet Noncompliance with Arms Control Agreements," *Congressional Record—Senate* 130, no. 8, 98th Cong., 2d sess., 1 February 1984, S-647-52. See also General Advisory Committee on Arms Control and Disarmament, *A Quarter Century of Soviet Compliance Practices Under Arms Control Commitments* (Washington, D.C., October 1984).

9. The CIA seems to be approaching a cogent analysis of Soviet objectives in general and the potential for ABM breakout in particular. [See testimony by Gates and

Gershwin, *Soviet Strategic Force Developments*, pp. 1–5.] The quotation about ABM capabilities of the SA-10 and the SA-X-12 appears on page 5.

10. *Soviet Military Power, 1985*, pp. 65–72, and 79–90; International Institute for Strategic Studies, *The Military Balance, 1985–1986* (London, 1985), p. 16–17, 21–30.

11. *Pravda*, 12 June 1985.

CHAPTER 8

1. For a comprehensive discussion of USSR views on protracted conflict, see Richard S. Soll, "The Soviet Union and Protracted Nuclear War," *Strategic Review* 8, no. 4 (Fall 1980): 15–28.

2. According to General Major S. Kozlov ("The Development of Soviet Military Science After World War II," *Military Thought*, no. 2 [February 1974]: 47), the change in USSR views on this issue seems to date from early 1964. This article appears to be the earliest statement recognizing that war with NATO could begin and continue for some time with both sides using only conventional weapons.

3. *Pravda*, 14 June 1977; *Krasnaia zvezda*, 27 May 1978.

4. Marshal of the Soviet Union N. I. Krylov, "Raketnye voiska strategicheskogo naznacheniia," *Nedelia*, no. 36 (27 August–2 September 1967): 8.
The same target categories are repeated in all three editions of Marshal V. D. Sokolovskii's *Voennaia strategiia* and in various articles published by *Military Thought*. They also appear on p. 139 of General Colonel N. A. Lomov, General Major I. I. Anureev, and Colonel M. I. Galkin, eds., *Nauchno-tekhnicheskii progress i revoliutsiia v voennom dele* (Moscow: Voenizdat, 1973) and on p. 41 of A. A. Grechko, *Na strazhe mira i stroitel'stva kommunizma* (Moscow: Voenizdat, 1971). The entry for "Rocket Forces of Strategic Designation" in *Sovetskaia voennaia entsiklopediia* (Moscow, 1979), 7: 52, does not spell out the target categories for the SRF. On the next page, however, enemy strategic missile forces are said to target the traditional USSR categories (a typical example of mirror imaging).

5. Colonel M. Shirokov, "The Question of Geographic Influences on the Military and Economic Potential of Warring States," *Military Thought*, no. 4 (April 1968): 38.

6. As an editorial ("The 51st Anniversary of the Soviet Armed Forces," ibid., no. 2 [February 1969]: 2) phrased it, the "wicked and crafty" class enemy is willing to commit any crime for the sake of his mercenary interests. Not having a future themselves, the imperialists want to "take the future from all peaceloving peoples, above all from the peoples building a new world—the world of socialism." The context is the alleged propensity of "imperialism" to wage war on "socialism," but the sentiment seems equally applicable to Soviet attitudes toward "maximum fatality" targeting.

7. Shirokov, "Geographic Influences," p. 34. Most USSR sources do not specify

types of industries to be attacked, beyond those producing weapons. The few singled out are power, petroleum, and chemical plants.

8. General Lieutenant G. Semenov and General Major V. Prokhorov, "Scientific Technical Progress and Some Questions of Strategy," *Military Thought*, no. 2 (February 1969): 23; General Major Kh. Dzhelaukhov, "Infliction of Deep Strikes," ibid., no. 2 (February 1966): 42–45; General Major V. Kruchinin, "Contemporary Strategic Theory," ibid., no. 10 (1963): 17; Colonel M. Skovorodkin, "Some Questions on Coordination," ibid., no. 2 (February 1967): 39–40; General Major I. Anureev, "Mathematical Methods in Military Affairs," ibid., no. 9 (September 1966): 50; General Major S. Bronevskii, "The Factors of Space and Time in Military Operations," ibid., no. 7 (July 1963): 35–38 and 40; Lomov, *Nauchno-technicheskii progress*, pp. 33, 139, and 144; Marshal V. D. Sokolovskii, ed., *Voennaia strategiia*, 3d ed. (Moscow: Voenizdat, 1968), pp. 297 and 349; Colonel M. Shirokov, "Military Geography at the Present Stage," *Military Thought*, no. 11 (November 1966): 50, 57, and 59; idem, "The Question of Geographic Influences," ibid., no. 4 (April 1968): 34, 36, and 37–40; and General Colonel A. S. Zheltov, Lieutenant Colonel T. R. Kondratkov, and Colonel E. A. Khomenko, eds., *Metodologicheskie problemy voennoi teorii i praktiki*, 2d rev. ed. (Moscow: Voenizdat, 1969), pp. 120–21.

The above sources span more than a decade of Soviet literature. General Colonel Lomov's book was written by a group of political and line officers. Zheltov was head of the Political-Military Academy named after V. I. Lenin. These principles of nuclear targeting, therefore, appear to reflect a military-political consensus. The practices of equipping missiles with a variety of yields, minimum yields required to destroy the targets, yield-accuracy tradeoffs, and of reducing warhead yields as missile accuracy is improved have appeared in at least one ballistic-missile design book. See A. M. Siniukov and N. I. Morozov, *Konstruktsiia upravliaemykh ballisticheskikh raket* (Moscow: Voenizdat, 1969), pp. 9–10.

9. Edgar Ulsamer ("USSR's Military Shadow," *Air Force Magazine* [March 1977], p. 36) reported that Soviet silos were being hardened to 3,000 psi, or roughly double the hardness of Minuteman silos.

These factors have been analyzed by John Shannon and his colleagues at Science Applications, Inc. The effectiveness calculations presented herein are based both on this research and on reconstruction of USSR measures of effectiveness derived from Soviet sources.

10. I. I. Anureev, "Nadezhnost' porazheniia," *Sovetskaia voennaia entsiklopediia* 5: 477; A. I. Aver'ianov, "Porazhenie ob"ektov," ibid. 6: 455.

11. The accuracy of inertial guidance systems varies with the range from launch point to target. Other factors, of course, contribute to total missile system accuracy. Inevitably, guided missiles are much more accurate at half range than at full range.

12. B. T. Surikov, *Boevoe primenenie raket* (Moscow: Voenizdat, 1965), Joint Press Research Survey translation (dated 3 November 1965), p. 32.

13. Siniukov and Morozov, *Konstruktsiia upravliaemykh*, pp. 9–10.

14. For MIRVed missiles, the re-entry vehicle's dispensing system, or "bus," usually accounts for some 40 to 50 percent of the total throw-weight.

15. Two or three small warheads will not only be more efficient in providing coverage of large area targets but will also cause much less collateral damage outside the target area.

16. V. F. Tolubko, *Nedelin: Zhizn' zamechatel'nykh liudei* (Moscow: Voenizdat, 1979), pp. 171–203.

17. Surikov, *Boevoe primenenie raket* (*Combat Employment of Missiles*), p. 23.

18. International Institute of Strategic Studies (IISS), *The Military Balance, 1979–1980* (London: IISS, 1979), p. 60.

19. John M. Collins, *U.S.-Soviet Military Balance: Concepts and Capabilities, 1960–1980* (New York: McGraw-Hill, 1980), p. 461.

20. The SS-7s and SS-8s were probably never assigned to Minuteman targets. These missiles had been marginally effective only against hardened Atlas and Titan ICBM launchers. All but 54 Titan II silos, however, were phased out of the U.S. inventory after 1,000 Minutemen had been deployed.

21. I. I. Anureev, "Nadezhnost' porazheniia," *Sovetskaia voennaia entsiklopediia* 5 (1978), p. 477 and A. I. Aver'ianov, "Porazhenie ob'ektov," ibid., 6 (1978), p. 455.

22. Collins, *U.S.-Soviet Military Balance*, p. 466, specifies the yield of the SS-18 mod 4 as 0.5 megatons and gives it a CEP of about 260 meters. The SS-19 mod 1 yield is given as 0.55 megatons and the accuracy of the SS-19 mod 2 as 260 meters (or the same as for the SS-18 mod 4). The yield of the SS-19 mod 3 is assumed to be the same as for the mod 1 and its accuracy the same as for the mod 2.

23. A representative example of this attitude appeared in *The Washington Post*, 4 May 1981. Michael Getler cited Harvard professor Stanley Hoffman in an appearance on "Bill Moyers' Journal." Professor Hoffman reportedly "wondered aloud if the only purpose of the MX or a reopened ABM system was to reassure ourselves rather than to combat a real threat."

24. Private observation to coauthor W. T. Lee. Mr. Metcalf has presented the detailed argument in editorials for *Strategic Review*.

25. Unlike American ICBMs, which are launched only on test ranges regardless of whether the objective is R&D or training for operational crews, the Soviets routinely launch missiles from both test ranges and operational launchers. In 1967 Marshal Krylov, commander of the SRF, reported that launches both from test ranges and from operational launchers demonstrated missile accuracy sufficient to destroy targets. (See page 15 of his article, "The Nuclear-Missile Shield of the Soviet State," *Military Thought*, no. 11 [November 1967].) Marshal Krylov also claimed that these training launches demonstrated not only a high degree of reliability but also the capability to launch "at the assigned time," which is vital to the fulfillment of the combat mission. The type of combat mission referred to probably consists of closely coordinated launches against hard targets, bomber bases, and command-control facilities. Nevertheless, even these launches by operational units on northern trajectories have not demonstrated USSR missile accuracy for targets as far away as U.S. Minuteman silos.

As the Soviets replaced their SS-11s with MIRVed SS-17s and SS-19s in the latter half of the 1970s, they presumably fired the SS-11s from their silos along northern trajectories (Clarence A. Robinson, Jr., SALT 1 & 2 in *Aviation Week and Space Technology* (1976), special issue, p. 37.

26. Robinson, ibid., p. 41, writes about terminal guidance development. Improved inertial guidance systems will be incorporated in the new generation of ICBMs reported to be under development.

27. General of the Army S. Ivanov, "Soviet Military Doctrine and Strategy," *Military Thought*, no. 5 (1969): 48.

28. N. I. Akimov, ed., *Grazhdanskaia oborona* (Moscow: Kolos, 1969), Oak Ridge National Laboratory translation (1971), p. 68, states that evacuation or dispersal could reduce urban population losses from 90 percent to between 5 and 8 percent.

CHAPTER 9

1. Central Intelligence Agency, *CPSU Central Committee and Central Auditing Commission: Members Elected at the 26th Party Congress*, CR 81–111349 (Washington, D.C.: GPO, May 1981), pp. 3–43.

2. Caspar W. Weinberger, "Preface," in *Soviet Military Power, 1985* (Washington, D.C.: The Pentagon, April 1985), p. 4.

3. This section is based on the Appendix.

4. In 1980 prices the current military burden is probably about 16 percent of Soviet GNP. The figure is lower than in 1970 prices because of economies of scale in weapons production that are passed on to the Ministry of Defense in the form of lower prices. *Narodnoe khoziaistvo 1978 goda*, p. 138, shows a differential of about 21 percent (lower) between the value of USSR machinery output in current prices and Soviet constant prices.

These are W. T. Lee's estimates, which are the only ones for Soviet military expenditures that were corroborated by the evidence that forced the CIA to double its figures. U.S. Congress, Joint Economic Committee, Subcommittee on International Trade, Finance, and Security Economics, Statement by Robert Gates, CIA deputy director for intelligence, *The Allocation of Resources in the Soviet Union and China, 1984*, 98th Cong., 2d sess. (Washington, D.C.: GPO, 21 November 1984, Mimeographed), 9.

5. John M. Collins, *U.S.-Soviet Military Balance, 1980–1985* (Washington, D.C.: Pergamon-Brassey's International Defense Publishers, 1985), table 54, p. 289. The evidence on the 10,000 warheads is taken from U.S. intelligence sources, according to an aide of Senator James A. McClure interviewed by the *New York Times*, 22 March 1985.

6. U.S. Department of Defense, *Soviet Military Power, 1985* (Washington, D.C.: The Pentagon, April 1985), pp. 30–31.

7. Joel S. Wit, "Advances in Anti-Submarine Warfare," *Scientific American* 224, no. 2 (February 1981): 31–41.

8. V. I. Korolev, ed., *Grazhdanskaia oborona SSSR*, 6th ed. (Moscow: Voenizdat, 1984). A total of 1.5 million copies were published.

9. United States Arms Control and Disarmament Agency, *Arms Control and Disarmament Agreements* (Washington, D.C.: GPO, 1982), Article 15, p. 142.

10. *Soviet Military Power, 1985*, p. 4.

11. A British source estimates that the USSR spends $18 to $19 billion on all kinds of planning for defense, as compared to $1.3 billion per year by the United States for the R&D on the Strategic Defense Initiative (SDI). *The Economist*, 23 March 1985, p. 47.

12. Marshal of the Soviet Union and Chief of the General Staff S. Akhromeev, "Agreement on SDI—A Barrier Against the Strategic Arms Race," *Pravda*, 4 June 1985, p. 4.

13. Hans Ruehle, "Gorbachev's 'Star Wars'," *NATO Review*, vol. 33, no. 4 (August 1985), pp. 26–32.

14. *Washington Post*, 29 September 1985.

15. *New York Times*, 9 October 1985.

16. U.S. Government, Department of Defense, *Annual Report FY 1981* (Washington, D.C.: GPO, 1980), p. 73.

17. Ibid.

18. See speech by Gorbachev in *Pravda*, 9 May 1985, for his contention that the United States is the successor to Nazi Germany.

APPENDIX

1. John Newhouse, *Cold Dawn: The Story of SALT* (New York: Holt, Rinehart and Winston, 1973), pp. 92 and 104.

2. Wayland Young (Lord Kennet), "Disarmament: Thirty Years of Failure," *International Security* 2, no. 3 (Winter 1978): 45.

3. Raymond L. Garthoff, "Mutual Deterrence and Strategic Arms Limitation in Soviet Policy," ibid. 3, no. 1 (Summer 1978): 129, citing General Major V. I. Zemskov, "Wars of the Modern Era," *Military Thought*, no. 5 (May 1969): 59. Dr. Garthoff perceives a "clear relationship" between the USSR fear of an effective ABM defense and the (prior) Soviet decision to seek limited ABM forces on both sides "so as not to risk restoring the United States to a position of superiority that could imperil the *still unstable state of mutual assured destruction and mutual deterrence*." (Emphasis added.) One can agree that USSR fears were the basis for seeking a near ban on ABM deployments in SALT, without agreeing that the Soviets sought a stable MAD or "mutual" deterrence.

4. *Pravda*, 11 February 1967. Cited by Michael J. Deane, *The Role of Strategic Defense in Soviet Strategy*, Monographs in International Affairs (Washington, D.C.: Advanced International Studies Institute; Coral Gables, Fla.: University of Miami, 1980), p. 32.

5. *Washington Post*, 26 June 1967. Cited in Deane, *Strategic Defense in Soviet Strategy*, p. 33.

6. Thomas W. Wolfe, *The SALT Experience* (Cambridge, Mass.: Ballinger Publishing Co., 1979).

7. Newhouse, *Cold Dawn*, pp. 56 and 192.

8. Igor S. Glagolev, "The Soviet Decision-Making Process in Arms-Control Negotiations," *Orbis* 21, no. 4 (Winter 1978): 767–76.

9. Wolfe, *The SALT Experience*, p. 51.

10. According to Glagolev ("Soviet Decision-Making Process," p. 770), the Academy of Sciences' commission on disarmament matters was headed by V. Emelianov, who "did everything in his power to persuade Khrushchev not to conclude a treaty on the partial prohibition of nuclear weapons tests, and he has not convened his commission even once during the past ten years."

11. For a discussion of the supreme command structure, see Harriet Fast Scott and William F. Scott, *The Armed Forces of the USSR*, 3d rev. ed. (Boulder, Colo.: Westview Press, 1984), pp. 105–40; General Major N. Komkov and Colonel P. Shemanskii, "Certain Historic Trends in the Development of Troop Control," *Military Thought*, no. 10 (October 1964): 4, 6, and 13; and General Major Kh. Dzhelaukhov, "The Infliction of Deep Strikes," ibid., no. 2 (February 1966): 48.

12. General of the Army V. F. Tolubko, "Raketnye Voiska Strategicheskogo Naznacheniia," *Voenno-istoricheskii zhurnal* 17, no. 4 (1975): 54; and article by Tolubko under same title in ibid. 18, no. 10 (1976): 20–21. See also Tolubko's biography of Marshal Nedelin (*Nedelin: Pervyi glavkom strategicheskikh* [Moscow: Molodaia gvardiia, 1979]).

13. Newhouse, *Cold Dawn*, pp. 251–52.

14. General Major of Engineering-Technical Services I. I. Anureev, "Determining the Correlation of Forces in Terms of Nuclear Weapons," *Military Thought*, no. 6 (1967): 35–45. Anureev was one of the senior research analysts and instructors at the General Staff Academy for many years (see General of the Army V. G. Kulikov, ed., *Akademiia General'nogo Shtaba* [Moscow: Voenizdat, 1976], p. 145) and is the author of several books and articles on operations research (cited in I. I. Anureev, "Issledovanie operatsii," *Sovetskaia voennaia entsiklopediia* 3: 619–21).

15. Coauthor W. T. Lee is indebted to John Shannon of Science Applications, Inc. for noting the error in Anureev's equation.

16. General Colonel A. S. Zheltov, Lieutenant Colonel T. R. Kondratkov, and Colonel E. A. Khomenko, eds., *Metodologicheskie problemy voennoi teorii i praktiki*, 2d rev. ed. (Moscow: Voenizdat, 1969), p. 67. This manuscript was sent to the editor in September 1968 and typeset in June 1969.

17. Ibid., p. 68. Judging from the relatively small size of this vehicle, it may be a scale model only. A photograph appears in *Soviet Military Power, 1985*, p. 55. See also *New York Times*, 18 September 1985, p. 10, for an account of the SOIUZ T-14 transport ship whose crew repaired the SALIUT 7 space station.

18. V. I. Varfolomeev and M. I. Kopytor, eds., *Proektirovanie i ispytaniia ballisticheskikh raket* (Moscow: Voenizdat, 1970).

19. Ibid., p. 15.

20. Ibid., pp. 15–16 specifies penetration of ABM defenses as one criterion of ballistic missile effectiveness. For a description of weapons system testing to ensure that design criteria are met, see General Colonel N. N Alekseev, "Ispytaniia voennoi tekhniki," *Sovetskaia voennaia entsiklopediia* 3: 616–18. Alekseev served as one of two General Staff officers in the Soviet delegation to SALT I. He was subsequently promoted to deputy minister of defense with responsibility for arms development (see Wolfe, *The SALT Experience*, p. 69).

21. The maneuvering of RVs, or a combination of maneuver and exhaustion, are also high-confidence penetration aids or tactics. These are the approaches the United States chose after spending several billion dollars investigating the feasibility of various types of atmospheric decoys and finding them inadequate.

22. These are the ICBM launchers referenced in the common understanding to Article 2 of the SALT II agreement. U.S. Arms Control and Disarmament Agency, *Arms Control and Disarmament Agreements* (Washington, D.C., 1982), p. 247.

23. Zemskov, "Wars of the Modern Era," p. 60. The phrase "nuclear balance of power" rarely appears in this literature. Zemskov quotes it from Western sources throughout the article. To coauthor W. T. Lee's knowledge, this is the only one of Zemskov's many articles and other writings in which he does so. Other contributors to this journal apparently have not used the term.

24. See also General Major V. I. Zemskov, "Characteristic Features of Modern Wars and Possible Methods of Conducting Them," ibid., no. 7 (July 1969): esp. p. 19.

25. When the Soviets first agreed to engage in SALT, effective enemy air and missile defenses were specified as one of the conditions for a surprise attack on the USSR by a prudent aggressor. General Major N. Vasendin and Colonel N. Kuznetsov, "Modern Warfare and Surprise Attack," ibid., no. 6 (June 1968): 42–48.

26. Newhouse, *Cold Dawn*, p. 126.

27. Henry A. Kissinger, "The Future of NATO," in Kenneth A. Myers, ed., *NATO: The Next Thirty Years* (Boulder, Colo.: Westview Press, 1980), p. 11.

28. Varofolomeev and Kopytor (*Proektirovanie i ispytaniia*, p. 269) define strategic missiles as those with a range of 1,000 kilometers or more. Clearly, this definition includes all Soviet IR/MRBMs, medium bombers, and the SS-N-5 SLBMs.

29. As an attempt to provide a Soviet perspective to the U.S. assistant secretary of defense for international security affairs, a "Red Team" was formed early in the negotiations. It was, however, quickly discontinued. If this "Red Team" had been allowed to function—that is, if it had been given access to *Military Thought* and to the positions of both sides as the negotiations proceeded—the history of SALT might have been quite different.

30. Newhouse, *Cold Dawn*, p. 265.

31. Dotsent V. Dmitriev, "Diplomacy and Military Strategy," *Military Thought*, no. 7 (July 1971): 48–52, 55, 57–58, and 61.

32. Newhouse, *Cold Dawn*, pp. 214–19.

33. According to U.S. estimates, the Soviets have 441 SS-20 launchers already deployed, and about 100 of these are targeted against Asia. *New York Times*, 27 September 1985.

34. Newhouse, *Cold Dawn*, p. 23.

35. On the question of U.S. forecasts of Soviet weapons development, see the debate between Congressman Les Aspen and coauthor William T. Lee ("A Poor Record," *Strategic Review* 8, no. 3 (Summer 1980): 29–43 and 44–57.

According to Newhouse (*Cold Dawn*, pp. 70 and 118), the CIA has been an advocate of SALT. How advocacy of a specific policy can be consistent with CIA responsibility to provide impartial evaluations of Soviet intentions, capabilities, and vulnerabilities is an interesting question. For a discussion of general intelligence community failures to anticipate USSR strategic missile programs, see David S. Sullivan, "The Legacy of SALT I: Soviet Deception and U.S. Retreat," *Strategic Review* 7, no. 1 (Winter 1979): 26–41. For Soviet overstatements on the numbers of both their operational SSBNs and those under construction and for the U.S. failure to forecast the range of the SS-N-8, see David S. Sullivan, "A SALT Debate: Continued Soviet Deception," ibid., 7, no. 4 (Fall 1979): 29–38, esp. 31–32.

Bibliography

Akimov, N. I.; Vasilevskii, M. L.; Makarov, I. D.; Rusman, L. P.; and Umnov, M. P. *Grazhdanskaia oborona*. Edited by N. I. Akimov. Moscow: Kolos, 1969. Translated by S. J. Rimshaw and edited by Joanne Gailar and Cresson H. Kearny. *Civil Defense*. Oak Ridge, Tenn.: Oak Ridge National Laboratory, U. S. Atomic Energy Commission, 1971.

Bely, Colonel V., et al. *Marxism-Leninism on War and Army*. Moscow: Progress Publishers, 1972. Published under the auspices of the United States Air Force. Soviet Military Thought, no. 2. Washington, D.C.: GPO, 1978.

Boinov, A. A., ed. *Sovetskie vooruzhennye sily: Istoriia stroitel'stva*. Moscow: Voenizdat, 1978.

Bonds, Ray, ed. *Soviet War Machine: An Encyclopedia of Russian Military Equipment and Strategy* (New York: Hamlyn, 1977).

Bublik, L. A., et al. *Partiino-politicheskaia rabota v sovetskoi armii i voenno-morskom flote*. Moscow: Voenizdat, 1982.

Chuev, Iu. V., and Mikhailov, Iu. B. *Prognozirovanie v voennom dele*. Moscow: Voenizdat, 1975. Translated by the DGIS Multilingual Section, Translation Bureau, Secretary of State Department, Ottawa, Canada. Published under the auspices of the United States Air Force. *Forecasting in Military Affairs: A Soviet View*. Soviet Military Thought, no. 16. Washington, D.C.: GPO, 1980.

Collins, John M. *American and Soviet Military Trends Since the Cuban Missile Crisis*. Washington, D.C.: The Center for Strategic and International Studies, Georgetown University, 1978.

————. *U.S.-Soviet Military Balance: Concepts and Capabilities, 1960–1980*. New York: McGraw-Hill, 1980.

————. *U.S.-Soviet Military Balance, 1980–1985*. Elmsford, N.Y.: Pergamon-Brassey, 1985.

Collins, John M., and Cronin, Patrick M., *U.S.-Soviet Military Balance, Statistical Trends, 1970–1983*. Report no. 84-1635. Washington, D.C.: Congressional Research Service, 27 August 1984.

Danchenko, Colonel A. M., and Vydrin, Colonel I. F., eds. *Voennaia pedagogika*. Moscow: Voenizdat, 1973. Translated and published under the auspices of the United States Air Force. *Military Pedagogy: A Soviet View*. Soviet Military Thought, no. 7. Washington, D.C.: GPO, 1976.

Dash, Barbara. *A Defector Reports: The Institute of the USA and Canada*. Falls Church, Va.: Delphic Associates, 1982.

Deane, Michael J. *The Role of Strategic Defense in Soviet Strategy*. Monographs in International Affairs. Washington, D.C.: Advanced International Studies Institute; Coral Gables, Fla.: University of Miami, 1980.

Dinerstein, Herbert S. *War and the Soviet Union*. New York: Praeger, 1959.

Douglass, Joseph D., Jr. *Soviet Military Strategy in Europe*. An Institute for Foreign Policy Analysis Book. New York: Pergamon, 1980.

Douglass, Joseph D., Jr., and Hoeber, Amoretta M. *Conventional War and Escalation: The Soviet View*. New York: Crane Russak for the National Strategy Information Center, 1981.

————, comps. *Selected Readings from Military Thought, 1963–1973*. Studies in Communist Affairs, vol. 5, pts. 1 and 2. Washington, D.C.: U.S. Air Force, GPO, 1982.

Druzhinin, V. V., and Kontorov, D. S. *Ideia, algoritm, reshenie: Priniatie reshenii i avtomatizatsiia*. Moscow: Voenizdat, 1972. Translated and published under the auspices of the United States Air Force. *Concept, Algorithm, Decision: Decision Making and Automation; A Soviet View*. Soviet Military Thought, no. 6. Washington, D.C.: GPO, 1978.

Egorov, P. T.; Shiakhov, I. A.; and Alabin, N. I. *Grazhdanskaia oborona*. 2d ed. Moscow: Vysshaia shkola, 1970. Translated and published under the auspices of the United States Air Force. Original translation and editing by Oak Ridge National Laboratory. *Civil Defense: A Soviet View*. Soviet Military Thought, no. 10. Washington, D.C.: GPO, 1976.

Epishev, General Colonel A. A., ed. *KPSS i voennoe stroitel'stvo*. Moscow: Voenizdat, 1982.

————. *Partiia i armiia*. Moscow: Politizdat, 1977.

Eustace, Harry F., ed. *The International Countermeasures Handbook, 1977–1978*. 3d ed. Palo Alto, Calif.: EW Communications, 1977.

Fedorov, G. A.; Sushko, N. Ia.; and Belyi, B. A., eds. *Marksizm-Leninizm o voine i armii*. 2d rev. ed. Moscow: Voenizdat, 1961.

Friedman, Norman. *Soviet Responses to U.S. Naval Initiatives.* HI-2901/4-RR. Croton-on-Hudson, N.Y.: Hudson Institute, 1979.

Garthoff, Raymond L. *The Soviet Image of Future War.* Washington, D.C.: Public Affairs Press, 1959.

Gorshkov, Fleet Admiral S. G. *Morskaia moshch' gosudarstva.* Moscow: Voenizdat, 1976.

————. *Morskaia moshch' gosudarstva.* 2d ed. Moscow: Voenizdat, 1979.

Gouré, Leon. *War Survival in Soviet Strategy: USSR Civil Defense.* Monographs in International Affairs. Coral Gables, Fla.: Center for Advanced International Studies, University of Miami, 1976.

————. *Shelters in Soviet War Survival Strategy.* Monographs in International Affairs. Washington, D.C.: Advanced International Studies Institute, 1978.

Gowa, Joanne, and Wessell, Nils H. *Ground Rules: Soviet and American Involvement in Regional Conflicts.* Philadelphia Policy Papers. Philadelphia, Pa.: Foreign Policy Research Institute, 1982.

Grechko, Marshal A. A. *Na strazhe mira i stroitel'stva kommunizma.* Moscow: Voenizdat, 1971.

————. *Vooruzhennye sily sovetskogo gosudarstva.* 2d ed. Moscow: Voenizdat, 1975. Translated and published under the auspices of the United States Air Force with the approval of the All-Union Copyright Agency of the USSR. *The Armed Forces of the Soviet State: A Soviet View.* Soviet Military Thought, no. 12. Washington, D.C.: GPO, n.d.

International Institute for Strategic Studies, *The Military Balance, 1971–1972.* London: IISS, 1971. All subsequent issues through *1985–1986.*

————. *Strategic Survey, 1984–1985.* London: IISS, 1985.

Ivanov, D. A.; Savel'ev, V. P.; and Shemanskii, P. V. *Osnovy upravleniia voiskami v boiu.* 2d ed. Moscow: Voenizdat, 1977. Translated and published under the auspices of the United States Air Force with the approval of the All-Union Copyright Agency of the USSR. *Fundamentals of Tactical Command and Control: A Soviet View.* Soviet Military Thought, no. 18. Washington, D.C.: GPO, n.d.

Katukov, A. M., and Tsvetaev, E. N. *Voenno-patrioticheskoe vospitanie uchashchikhsia na zaniatiiakh po nachal'noi voennoi podgotovke.* Biblioteka rukovoditelia nachal'noi voennoi podgotovki. Moscow: Prosveshchenie, 1984.

Khrushchev, N. S. *Disarmament for Durable Peace and Friendship.* Moscow: Foreign Languages Publishing House, 1960.

Kintner, William R., and Scott, Harriet Fast, trans. and eds. *The Nuclear Revolution in Soviet Military Affairs.* Norman: University of Oklahoma Press, 1968.

Kir'ian, M. M., ed. *Voenno-tekhnicheskii progress i vooruzhennye sily SSSR: Analiz razvitiia vooruzheniia, organizatsii i sposobov deistvii.* Moscow: Voenizdat, 1982.

Kommunisticheskaia Partiia Sovetskogo Soiuza. *XXII s''ezd Kommunisticheskoi Partii Sovetskogo Soiuza: 17–31 oktiabria 1961 goda, stenograficheskii otchet.* Vol. 2. Moscow: Politizdat, 1962.

———. *XXV s"ezd KPSS: 28 fevralia-5 marta 1976 goda, stenograficheskii otchet.* Vol. 2. Moscow: Politizdat, 1976.

Koriagin, A. G., et al., eds. *Sotsialisticheskoe vosproizvodstvo: Dinamizm i rezul'tativnost'.* Moscow: Mysl', 1983.

Korolev, V. I., ed. *Grazhdanskaia oborona SSSR.* 6th ed. Moscow: Voenizdat, 1984.

Kozhevnikov, M. N. *Komandovanie i shtab VVS Sovetskoi Armii v Velikoi Otechestvennoi Voine, 1941–1945 gg.* Moscow: Nauka, 1977. Translated and published under the auspices of the United States Air Force with the approval of the All-Union Copyright Agency of the USSR. *The Command and Staff of the Soviet Army Air Force in the Great Patriotic War, 1941–1945: A Soviet View.* Soviet Military Thought, no. 17. Washington, D.C.: GPO, n.d.

Kozlov, General Major S. N., ed. *Spravochnik ofitsera.* Moscow: Voenizdat, 1971. Translated by the DGIS Multilingual Section, Translation Bureau, Secretary of State Department, Ottawa, Canada. Published under the auspices of the United States Air Force. *The Officer's Handbook: A Soviet View.* Soviet Military Thought, no. 13. Washington, D.C.: GPO, 1977.

Krasovskii, S. A., et al. *Aviatsiia i kosmonavtika SSSR.* Moscow: Voenizdat, 1968.

Kulikov, Marshal V. G. *Kollektivnaia zashchita sotsializma.* Moscow: Voenizdat, 1982.

———, ed. *Akademiia General'nogo Shtaba.* Moscow: Voenizdat, 1976.

Kulish, Colonel V. M. *Raskrytaia taina: Predistoriia vtorogo fronta v Evrope.* Moscow: Voenizdat, 1960.

Lee, William T. *Inventories in the Soviet Economy: Some Implications for Targeting.* Washington, D.C.: Center for Planning and Research, December 1978.

———. *The Estimation of Soviet Defense Expenditures, 1955–75: An Unconventional Approach.* Praeger Special Studies in International Politics and Government. New York: Praeger, General Electric Tempo Center for Advanced Studies, 1977.

———. *Soviet Defense Expenditures in an Era of SALT.* USSI Report 79-1. Washington, D.C.: United States Strategic Institute, 1979.

———. *Trends in Soviet Defense Expenditures.* Report no. AAC-TR-10001/79. Washington, D.C.: Analytical Assessments Co., 1979.

———. *Understanding the Soviet Military Threat: How CIA Estimates Went Astray.* Agenda Paper no. 6. New York: National Strategy Information Center, 1977.

———. *Viability of the ABM Treaty in the 1980s: A Note on the Issue.* DNA-4769T-1. Vol. 1. Washington, D.C.: Center for Planning and Research, 1980.

Levanov, I. N., et al., eds. *Marksizm-Leninizm o voine i armii.* Moscow: Voenizdat, 1957.

Lomov, General Colonel N. A., ed. *Nauchno-tekhnicheskii progress i revoliutsiia v voennom dele.* Moscow: Voenizdat, 1973. Translated and published under the auspices of the United States Air Force. *Scientific-Technical Progress and the Revolution in Military Affairs: A Soviet View.* Soviet Military Thought, no. 3. Washington, D.C.: GPO, 1980.

Malinovskii, Marshal R.I. Speech to the Twenty-second Congress of the CPSU. Stenographic report, vol. 2. Published separately as *Bditel 'no stoiat' na strazhe mira*. Moscow: Voenizdat, 1962.

Mal'tsev, E. E. *KPSS: Organizator zashchity sotsialisticheskogo otechestva*. Moscow: Voenizdat, 1974.

Milovidov, A. S., and Kozlov, V. G., eds. *Filosofskoe nasledie V. I. Lenina i problemy sovremennoi voiny*. Moscow: Voenizdat, 1972. Translated and published under the auspices of the United States Air Force. *The Philosophical Heritage of V. I. Lenin and Problems of Contemporary War: A Soviet View*. Soviet Military Thought, no. 5. Washington, D.C.: GPO, 1977.

Moore, Captain John E., RN, ed. *Jane's Fighting Ships, 1973–74*. London: Macdonald and Jane's Publishers Limited, 1973.

————. *Jane's Fighting Ships, 1975–76*. London: Macdonald and Jane's Publishers Limited, 1975. All subsequent volumes through *1985–1986*.

Murphy, Paul J., ed. *Naval Power in Soviet Policy*. Washington, D.C.: GPO, 1978.

Myers, Kenneth A., ed. *NATO: The Next Thirty Years*. Boulder, Colo.: Westview Press, 1980.

Newhouse, John. *Cold Dawn: The Story of SALT*. New York: Holt, Rinehart and Winston, 1973.

Ogarkov, Marshal N. V. *Vsegda v gotovnosti k zashchite otechestva*. Moscow: Voenizdat, 1982.

————, ed. *Voennyi entsiklopedicheskii slovar'*. Moscow: Voenizdat, 1983.

Pavlenko, V. F., ed. *Boevaia aviatsionnaia tekhnika: Letatel'nye apparaty, silovye ustanovki i ikh ekspluatatsiia*. Moscow: Voenizdat, 1984.

Polmar, Norman. *Strategic Weapons: An Introduction*. Rev. ed. New York: Crane Russak for the National Strategy Information Center, 1982.

Prados, John. *The Soviet Estimate: U.S. Intelligence Analysis and Russian Military Strength*. New York: The Dial Press, 1982.

Pretty, R. T., ed. *Jane's Weapons Systems, 1969–70*. New York: Franklin Watts, 1969.

————. *Jane's Weapons Systems, 1979–80*. New York: Franklin Watts, 1979.

Radzievskii, General Colonel A. I., senior ed. *Dictionary of Basic Military Terms*. Moscow: Voenizdat, 1965. Translated by the DGIS Multilingual Section, Translation Bureau, Secretary of State Department, Ottawa, Canada. Soviet Military Thought, no. 9. Washington, D.C.: GPO, 1976.

Raupach, Hans, ed. *Jahrbuch der Wirtschaft Osteuropas* [Yearbook of East European Economics]. Vol. 8. Munich and Vienna: Guenter Olzog Verlag, 1979.

Record, Jeffrey. *Sizing Up the Soviet Army*. Washington, D.C.: Brookings Institution, 1975.

Rosefielde, Steven, ed. *World Communism at the Crossroads: Military Ascendancy, Political Economy, and Human Welfare*. Boston: Martinus Nijhoff Publishing, 1980.

"SALT 1-2," special issue, *Aviation Week and Space Technology* (1976).

Saltykov, N. D. *Dokladyvaiu v General'nyi Shtab.* Moscow: Voenizdat, 1983.

Savkin, V. E. *Osnovnye printsipy operativnogo iskusstva i taktiki.* Moscow: Voenizdat, 1972. Translated and published under the auspices of the United States Air Force. *The Basic Principles of Operational Art and Tactics: A Soviet View.* Soviet Military Thought, no. 4. Washington, D.C.: GPO, 1982.

Scott, Harriet Fast, and Scott, William F. *The Armed Forces of the USSR.* 3d rev. ed. Boulder, Colo.: Westview Press; London: Arms and Armour Press, 1984.

———. *The Soviet Control Structure: Capabilities for Wartime Survival.* New York: Crane Russak for the National Strategy Information Center, 1983.

———, eds. *The Soviet Art of War: Doctrine, Strategy, and Tactics.* Boulder, Colo.: Westview Press, 1982.

Scott, Colonel William F. (USAF, ret.), ed. *Selected Soviet Military Writings, 1970–1975: A Soviet View.* Translated and published under the auspices of the United States Air Force. Soviet Military Thought, no. 11. Washington, D.C.: GPO, 1979.

———. *Soviet Sources of Military Doctrine and Strategy.* New York: Crane, Russak, 1975.

Shavrov, I. E. *Lokal'nye voiny: Istoriia i sovremennost'.* Moscow: Voenizdat, 1981.

Sheliag, V. V.; Glotochkin, A. D.; and Platonov, K. K., eds. *Voennaia psikhologiia.* Moscow: Voenizdat, 1972. Translated and published under the auspices of the United States Air Force. *Military Psychology: A Soviet View.* Soviet Military Thought, no. 8. Washington, D.C.: GPO, 1976.

Shields, Johanna Nicol, ed. *SALT II and American Security.* Proceedings from the John Sparkman Symposium on United States Foreign Policy. Huntsville, Ala.: University of Alabama in Huntsville, 1979.

Sidorenko, A. A. *Nastuplenie.* Moscow: Voenizdat, 1970. Translated and published under the auspices of the United States Air Force. *The Offensive: A Soviet View.* Soviet Military Thought, no. 1. Washington, D.C.: GPO, 1984.

Simon, Jeffrey. *Warsaw Pact Forces: Problems of Command and Control.* Westview Special Studies in Military Affairs. Boulder, Colo.: Westview Press, 1985.

Siniukov, A. M., and Morozov, N. I. *Konstruktsiia upravliaemykh ballisticheskikh raket.* Moscow: Voenizdat, 1969.

Skirdo, Colonel M. P. *Narod, armiia, polkovodets.* Moscow: Voenizdat, 1970. Translated by the DGIS Multilingual Section, Translation Bureau, Secretary of State Department, Ottawa, Canada. Published under the auspices of the United States Air Force. *The People, the Army, the Commander: A Soviet View.* Soviet Military Thought, no. 14. Washington, D.C.: GPO, n.d.

Sobolev, M. G., ed. *Partiino-politicheskaia rabota v sovetskoi armii i flote.* 2d rev. ed. Moscow: Voenizdat, 1984.

Sokolovskii, Marshal V. D., ed. *Soviet Military Strategy.* Edited by Harriet Fast Scott. 3d ed. New York: Crane, Russak & Co., 1975.

———. *Voennaia strategiia.* 2d rev. ed. Moscow: Voenizdat, 1963.

————. *Voennaia strategiia.* 3d rev. ed. Moscow: Voenizdat, 1968.

Sovetskaia voennaia entsiklopediia. 8 vols. Moscow: Voenizdat, 1976–1980. Vols. 1 and 2 edited by A. A. Grechko; vols. 3–8 edited by N. V. Ogarkov.

Staar, Richard F. *Communist Regimes in Eastern Europe.* 4th rev. ed. Stanford: Hoover Institution Press, 1982.

————. *USSR Foreign Policies After Détente.* Stanford: Hoover Institution Press, 1985.

————, ed. *Arms Control: Myth Versus Reality.* Stanford: Hoover Institution Press, 1984.

Surikov, B. T. *Raketnye sredstva bor'by s nizkoletiashchimi tseliami.* Moscow: Voenizdat, 1973.

————. *Boevoe primenenie raket.* Moscow: Voenizdat, 1965. Joint Press Research Survey translation (dated 3 November 1965).

Sushko, N. Ia., and Kondratkov, T. R., eds. *Metodologicheskie problemy voennoi teorii i praktiki.* Moscow: Voenizdat, 1966.

Sushko, N. Ia.; Kondratkov, T. R.; and Khomenko, E. A., eds. *Metodologicheskie problemy voennoi teorii i praktiki.* 2d ed. Moscow: Voenizdat, 1969.

Suvorov, Viktor. *Inside the Soviet Army.* New York: Macmillan, 1982.

Swanborough, Gordon. *Military Aircraft of the World.* New York: Charles Scribner's Sons, 1981.

Taylor, John W. R., ed. *Jane's All the World's Aircraft, 1973–74.* London: Jane's Publishing Co., 1974.

————. *Jane's All the World's Aircraft, 1979–80.* London: Jane's Publishing Co., 1979. All subsequent issues through *1981–1982.*

Tel'pukhovskii, B. S. *KPSS vo glave stroitel'stva vooruzhennykh sil SSSR: Oktiabr' 1917–1982 gg.; Istorlcheskii ocherk.* Moscow. Politizdat, 1983.

Tiushkevich, S. A. *Filosofiia i voennaia istoriia.* Moscow: Nauka, 1975.

————. *Sovetskie vooruzhennye sily: Istoriia stroitel'stva.* Moscow: Voenizdat, 1978. Translated by the CIS Multilingual Section, Translation Bureau, Secretary of State Department, Ottawa, Canada. Published under the auspices of the United States Air Force with the approval of the All-Union Copyright Agency of the USSR. *The Soviet Armed Forces: A History of Their Organizational Development; A Soviet View.* Soviet Military Thought, no. 19. Washington, D.C.: GPO, n.d.

————, chief ed. *Filosofiia i voennaia istoriia.* Moscow: Nauka, 1979.

Tolubko, V. F. *Nedelin: Pervyi glavkom strategicheskikh.* Moscow: Molodaia gvardiia, 1979.

Truman, Harry S. *Memoirs by Harry S. Truman: Year of Decisions.* Vol. 1. Garden City, N.Y.: Doubleday, 1955.

Tsentral 'noe statisticheskoe upravlenie SSSR. *Narodnoe khoziaistvo SSSR v 1978 g.: Statisticheskii ezhegodnik.* Moscow: Statistika, 1979.

———. *Narodnoe khoziaistvo SSSR v 1979 g.: Statisticheskii ezhegodnik.* Moscow: Statistika, 1980.

———. *Narodnoe khoziaistvo SSSR v 1982 g.: Statisticheskii ezhegodnik.* Moscow: Statistika, 1983.

U.S. Congress. Congressional Budget Office. *Counterforce Issues for the U.S. Strategic Nuclear Forces.* Background Paper. Prepared by Robert R. Soule. January 1978. Washington, D.C.: GPO, 1978.

———. Joint Economic Committee. Subcommittee on International Trade, Finance, and Security Economics. *The Allocation of Resources in the Soviet Union and China, 1984.* 98th Cong., 2d sess. Washington, D.C.: GPO, 1984.

———. Joint Session of the Subcommittee on Strategic and Theater Nuclear Forces of the Senate Armed Services Committee and the Defense Subcommittee on Appropriations. *Soviet Strategic Force Developments.* 99th Cong., 2d sess. 26 June 1985. Washington, D.C.: GPO, 1985.

U.S. Government. Arms Control and Disarmament Agency. *Arms Control and Disarmament Agreements: Texts and Histories of Negotiations.* Washington, D.C.: GPO, 1982.

———. ———. *World Military Expenditures and Arms Transfers 1985.*

———. Central Intelligence Agency. Directorate of Intelligence. *Directory of Soviet Officials: National Organizations.* CR 84-13894. November 1984.

———. National Foreign Assessment Center. *CPSU Central Committee and Central Auditing Commission: Members Elected at the 26th Party Congress.* CR 81-11349. May 1981.

———. ———. *USSR: Ministry of Defense Officials.* CR 85-11682. April 1985.

———. Department of Defense. *Annual Report, Fiscal Year 1980.* Report of Secretary of Defense Harold Brown to the Congress on the FY 1980 budget, FY 1981 authorization request and FY 1980–84 defense programs. 25 January 1979. Washington, D.C.: GPO, 1979.

———. *Annual Report, Fiscal Year 1981.* Report of Secretary of Defense Harold Brown to the Congress on the FY 1981 budget, FY 1982 authorization request and FY 1981–85 defense programs. 29 January 1980. Washington, D.C.: GPO, 1980.

———. *Annual Report, Fiscal Year 1982.* Report of Secretary of Defense Harold Brown to the Congress on the FY 1982 budget, FY 1983 authorization request and FY 1982–86 defense programs. 19 January 1981. Washington, D.C.: GPO, 1981.

———. *Annual Report to the Congress, Fiscal Year 1985.* Report of Secretary of Defense Caspar W. Weinberger to the Congress on the FY 1985 budget, FY 1986 authorization request and FY 1985–89 defense programs. 1 February 1984. Washington, D.C.: GPO, 1984.

———. *The FY 1982 Department of Defense Program for Research, Development, and Acquisition.* Statement by the Honorable William J. Perry, Undersecretary of

Defense, Research, and Engineering, to the 97th Cong., 1st sess., 1981. Washington, D.C.: The Pentagon, 1981.

————. *The FY 1985 Department of Defense Program for Research, Development, and Acquisition.* Statement by the Honorable Richard D. DeLauer, Undersecretary of Defense, Research, and Engineering, to the 98th Cong., 2d sess., 1984. Washington, D.C.: The Pentagon, 1984.

————. *The FY 1986 Department of Defense Program for Research, Development, and Acquisition.* Statement by the Honorable Richard D. DeLauer, Undersecretary of Defense, Research, and Engineering, to the 99th Cong., 1st sess., 1985. Washington, D.C.: The Pentagon, 1985.

————. "National Security Strategy of Realistic Deterrence," *Annual Defense Department Report, FY 1973.* Statement of Secretary of Defense Melvin R. Laird before the Senate Armed Services Committee on the FY 1973 defense budget and FY 1973–77 program, 15 February 1972. Washington, D.C.: GPO, 1972.

————. *Soviet Acquisition of Militarily Significant Western Technology: An Update.* Washington, D.C., September 1985.

————. *Soviet Military Power.* Washington, D.C.: The Pentagon, 1982.

————. *Soviet Military Power.* 2nd ed. Washington, D.C.: The Pentagon, 1983.

————. *Soviet Military Power.* 3d ed. Washington, D.C.: The Pentagon, 1984.

————. *Soviet Military Power.* 4th ed. Washington, D.C.: The Pentagon, 1985.

————. Organization of the Joint Chiefs of Staff. *United States Military Posture for FY 1982.* An Overview by General David C. Jones, USAF, chairman of the joint chiefs of staff. Washington, D.C.: GPO, 1981.

————. *United States Military Posture for FY 1983.* Washington, D.C.: GPO, 1982.

————. *United States Military Posture for FY 1984.* Washington, D.C.: GPO, 1983.

————. *United States Military Posture for FY 1986.* Washington, D.C.: GPO, 1985.

————. General Advisory Committee on Arms Control and Disarmament. *A Quarter Century of Soviet Compliance Practices under Arms Control Commitments.* Washington, D.C. October 1984.

————. Department of State. Bureau of Public Affairs. *SALT II Agreement.* Selected Document No. 12A. June 1979. Washington, D.C.: Dept. of State, 1979.

U.S. House of Representatives. Select Committee on Intelligence. Subcommittee on Oversight. *Hearings on CIA Estimates of Soviet Defense Spending.* 96th Cong., 2d sess. Washington, D.C.: GPO, 1980.

U.S. Senate. Committee on Aeronautical and Space Sciences. *Soviet Space Programs, 1966–70.* Senate Doc. No. 92–51. Prepared by Charles S. Sheldon, II et al. Washington, D.C.: GPO, 1971.

————. Committee on Armed Services. Subcommittee on General Procurement. *Hearings on Soviet Defense Expenditures and Related Programs.* 96th Cong. 1st and 2d sess. Washington, D.C.: GPO, 1980.

Ustinov, D. F. *Sluzhim rodine, delu kommunizma.* Moscow: Voenizdat, 1982.

Van Cleave, William R. *Fortress USSR: The Soviet Strategic Defense Initiative and the U.S. Strategic Defense Response.* Stanford: Hoover Institution Press, 1986.

Varfolomeev, V. I., and Kopytov, M. I., eds. *Proektirovanie i ispytaniia ballisticheskikh raket.* Moscow: Voenizdat, 1970.

Vasil'ev, B. A. *Dal'naia, raketonosnaia.* Moscow: DOSAAF, 1972. Translated by the DGIS Multilingual Section, Translation Bureau, Secretary of State Department, Ottawa, Canada. Published under the auspices of the United States Air Force. *Long-Range, Missile-Equipped: A Soviet View.* Soviet Military Thought, no. 15. Washington, D.C.: GPO, 1979.

Vernon, Graham D., ed. *Soviet Perceptions of War and Peace.* Washington, D.C.: National Defense University Press, Fort Lesley J. McNair, 1981.

Weeks, Albert T., and Bodie, William C., eds. *War and Peace: Soviet Russia Speaks.* New York: National Strategy Information Center, 1983.

Wolfe, Thomas W. *The SALT Experience.* Cambridge, Mass.: Ballinger, 1979.

———. *Soviet Power and Europe, 1945–1970.* Baltimore, Md.: Johns Hopkins Press, 1970.

Zheltov, A. S., ed. *Imeni Lenina: Kratkii istoricheskii ocherk o voenno-politicheskoi ordena Lenina krasnoznamennoi akademii imeni V. I. Lenina.* Moscow: Voenizdat, 1966.

Zheltov, A. S.; Kondratkov, T. R.; and Khormenko, E. A., eds. *Metodologicheskie problemy voennoi teorii i praktiki.* 2d rev. ed. Moscow: Voenizdat, 1969.

Zhilin, P. A., et al., eds. *Osvoboditel'naia missiia sovetskikh vooruzhennykh sil v Evrope vo vtoroi mirovoi voine: Dokumenty i materialy.* Moscow: Voenizdat, 1985.

Zimin, G. V., ed. *Razvitie protivovozdushnoi oborony.* Moscow: Voenizdat, 1976.

Index